MW00565511

To Dad,
Merry Christmas
2007.
Love,
Stephanie

Gloucester's Bargain with the Sea

Also by Chester Brigham

The Stream I Go A-Fishing In: Musical Adventures of Gloucester Schoonerman John Jay Watson

"The Fiddling Fisherman," a narrated musical excursion based on the career of John Jay Watson

Gloucester's Bargain with the Sea

The Bountiful Maritime Culture of Cape Ann, Massachusetts

There is more here than can be pictured
by the most ingenious pen

- George Procter,
Gloucester newspaper editor and author

CHESTER BRIGHAM

Whale's Jaw Publishing
www.whalesjaw.com

First Printing

ISBN 978-0-9740778-6-4 (*hardcover*)
ISBN 978-0-9740778-5-7 (*paperback*)

Library of Congress Control Number: 2006939968

 Published by Whales's Jaw Publishing, Gloucester, Massachusetts 01930. Address all inquiries to info@whalesjaw.com.

Published in Gloucester, MA by Whale's Jaw Publishing

Printed in the United States by King Printing Company, Lowell, MA

Cover and book design by Barry Rower

To

Anthea

Contents

Illustrations

Page

Page

Preface

A READER WHO IS of a true nautical bent might well pick up this book about a "maritime culture" with the comfortable expectation of being immersed exclusively in tales of the sea and ships. Well, there is much of that here. But what's this about high-wheeled bicycles, and pipe organs, and Folly Cove fabrics? And talk of Kipling, and T. S. Eliot, and Charles Olson, and Robert Frost? And of John Sloan and Edward Hopper, and of sculptors carving art from granite left behind by the quarrymen?

What is all that doing in a book that purports to be about the maritime culture of Cape Ann? There is a short answer, and a long answer. First the short answer. The life of the sea, and especially of fishing, has permeated every aspect of human existence on Cape Ann for the past four centuries. All these permutations constitute the maritime culture of Gloucester and vicinity – a remarkably fertile culture that has produced a broad array of writings and works of art. That is what we will be looking at in the chapters ahead.

For the longer answer, I will have to go back a few years, into the mid-1930s to be exact. That was when my parents began renting in the summers a little house in Bay View that was owned by my aunt and her husband, who was one of the Gott family once numerous along that stretch of Gloucester coastline. It was, to my brother and me, beginning age four and seven respectively, perfect bliss to climb barefoot over the granite wharves of Hodgkins Cove, pass the days amphibiously in woolen bathing suits always itchy with sand, dissect dead horseshoe crabs, fish for cunners that flapped, eyes staring, when tossed ashore.

It was an exotic life after our other existence in Melrose, where our father had a drugstore. He and my mother had strayed from the Marlborough-Sudbury area west of Boston that had been home to our forebears since the 1600s. Melrose was then a railroad suburb of Boston, and was of the America of steady habits, thrift, the dignity of labor, and early bedtimes. It lay a mere thirty miles from Gloucester, but was an hour away in those times over roads that led through one town's main street to the next.

Gloucester was a different world. Its grown men we saw did not wear vested suits and fedoras, but walked in rolled-over rubber boots, shaded their eyes from sea glare under long-billed "swordfishing" caps, wore faded work shirts under suspenders, stood in dories sculling them magically by one oar in a slot at the stern, sat on the ledges barefoot mending lobster pot webbing and talking among themselves with drawling humor, using words not often heard in Melrose. The mothers of our wharf chums were formidable in flowing dresses, wore their hair in buns, seemed fierce but were kindly underneath.

Our parents liked Gloucester, too. So much so that they bought a bit of shore on Goose Cove in the late '30s and built a tiny cottage, the "camp" we called it. That first summer was wonderful, but then my father died suddenly and unexpectedly. My mother, who had known only the role of homemaker, studied nights to become a pharmacist, while by day she learned first-hand how to run the business she would own long enough to put her sons through college. As we grew older, my brother and I spent more and more of our time on Goose Cove, in every kind of weather, all times of the year, especially after our mother winterized the house and moved in. Cape Ann became my home of the spirit, and would always remain so.

A sense that I had had from my earliest days there was reinforced and gradually took shape: that this was a very special place. Later – during years as an undergraduate at Colby College in Maine, stationed in Texas during the Korean War, and as a GI Bill graduate student in Mexico and Spain, and then free-lancing for years from the house my wife, Anthea, and I bought in Connecticut – I gained the perspective that only distance can provide as to just how unique the Gloucester area really was. The atmosphere was more pellucid on Cape Ann, sunlight glancing off coves edged by curves of granite bleached by the sun and washed by ten-foot tides. The naturescape and humanscape were in special harmony, where granite wharves stood out into inlets amid masts and working boats and circling gulls, and clapboard houses with steep Greek Revival roof lines backed up against boulder-strewn slopes, and black-white buffleheads bobbed in an out of the water at the edge of winter sea ice. The sounds were of draggers chugging down the Annisquam River from Ipswich Bay, and the squawk of a night heron before dawn, and the distant steam whistle that later became a diesel horn from a train pulling into the Gloucester depot. The people were different, scorning pretense, taking quiet pride in skills of woodworking and stoneworking and boatbuilding and fish harvesting. And reveling in the life, earning the high honor of being quoted among their peers for some original quip or demolishing appraisal. My home of the spirit again became my home in fact when Anthea and I moved back year-round to the house on Goose Cove in 1997.

A question had always hovered in my thinking about Cape Ann. Why was it that so many writers, painters and sculptors of the first rank had not just visited or vacationed in the Gloucester neighborhood, but were drawn there for their subject matter? Why was it that their work, taken all together, constituted a remarkable body of major artistic output? True, the area had its scenic beauties, and harbors for boaters, and beaches for sun worshipers. But so did other coastal locales.

I kept circling back to one thought: It all comes down to the maritime heritage. A working partnership with the North Atlantic, stretching back over four centuries, keeps Gloucester from becoming a hostage to tourism. Keeps vacationers and summer residents aware that the unique character of this place needs to be respected. Forms the enduring basis, reinforced by geographic and geologic separateness, and by the omnipresence of the ocean, for the words and images that seek to capture the special qualities of Cape Ann.

So that is the short and the long of it. There will still be those who insist that it's a bit of a stretch to call this a book about maritime culture. But I'll risk it.

Acknowledgments

MY SEARCH FOR DOCUMENTATION on Cape Ann's cultural riches began with the Gloucester shelf in Gloucester's Sawyer Free Library, from which I could check out a vast range of books on every aspect of Cape Ann, especially to do with Gloucester. When I could not find a book on the shelf, the research staff, with almost conspiratorial willingness, would be quick to retrieve it from the reserve stacks. The library of the Cape Ann Historical Museum has its own trove of works about Cape Ann, published or in manuscript form. I wandered happily at length through its stacks, sometimes in search of a specific title, other times stumbling upon a fascinating captain's log or a typewritten journal.

Of the people who have generously rendered information and suggestions, Ellen Nelson, former librarian-archivist at the Cape Ann Historical Museum, was invaluable in pointing me to much that I would have otherwise missed in its library. Stephanie Buck, the current librarian-archivist at the Historical, has been of particular assistance (with the volunteer help of her husband, Fred) in locating, in the museum's vast photo archives, a number of relevant images that have not previously appeared in print. In many discussions with former Gloucester mayor and philanthropist Robert L. French, I have had the benefit of his long, active involvement with Cape Ann institutions and the arts. Joseph E. Garland was encouraging and full of good suggestions, as he has been to countless writers generating books about the Gloucester area. Nick Parisi told me much about dragger fishing, and about the early economic hardships of the Sicilian community in the Fort. I would also like to thank Carol Gray, Assistant Director of the Sawyer Free Library, for early records of the Gloucester Lyceum; Paul Littlefield for information on his uncle, Foster Damon; Jean Young for her recollections of her father, "Bunt" Davis; Martha Oaks at the Sargent House Museum for access to editor-author Epes Sargent's poetic works, including *Songs of the* Sea and *The Light of the Light-House*; Robert Myers for information on the Hyatt and Mayor families; and, in the distant past, Neil Leonard for introducing me to all that T. S. Eliot had written about Cape Ann. On an adjacent stool at the counter of the Willow Rest coffee shop, Cal Cook filled me in on anecdotal history of the Goose Cove area, and reminded me of much that I had forgotten about the Squam area in the '40s.

Last and foremost, my wife, Anthea. Without her persevering involvement and unfailing enthusiasm, there would be no book here. Or, if there were, I would have had little or no fun in pulling it all together.

In addition to authors mentioned in the text, the following sources have been particularly useful:

Mary Angela Bennett's biography of Elizabeth Stuart Phelps is one of those circumspect personal histories of the 19th century that were guaranteed not to offend. It manages, nevertheless, to be highly informative.

C. E. Carrington's "Life" is a standard source for Rudyard Kipling. Angus Wilson offered a different perspective in *The Strange Ride of Rudyard Kipling – His Life and Works*. David McAveeney provides a valuable local focus on the author in his *Kipling in Gloucester*.

For the Epes Sargent era at *The Boston Transcript*, see Joseph Edgar Chamberlin, *The Boston Transcript – A History of its First Hundred Years*.

Howard Chapelle's expert studies of the evolution of the Essex fishing schooner are his *American Sailing Craft* and *The American Fishing Schooners*.

Tom Clark's *Charles Olson – The Allegory of a Poet's Life* chronicles the outsize career of that outsize poet.

A valuable but overlooked mine of information on the younger John Hays Hammond is John Dandola's *Living in the Past, Looking to the Future: The Biography of John Hays Hammond, Jr.*

The extensive correspondence of Judith Sargent Murray has been made available by Marianne Dunlop in her *Judith Sargent Murray: Her First 100 Letters*, and by Bonnie Hurd Smith in *From Gloucester to Philadelphia in 1790* and *Letters I Left Behind*.

Incidents from the neglected history of the Gloucester fisheries during World War II are documented in David S. Eldredge's "The Gloucester Fishing Industry in World War II," an article printed in *The American Neptune*.

A valuable source on the Folly Cove Designers is Barbara

Elleman's *Virginia Lee Burton: A Life in Art.*

There is rich material on T. S. Eliot's youthful Gloucester summers in Lyndall Gordon's *Eliot's Early Years*, which she followed later with her equally penetrating *Eliot's New Life*. Russell Kirk placed Eliot in the context of his time in *Eliot and His Age*. In "The Dry Salvages and the Thacher Shipwreck," published in *The American Neptune*, Samuel Eliot Morison analyzed the Cape Ann links found in a section of his kinsman T. S. Eliot's *Four Quartets*.

Dick Hill's *Sylvester Ahola – The Gloucester Gabriel* incorporates a biography, discography and orchestra photos of Gloucester's legendary big band trumpeter.

For Lucy Larcom's rise from child labor in the Lowell mills, see *The Worlds of Lucy Larcom* by Shirley Marchalonis.

Reverend John Wise's role as one of the intellectual forerunners of the American Revolution is detailed in Paul Simpson McElroy's "John Wise: The Father of American Independence," printed in the *Essex Institute Historical Collections*. Also valuable is a section on John Wise by Thomas Waters in "Two Ipswich Patriots," printed in *Publications of the Ipswich Historical Society*.

Helen Naismith fills in the blanks on Mason Walton's early years in her *The Hermit of Ravenswood*.

The most complete account of the Gloucester Fishermen's Institute is *The Gloucester Fishermen's Institute, 1891–1991* by Martha Oaks.

Philip L Barbour's *The Three Worlds of Captain John Smith* of 1964 was scoffed at for taking the adventurer's words at face value, but later research has tended to confirm certain of the captain's extravagant claims.

Cruel practices in early colonial Gloucester that lingered from the Middle Ages are detailed in articles by John C. Reilly, Priscilla O. Kippen-Smith and Edith M. Sparling in *Historical Gleanings from the Gloucester Archives*.

The role of the Reverend John White in organizing the Gloucester fishing settlement as predecessor to the Massachusetts Bay Colony was investigated by Frances Rose-Troup in her *John White – The Patriarch of Dorchester (Dorset) and The Founder of Massachusetts*.

Earl Smith is credited as author of *Yankee Genius – A Biography of Roger W. Babson*, but the subject is believed to have had more than a little to do with the content. Another admiring (but more balanced) word portrait of the remarkable Roger W. is Paul B. Kenyon's *Roger W. Babson, A Reminiscence*, written with Philip S. Weld.

It was Marshall W. S. Swan who wrote of Ralph Waldo Emerson's visits to Gloucester in his "Emerson and Cape Ann," *Essex Institute Historical Collections*. Records of the Gloucester Lyceum at Gloucester's Sawyer Free Library chronicle Emerson's many Lyceum talks in Gloucester.

A rounded, perhaps corpulent, picture of the Boston and Manchester-by-the-Sea publisher James T. Fields emerges from W. S. Tryon's *Parnassus Corner – A Life of James T. Fields*, supplemented by Fields's own *Yesterdays with Authors*, as well as *Authors and Friends* by his wife, Annie Fields.

Introduction:
The Contract

Whereas, the citizens of a certain place known as Gloucester, together with the nearby towns on Cape Ann to be known eventually as Rockport, Essex and Manchester-by-the-Sea, in the also eventual Commonwealth of Massachusetts, being of sound mind (flagrant eccentricities notwithstanding), do hereby enter into solemn agreement with His Serene Majesty Poseidon (a.k.a. Neptune), Ruler of the Seas, whereby said citizens do agree to spend their lives upon, or in close proximity to, the sea in this place, and commit themselves to maritime endeavors, at whatever cost in lives and property, in expectation that His Aquatic Highness will see fit to favor these, his loyal subjects, with fair winds, gentle seas and good fortune.

ADMITTEDLY, NO SUCH compact was ever put into writing. But the people of Cape Ann have behaved for upwards of four centuries as if they did have a contractual agreement to make their livelihood from the sea, whatever the consequences.

In case introductions are in order, be it known that Cape Ann is a boulder-strewn knob of granite jutting out into the Atlantic half way between Boston, Massachusetts and Portsmouth, New Hampshire. An island portion of the knob is occupied by a large portion of the city limits of Gloucester, and all of the town of Rockport which was a part of Gloucester for its first two centuries. To the north the Great Marsh begins, 20,000 acres of salt grass islands and barrier beaches that sweep to the mouth of the Merrimack River. At the end of a winding channel within that marsh is the town of Essex, long a well-sheltered shipbuilding center.

Inland from island Gloucester is West Gloucester, much of it still deep woods. For a century, from the 1830s to the 1930s, its ponds were harvested in the winter for the ice trade. Adjoining Gloucester's Magnolia section on the shore toward Boston is the town of Manchester, or Manchester-by-the-Sea if you will. Manchester bears the stamp of old money, as well as of more recent affluence. Still, the town's picture-perfect harbor is a working port for a score or more lobster boats, as well as a protected mooring ground for many summer sailing vessels. The launching of, storing and maintaining of those craft keeps the harbor boatyards busy throughout the benign months of the year.

Cape Ann lies only thirty-five miles from Boston, which would seem to make it perilously vulnerable to the influences of New England's capital city. Yet, as we shall see, the Gloucester district has developed a culture very unlike that of the Boston area – in fact, a maritime culture as distinctive and multi-dimensioned as any on America's Atlantic coast.

Some of the reasons are bound up in the history of Cape Ann, especially at its gravitational center in Gloucester. Gloucester began as a fishing station, then had a go at global sea commerce. After the Embargo of 1807 and War of 1812 had killed their sea trade, the merchants of the town scorned a turn to manufacturing and instead continued to face seaward and made fisheries their main industry. It was then that Gloucester achieved its greatest renown in the glorious and tragic era of the fishing schooners. Soon after 1900, Gloucester's fisheries went into a slow, century-long decline. Still, as of this writing, much of Cape Ann continues to busy itself with ocean-related occupations.

The singular culture of the Cape Ann area owes much to its geography as well. The villages that took hold in coves along its harsh granite shore were isolated enough over their first three centuries of settlement to develop a self-sufficient, independent spirit seasoned by long exposure to the ways and wiles of the sea. When the outside world did arrive on the cape, in the form of tourists and then summer residents drawn by the natural beauties, the character of the place was already sharply etched. The late-comers who were artists and writers offered fresh interpretations of this sea-girt land and society.

Their names will pop up in the chapters ahead, with some mention of their contributions. Among them are Rudyard Kipling, T. S. Eliot, Charles Olson, Robert Frost, Fitz Henry Lane, Winslow Homer, Edward Hopper, Walker Hancock, Anna Hyatt Huntington. And historians John J. Babson, Joseph E. Garland, Melvin Copeland & Elliott Rogers, and Herbert Kenny. And also a number of lesser knowns whose writings were secondary to their main interests. Such as Gordon Thomas, biographer of the fishing schooners. Dana Story, chronicler of the schooner shipyards in Essex. Barbara Erkkila, who wrote from close family knowledge of the granite quarries on the outer cape. Sea captains who confided more than weather conditions to their logs. Travelers and travel-advisors who recorded Cape Ann at its various stages of early isolation and later discovery by vacationers.

These and many other authors, painters, sculptors and musicians have found inspiration on this cape, have discovered valor, tragedy and cockeyed humor in the human record of the region. All have puzzled upon the profundities of man and sea in this little realm of stark reality and enchanting uncertainty that exists somewhere at the intersection of granite, surf and fantasy.

Map of Cape Ann. The U.S. Geodetic Survey map of 1886, revised in 1917.

CHAPTER I

"The Towne Called Glocester"

GLOUCESTER'S DESTINY as a maritime community was fixed from the day the first English settlers arrived in its harbor in 1623 in a small ship of fifty tons. They stumbled in, actually, in their quest for good fishing grounds, and decided this would be a well-sheltered harbor for setting up a year-round fishing station. They had no interest in exploring inland. They were there to face seaward and fish. And so it all began.

Prior to that, it seemed as if no one was going to get around to setting up housekeeping on Cape Ann. Various European explorers had sailed by without dropping in. It was not until 1602 that the English became interested in the neighborhood and a hopeful group of investors sent Bartholomew Gosnold off to America to trade to their advantage. Gosnold, in the bark *Concord*, made landfall along the southern Maine coast.

There, Gosnold was met by a boat manned by natives, one attired in "a waist-coat and breaches of black serdge," the others naked. They spoke some French and could make maps, having been taught by the Basque, and later French and English, fishermen who had been making yearly trips to the Newfoundland fishing grounds since the 1570s if not earlier. These Europeans had clearly fished as far as the lower Maine coast. But not so far south that the natives of the Massachusets tribe on Cape Cod knew them. Had they cast their lines off Cape Ann, and perhaps come ashore for fresh water? Very possibly, but if so they left no records or artifacts that anyone has come across. When these boats returned to harbors in the Bay of Biscay, their crews kept very quiet about where they had been and how they had happened to fill their holds with fish. Let their competitors find their own fishing grounds.

Gosnold returned with a profitable cargo of sassafras, and a year later, Martin Pring, a Devon skipper, set sail in the ships *Speedwell* and *Discoverer*, also commissioned to bring back a cargo of *Sassafras albidum*. What was the allure of sassafras? Pring explained that it was "a plant of sovereigne virtue for the French Poxe, and as some have learnedly written good against the Plague and many other Maladies." When the English of the day said "French poxe," they meant syphilis, unfairly blaming the French for a disease present in the Old World since antiquity. A virulent new strain had appeared in the 1500s, brought back, it was believed, by the Spaniards from their American colonies – along with chocolate, tomatoes and tobacco. The hope (soon dashed) was that New World sassafras would prove a cure. It was Pring who first described sighting Cape Ann, but it did not look like sassafras country and he kept to his course southwestward.

As it happened, the first European to set foot on Cape Ann and write about it was a man of France, Samuel de Champlain. In 1605 Champlain, then in his late thirties, was attached as Royal Geographer to an expedition under Sieur de Monts, Lieutenant General in command of the French presence in North America. The role of chart-maker in the age of exploration was one of great importance, and Champlain had earned his appointment through distinguished military service on land and sea under King Henri IV.

Sieur de Monts cruised along the coast in a small pinnace that could poke into shallow bays and estuaries, which Champlain charted. The party kept an eye out for likely sites to colonize (they had already planted a settlement under the fleur de lys at Mount Desert). They sailed down the wide swerve of Ipswich Bay and raised a headland jutting out into the sea. It was late in the afternoon so they hove to for the night.

Next day the French sailed past the future Straitsmouth, Thacher's and Milk Islands, and saw the breakers crashing over the Salvages. All those islands suggested to Champlain a name for the place: "We called it Cape of Islands (Nous nommasmes ce lieu le cap aux Isles)". On the shore were natives, who went into a ritual dance when they saw the French. Champlain decided to go ashore to meet them. ("Je fus a terre pour les voir.") And so European man took his first recorded steps on Cape Ann. It was Thursday, July 16, 1605.

The French did not linger on Cape Ann that trip, but a year later Champlain was again off Cape Ann in another pinnace. This expedition was commanded by Jean de Biencourt, Sieur de Poutrincourt, Lieutenant-Governor of Port Royal in Acadia (today Nova Scotia's Annapolis Basin). In late September they entered Gloucester harbor, anchoring near what was later named Ten Pound Island. "This port is a very good one," wrote Champlain, "having sufficient water for vessels, and affording shelter behind some islands. It is in the latitude of 43 degrees, and we have named it Le Beau Port."

He set to drawing a harbor map, including a sketch of an encounter that led the French to question the intentions of the inhabitants. Members of the crew were attending to laundry chores on the shore at Rocky Neck when Champlain observed a band of armed natives stealing up on them. However, the Indians then saw "the Sieur de Poutrincourt within the wood, with eight arquebusiers [soldiers armed with blunderbusses], which astonished them. They . . . retired from one side and the other, with apprehension that we should do them some harm."

The natives gestured that they had never meant to suggest any ill will, and that two thousand more of their tribe would be arriving soon who were eager to meet the French. De Poutrincourt and Champlain, not liking the odds, made sail out of the harbor. This rocky cape, they concluded, was not yet ripe for settlement.

Champlain's *Journal* is not the only account of the French on Cape Ann in 1606. Marc Lescarbot, Paris lawyer, poet and bon vivant, was at Port Royal with Champlain and Poutrincourt. Classically educated, with some repute already as a translator of Latin histories, Lescarbot was intent on making literature of his adventures in North America.

He did not join Champlain and Poutrincourt on the cruise to Cape Ann, but his account of that voyage, in his *Nova Francia – A Description of Acadia*, has a special élan. "Monsieur de Poutrincourt following on his course, found a certain Port [Gloucester harbor] very delightful...."

Throughout the pages of *Nova Francia* Lescarbot conveys the panache with which the French preserved a sophisticated lifestyle in primitive North America: "All this month we made merry . . . . Monsieur de Poutrincourt did set up and opened a hogshead of wine, one of them that was given him for his own drinking, giving leave to all comers to drink as long as it should hold, so that some of them drunk until their caps turned round." Ah, and the cuisine. Every two weeks it was the turn of one or another of the French expedition to be steward and caterer whose "care was that we should have good and worshipful fare." The repasts, says Lescarbot, might not have been as sumptuous as those at La Rue aux Ours, a street in Paris then famed for its butchers. But these true Frenchmen, surviving on a wild shore at the edge of the howling wilderness, still dined in good cheer. And, Lescarbot adds with true French frugality, the dinner tabs were far cheaper than in Paris.

Always enthusiastic and bubbling with optimism, Lescarbot describes a day crossing the Grand Bank: "The dawn of day being come, which was Saint John Baptist's Eve, in God's name we pulled down sails, passing that day a-fishing of cod-fish, with a thousand mirths and contentments." In his *Mythologos*, poet Charles Olson called *Nova Francia* "one of the greatest books . . . more interesting than Champlain's report." True, Lescarbot is a delight to read – when he is not straying into medieval speculations on natural history, or drawing on Herodotus or the Bible for labored analogies. But his account of Cape Ann was second-hand. Champlain, on the other hand, had been there.

The French never did return to Gloucester. They shifted their attention north, and four years later Champlain would found French Quebec. Still, it is tempting to speculate what Cape Ann might have looked like as a French Cap aux Isles, with le Beau Port as its provincial capital. Would there have been boulevardiers in berets, lingering over a café espress at a downtown sidewalk terrace, scanning the *Beau Port Daily Figaro*, with a wink at a comely meter maid? Would there have been some massive chateau on Banner Hill? Would local restaurants feature *sole meunier* instead of *boiled lobster with drawn butter*? We will never know. A Gallic Gloucester was not to be.

After Pring's sassafras commission, Englishmen lost interest in North America. Until 1616, that is, when Captain John Smith penned *A Description of New England*, in which he recommended maritime pursuits as a promising enterprise for Cape Ann and the neighboring

Capt. John Smith. Frontispiece of his *A Description of New England*, with the tribute to rough-and-ready John Smith: "Thou art Brasse without, but Golde within."

coast. What would be the basis of New England's trade with England and the rest of Europe? Smith considered whaling, fur trading and mining gold or copper. But practically speaking: "The maine Staple, from hence to be extracted for the present to produce the rest, is fish;

which however it may seeme a mean and a base commoditie: yet who will but truly take the paine and consider the sequel, I think will allow it well worth the labour."

Hardly any labor, as Captain Smith described it: "Scarce any place, but Cod, Cuske, Holybut, Mackerell, Scate, or such like, a man may take with a hook or line where he will." It paid well, too: "And is it not pretty sport to pull up twopence, sixpence, and twelvepence, as fast as you can haul and veer a Line? And what sport doth yield a more pleasing content, and less hurt or charge, than angling with a hook, and crossing the sweet air, from isle to isle, over the silent streams of a calm sea?"

After his frustration with aristocratic idlers in the Jamestown Colony, Smith had a fresh vision for the shores he named "New-England" (previously it had always been "North Virginia"). He saw it as a place for a new start, where a man could succeed on his own if he had the will and the skill, free of the fetters of the Old World. "Here every man may be master and owne labour and land; or the greatest part in a small time. If hee have nothing but his hands, he may set up his trade; and by industrie quickly grow rich . . . ."

Captain Smith's enthusiasm was based upon a three-month cruise along New England shores. He sailed close inshore, plotting what would survive as a definitive map. South from the estuaries of the Kennebec and the Saco he sailed, along the barrier dunes of the Great Marsh. And after the outer beaches, his lookouts spied that same great shoulder of granite Champlain had charted: "From hence doth stretch into the Sea the faire headland Tragabigzanda, fronted with three Isles called the three Turks heads . . . ."

"Tragabigzanda," mercifully for anyone trying to spell or pronounce the word, would become Cape Ann, and the "Turks heads" would become Straitsmouth, Thacher's and Milk Islands. Smith had given them their original names to keep alive the fame of exploits in his earlier career. As a young soldier of fortune he had joined an Austrian army fighting Turks in Transylvania. On a dull day between battles a Turk champion thought to impress the ladies by taking on one of the opposition in single combat. Several of the Christian lads volunteered, and John Smith won the toss. Short, stocky, sinewy and reckless, he slew not only the first challenger, but two who followed, and took their heads as souvenirs. All this was recorded in the army minutes, it was said, and John Smith earned the right to display on his shield a crest representing the three Turks' heads. Doubters have dismissed the story as preposterous. But if so, it was a gloriously inspired fabrication, worthy of a Cervantes.

There was more. When he was enslaved as a prisoner of war, John Smith was presented as a gift to a young Turkish, or perhaps Greek, princess, Charatza Tragabigzanda. She was fascinated by this fearless infidel and "took much compassion on him," however that may be interpreted. She loaned him to her brother for safekeeping until she came of age and could own human chattel in her own right. But John chose freedom over future bliss as a kept man, and made his escape.

Years later Captain Smith must have been impressed indeed with a wild cape on his New England coast, to name it after his princess. And to honor, in his name for those three islands, the memory of his splendid victory over his hapless, and subsequently headless, Turk adversaries. "Turk's Head" lived on in the name of a summer hotel, and later of a motel built upon the ashes of the hotel.

Smith was never again able to get backing for a voyage to New England. He slipped into disgruntled obscurity complaining that, for all his services in opening up the territory for successful colonization, the New England Council granted him nothing but a small cluster of islands "which are a many of barren rocks . . . without either grass or wood." He never visited his Smith's Islands, which were within sight of Cape Tragabigzanda on a clear day. Later they even ceased to bear his name. They are known today as the Isles of Shoals, divided between the hegemony of New Hampshire and Maine.

If John Smith's proposals for establishing permanent trading and fishing communities in New England had anything to do with that first English fishing enterprise in Gloucester harbor, its sponsors were mum on the subject. The Reverend John White, leader of worthy investors in the Dorchester Company in England, said that the plan for a fishing plantation was that of "some Westerne *Merchants* (who had continued a trade of fishing for Cod and bartering for Furres in those parts for divers yeares before conceiving that a Colony planted on the Coast might further them in those employments ...)." These merchants from the West of England were doubtless among those who, for a century or more, had been dispatching vessels for seasonal fishing on the Newfoundland Banks. And, like the Basque fishermen, keeping very quiet about it, lest competitors be drawn to their bonanza.

White was Puritan pastor of two principal parishes of Dorchester in Dorset, and was considered broad-minded and tolerant as Puritans went. But Puritan leniency had its limits. Woe betide a parishioner who skipped one of John White's sermons with the excuse that she had to stay home "a-mending her stockings."

While White was a man of the cloth, the proposed fishing venture was first and foremost commercial. John White combined piety with a passion for commercial enterprise – the same fusion of the worldly and godly that would plant enduring Puritan communities all over New England by the end of the seventeenth century. (The Pilgrims at the Plymouth Plantation were, by contrast, religious idealists whose unfamiliarity with such practical matters as how to deploy a fishhook caused them great suffering.)

White made a strong case for a fisheries-based plantation, echoing many of John Smith's arguments. The ships would be double-manned so that, after the main party returned to England at the close of the fishing season, some of the men would winter-over to plant crops. In time the colony would provide employment for the surplus population idling about the streets of English towns. Colonists would ship to England timber, flax, hemp and dye-stuffs. And, in turn, buy English manufactures, providing "a vent for oure clothes and other stuffes."

In recruiting merchants to invest in a joint stock company, Reverend White would have brought to bear his undisputed powers of persuasion. In an age when English men and women flocked for their entertainment to the "lectures" of inspired clergymen whose sermons might go on for five hours on a Sunday, John White preached twice, then three times a week to meet the demand.

In his words to the West Country merchants, White understandably emphasized profits over piety. He included religion in his sales prospectus only to the extent of urging that clergy be included aboard their vessels to minister to the spiritual needs of the fishing crews, "whereas otherwise being usually upon those Voyages nine or ten moneths of the yeare, they were left all the while without any meanes of instruction at all." This argument softened the hearts of the most

was almost completely denuded of trees. They did what farming they could upon thin soil resting on granite ledges and peppered with boulders deposited by glaciers. They built their first rudimentary village center, complete with meeting house and tavern, at the head of a marsh remote from the open sea.

Ultimately, the claim of the sea upon the settlers could not be denied. The harbor became active again, and a maritime community began to grow along its shores. Boats were built to float lumber from the felled trees along the coast to meet demand elsewhere, and other trade followed the same routes. By 1660 Samuel Maverick, Episcopalian maverick in Puritan Boston, could write: "There is a passage cutt through a Marsh between Cape Ann Harbour and Manisquanne [Annisquam] Harbour where stands the Towne called Glocester very comodious for building of shipping and ffishing."

On Cape Ann early generations of settlers lived out earthy, sometimes bawdy, 17th century lives much as they would have back in England. One of them was Christopher Avery, often elected as selectman, but whose reputation was sullied when it was charged that he lived away from his wife, spoke with disrespect of the minister, and once was said to have drunk so much rum that he "took another man's wife upon his knee, and dandled her, ye foolish man, her husband looking on therewhile."

The wheels of government always seemed to require generous lubrication. As when a newly sworn-in slate of town selectmen ran up a substantial bill at James Stevens's tavern at the old Green, a hostelry that Stevens was in the process of selling to Captain Ellery (the structure has since been known as the Ellery House, now owned by the Cape Ann Historical Association). The town balked, voting to require the selectmen to pay for their own refreshments. But official business apparently ground to a halt, because the town soon reversed its hasty decision. The selectmen, scarcely chastened, celebrated by running up a far higher tab when next they convened at the aforesaid tavern.

Somehow or other, government did function, and business did get conducted, and by the time of the American Revolution, Gloucester had become a considerable port, crowded with coasting vessels, sending its own ships off to distant ports. Its bargain with the sea, no longer tentative, was strongly in force.

CHAPTER 2

Revenge of the Privateers

CAPE ANN'S run-up to the American Revolution had begun a century before the battle on Lexington Green. In 1687 Sir Edmund Andros, James II's autocratic new royal governor of the Massachusetts province, slapped taxes on the Colonials by edict. Essex County rallied in support of John Wise, pastor of Chebacco parish (later the town of Essex), who raised the cry of no taxation without representation.

Informed of this insolent disobedience, Andros was in high dudgeon. Reverend Wise and several of his parishioners were rounded up and brought to Boston, where Wise protested his rights as an English citizen. In Andros's kangaroo court one of the judges said it was absurd of Wise to think the laws of England would follow him to the ends of the earth. "Mr. Wise, you have no more privilege left you, than not to be sold as slaves." Wise demanded habeas corpus. It was denied and he was sentenced to some weeks in Boston's stone jail, suspended from his ministry and assessed a heavy fine.

The Stuart dynasty was deposed and, in 1689, Boston rose up against Andros and his myrmidons and marched them to the dock from whence they were to take ship back to England. When the procession reached Boston Town House, John Wise's demand for liberties guaranteed by the Magna Carta was read to the crowd. Boston cheered. Arbitrary rule by agents of a British king had been thwarted, at least for the time being.

This Reverend John Wise was born a Massachusetts man in 1652, in Roxbury, worked his way through Harvard (Class of 1673), and married a Roxbury parish girl. They had six children and John preached in Connecticut for a time until called to the new Chebacco

Homestead of Rev. John Wise, Essex trouble-maker who raised the cry of "no taxation without representation" a century before the Revolution.

parish, which had split off from cleric-historian William Hubbard's Ipswich congregation. They lived in a saltbox house, which still stands, just back from the broad stretches of salt marsh and well within whiff of the sea. Wise would occupy the Chebacco pulpit for the next forty-five years. Dominate that pulpit, might be a better way to put it. He was a massive man by all accounts, leonine in presence with a stentorian voice that thundered the verities.

Historian Vernon Parrington said that John Wise was the first

New England minister to break with the literal interpretation of the Bible that was at the core of Calvinist Puritanism. Wise had the audacity to venture beyond Christian orthodoxy as well. He knew his Greek and Latin authors and, from their speculations on the nature of the universe and man and beauty, imbibed the spirit of pragmatic inquiry that was gnawing at the underpinnings of received religious beliefs. When he heard complaints that the elders of the Chebacco parish were not elderly enough, that a young crowd was taking over, Wise replied from the pulpit that if the length of a beard was any measure of wisdom, they would all be ruled by billy goats. He was quoting the reply of the Athenians to the Persians who grumbled about the youthfulness of the Greek emissaries. But the analogy made perfect sense to John Wise's farming parishioners, who were well acquainted with billy goats.

Wise was first to compare Cape Ann to Tyre, the flourishing Phoenician seaport that remained safely buttressed by the Mediterranean until overwhelmed and sacked by Alexander the Great. Tyre, said Wise, "was but a Rock . . . Yet by Merchandize became the Queen of the Seas, the Metropolis of the World." A comparable glory could be expected for the granite shores of Cape Ann: "Then what a perfection may Cape Ann or Gloucester, a Promontory thrust so far into the Sea . . . be brought to, by Commerce and Merchandize, in a few Ages more." If Gloucester never quite lived up to Reverend Wise's mercantile expectations, it achieved glories of a different sort.

Wise's inflammatory sermons were printed, and on the eve of the Revolution were re-issued. They were subscribed to by some of the early agitators for secession from the Crown, including John Scollay, a sponsor of the social event that became known as the Boston Tea Party. And when in Philadelphia in 1776 John Adams nominated articulate young Thomas Jefferson to draft the Declaration of Independence, it is just possible he dropped off a copy of John Wise's *Vindication of the Government of the New England Churches.* Tom might find some useful wording in a tract that said "The end of all good government is to cultivate humanity and promote the happiness of all, and the good of every man in all his rights, his life, liberty, estate, honor, etc., without injury or abuse done to any." The sentiments echo those in Pufendorf's *De Jure Naturae et Gentium* of 1672, suggesting that books by natural-rights philosophers shared space on the shelves of Reverend Wise's library in the Chebacco parsonage.

When the Revolution did come to Cape Ann it arrived, almost inevitably, by sea. After the British blockaded Boston harbor in retaliation for the Boston Tea Party, a town meeting was called in Gloucester. The citizens unanimously approved a resolution that asserted: "We will hold ourselves in readiness to join the town of Boston, and all other towns, in all measures to extricate ourselves from tyranny and oppression."

Gloucester had not hesitated to commit to the side of rebellion. After the fighting broke out at Concord and Lexington in April of 1775, followed by the Battle of Bunker Hill two months later, the people of Cape Ann knew they were achingly vulnerable to attack by the British Navy. There was no American sea force to defend Gloucester, nor would there be throughout the years of the Revolution. John Adams wrote in his autobiography about his efforts to organize a navy, drawing upon the region's reserves of experienced seamen. But the American naval vessels that were built during the war fought far at sea, and none too successfully. Ports like Gloucester remained nakedly exposed.

Attack came in August in what became known as "The Battle of Gloucester Harbor." The British sloop-of-war *Falcon*, commanded by Captain John Linzee (or Lindsay), after supporting the British attack at Bunker Hill, was cruising in Cape Ann waters inflicting assorted mischiefs. The *Falcon* then chased into Gloucester harbor a schooner returning well-laden from the West Indies, and the townspeople turned out to save the American vessel from capture. They had little ammunition and only a pair of old swivel cannons which they mounted onto gun carriages.

When Captain Linzee observed through his glass that these colonial ruffians had the effrontery to fire upon the small boat he had sent in to seize the schooner, he retaliated by pouring broadsides into the town. A few houses were hit, and one cannonball lodged in the First Parish Church. It now reposes in a display case in the Cape Ann Historical Museum, alongside other balls fired from the guns of the

Falcon in the engagement. One of these had struck the house of the prosperous Mansfields on Front Street. Another bumped down onto Daniel Rogers's wharf.

But all of Captain Linzee's maneuvers were frustrated. He sent a party to land at Fort Point to incinerate the fish flakes. Result: all members of the landing force captured. He sent another boat to board and secure the schooner he had pursued. Result: it was seized by the Gloucestermen, who took thirty-five prisoners, some badly wounded. Gloucester's losses during the entire fracas: two men killed by musket fire, one pig sent to hog heaven by a cannonball. Gloucester slept uneasily that night, wondering what a frustrated Captain Linzee might be planning to do to the town with all his firepower come daybreak. But next day the *Falcon* made sail and left the harbor. Historian John J. Babson, who in his *History of the Town of Gloucester* of 1860, wrote the first reliable account of the battle, wondered why Linzee left Gloucester unpunished. That question would go unanswered for more than a century.

As an irony of history, Captain Linzee was not only routed in Gloucester harbor. In a later skirmish he surrendered his heart to a Boston girl, Susanna Inman. They were married and after the Revolution settled in Boston. Two generations later, historian William Prescott, grandson of Colonel Prescott who commanded the rebels Linzee fired upon at Bunker Hill, married Susan Amory, granddaughter of Captain Linzee and his Boston bride. The swords of both ancestors were mounted on the wall of the historian's library. British author William Makepeace Thackeray stopped by to visit Prescott during an American tour, was intrigued by the story, and wove the symbolism of the swords into his novel *The Virginians*. Today the Linzee and Prescott swords are crossed in enduring amity at the Massachusetts Historical Society.

It was Joseph E. Garland who solved the problem that had perplexed John Babson: Why, after humiliating the British Navy, was Gloucester spared retaliatory attacks that might obliterate the town? After all, the Gloucester defenders had tugged the lion's tail with unbelievable success. Yet the reprisals never came.

Thanks to his access to naval documents not available in Babson's day, Garland learned that indeed a devastating attack had been

James Babson, school dropout who wrote the first scrupulously researched history of Cape Ann. *Courtesy Cape Ann Historical Museum*

ordered against Gloucester harbor by British Admiral Samuel Graves, both in retribution for the humbling of the *Falcon*, and as a preemptive strike against a port that commanded the sea approaches to Boston.

It was just dumb luck that the order was never carried out. Lieutenant Henry Mowat, assigned to burn Gloucester and its vessels, set sail toward Cape Ann but was forced out to sea by a gale.

Instead of waiting for a wind change, he continued up the coast to another target of opportunity, Falmouth, Maine (today's Portland). The harbor was undefended and bombardment by the British ships continued until a large part of the town was reduced to cinders. This was the punishment intended for Gloucester. Garland marshaled the evidence in his *Guns Off Gloucester* (1975), that ranks with Ronald Tagney's *The World Turned Upside Down* as a narrative of heroism, suffering and endurance in Essex County during the American Revolution.

As sources in addition to Garland confirm, Gloucester had good reason to fear additional British attacks during the eight long years of the war. Colonial Secretary Lord George Germain was determined to raid and burn every American seaport. The turncoat adventurer Benjamin Thompson from North Reading, Massachusetts was at Germain's side, providing local intelligence. (Thompson became better known as Count Rumford, knighted in England, pioneer physicist and founder of the scientific Royal Institution in London, generalissimo of the Bavarian armies, inventor of the Rumford stove.) But Germain's orders could never be carried out. The French navy kept the British men-of-war bottled up in home waters.

Things were bad enough on Cape Ann without further enemy attacks. The latter 1770s and early 1780s were what Marshall Swan called Cape Ann at its nadir. In *Guns Off Gloucester* Garland speaks of the disasters that combined to devastate the town: the destitution of a fishing community that could no longer venture from its shores, unusually bitter winters, epidemics of smallpox that ravaged family after family and spread general consternation.

The battle of Gloucester harbor was to be the only engagement of the war fought on Gloucester shores, but many volunteers marched off to serve in the Continental army. Enterprising members of the community also sought their revenge against Captain Linzee, and otherwise serve the cause of liberty, by means of privateering. They preyed upon British cargo vessels in armed vessels, and sometimes sent rich cargoes back to Gloucester. To be sure, privateering seldom paid in the long run. Most of the little vessels that fitted out for offshore robbery were eventually taken by the British. It was not an enviable fate to be consigned to the hell of prison ships, or to wander penniless in foreign lands. William Ellery, an officer on a privateering vessel taken by the British, survived a year in a prison ship in New York harbor until he either escaped or was let go and walked home to Gloucester barefoot, begging food along the way.

Privateering also scuttled recruiting efforts for the regular navy. As William Fowler says in *Rebels Under Sail*, those who went into privateering were an independent lot who were not accustomed to military discipline. What's more, if they took part in the capture of a valuable vessel, they could hope for a share of the prize that would far exceed the wages of a navy seaman. So why enlist when you could hope for a fine share of booty that would allow you to live in handsome style ashore? Provided you avoided capture.

Privateersmen have been confused with pirates, and sometimes there were only fine distinctions between the two. But privateersmen sailing out of Gloucester and other American ports did not go about violating the daughters of British passengers, or holding the wives for ransom, or cutting throats in the process of burying chests of gold on desert islands. That was the business of pirates. Privateers, instead, were licensed to prey upon enemy shipping, and could not share in the proceeds until the goods were brought into an approved port and certified as legal loot. Any misconduct toward those aboard the captured vessel would mean forfeit of the cargo and a criminal trial.

Still, armed robbery of lightly protected merchant vessels was troubling to many, although there was a lighter side to privateering. Consider the heart-rending frustration of the captain of the English ship *Sarah and Elizabeth*, bound richly laden from Jamaica to London. She was challenged in the night by the Gloucester privateer *Warren*, Captain William Coas. The captain's wife and other passengers on board the *Sarah and Elizabeth* were so convinced they would be murdered – or worse – by the Yankees, they begged the captain to surrender the vessel. He did so, without firing a shot. Next morning, when he saw that he had yielded his splendid ship to a pitifully small and lightly armed raider, the captain of the *Sarah and Elizabeth* was reduced to sobs of humiliation. At least he could take consolation in reflecting that his fair passengers had not been scalped or otherwise misused by the barbarous Yankees.

In the years after the Revolution, the former practitioners of privateering enjoyed the status of patriotic heroes. Isaac Trask, for one. Trask was one of the crew of a Gloucester privateer captured by the British. He escaped from a prison ship and after the war became a sailing ship master and finally a prosperous owner of vessels. "It was only a few days before his death," said Babson, "that his erect form and agile step were missed from our streets. He gave much attention to intellectual cultivation, and could speak several foreign languages with fluency; but he is best remembered by townsmen as a man of pure morals, of benevolent heart, and very courteous manners." Thus Isaac Trask, who had once been the scourge of shipping on the high seas, ended his days revered and beloved by all.

The years of Revolution had been hard ones on Cape Ann. But the citizens emerged with their pride intact. They had been loyal Colonials for a century and a half, then had risen up with the citizens of Boston and the other Massachusetts towns in defiance of the crushing edicts of King George. They held on through attack and privation until they could, at last, share the satisfactions of national independence.

CHAPTER 3

Stirrings of Mind and Spirit

THE TIMES after the Revolution were ones of wrenching but liberating change on Cape Ann. Some of the usages that endured from the past now seem bizarre indeed. Most troubling is the attitude toward slavery, not seriously challenged until the 18th century, by which it was casually accepted that human beings of African extraction could be bought and sold like a horse or a plow. Those few prosperous members of the community who did own slaves saw to it that their "servants" were baptized, thanks to an odd quirk of religious reasoning. The Bible was interpreted as decreeing that, if the slave-owner did not have his human property baptized, he would be condemned to eternal damnation.

There was also the cruel practice, often motivated by desperate need, of apprenticing a child out until twenty-one if a boy, or eighteen if a girl. The sons of lost fishermen were frequently "bound over" – essentially sold into servitude until adults – "to learn the trade of mariner or fisherman." For example, "Isaac Dade . . . a poor child unable to maintain himself, bound to David Babson to learn the trade of Fisherman." Isaac was thirteen. Or a surplus child might be bound over simply as a cash deal. The price negotiated for James Gott was $50. Upon receipt of that amount from John Butler, James's father duly transferred title to his son to Butler "to learn the trade of mariner." The terms of apprenticeship imposed a heavy moral obligation on a bound-over lad: "At Cards, Dice, or any other unlawful Game or Games he shall not play: Fornication he shall not committ: Matrimony he shall not contract: Taverns, Ale-Houses or Places of Gaming he shall not haunt or frequent."

The 'prenticed white children differed from slaves in that these bound-over boys and girls would obtain their release when adults, and be set on their way "with Two Suits of Apparel from head to foot suitable for such an Apprentice one of which to Be New." Their freedom might be brief, though. A boy apprenticed as a mariner would have credentials only in that hazardous calling, and might soon turn up on the crew roster of a lost ship.

Penalties for all sorts of misdemeanors were harsh, and seldom subject to appeal. Anyone caught intentionally setting fire to a barn or stable would be "whipt" and fined double damages. If the building set afire was a residence or meeting house, the fire bug would be afforded a just and speedy trial. Then hung. Such were the standards of righteousness passed down through the Colonial generations.

But new thinking was in the wind, as in the breezes that blew Reverend John Murray's vessel from England. Murray, as it turned out, would play as important a role as John Wise in setting precedents of freedom and self-determination not only for Cape Ann, but for the new nation. Murray had come to America not with any ambition to prosper. On the contrary, he was passively suicidal and hoped that, with a little luck, he might meet an early death in the wilderness. In England Murray had been devastated by the death of his year-old-son, followed soon after by that of his young wife. He was intentionally taking late night walks on lanes notorious for cutthroat footpads. His friends suggested America and he came, not caring.

The all-embracing Universalist faith had been espoused in Gloucester by the town's merchant trading families, a class not typically associated with innovative social or religious views. Members of Gloucester's independent-minded Sargent clan and their friends had been introduced to the Universalist writings of James Relly by an itinerant preacher named Gregory. When, in 1774, they heard that the Reverend John Murray, also of the Relly-ist persuasion, was to speak in Boston, Winthrop Sargent traveled to that hotbed of rebellion and invited Murray to preach in Gloucester. Murray came to stay with the Sargents twice, and wrote in his journal "To my great astonishment, there were a few persons, dwellers in that remote place, upon whom the light of the gospel had *more than dawned.*"

Murray decided that Gloucester would be just the place to take pause from his wanderings. "Here my God grants me rest from my toils; here I have a taste of heaven." Gloucester might well have seemed like paradise after the treatment Murray was getting in Boston. On one of his appearances there, "The audience were incommoded by a profusion of water thrown over them, and an egg was aimed at me in the pulpit, which however happened to miss me."

The small but earnest congregation of Gloucester Universalists met Sundays at Winthrop Sargent's mansion on the corner of Spring and Duncan Streets in the months before the Revolution. After Bunker Hill, Murray left no doubt that he was now a New England patriot. He volunteered as chaplain of a Continental Army brigade then in quarters at Jamaica Plain. The other chaplains were indignant and petitioned for removal of this heretic Universalist who would poison the minds of the troops. But General George Washington confirmed Murray's appointment, and that was that.

After he had served nearly a year, Murray was forced by illness to leave the camp. Back in Gloucester he was shocked at the poverty and suffering the war had brought upon Cape Ann. He appealed to his friends in the Continental Army for aid. George Washington opened his purse to Murray's Gloucester relief appeal, as did many of his senior officers, along with some wealthy citizens of Boston. In 1776 Gloucester's Town Council voted unanimously to offer "their sincere thanks to the compassionate donors of a sum of money sent by the hands of Mr. John Murray for the relief of our poor."

But the Universalist doctrine of eventual salvation for all provoked much suspicion and opposition. Reverend John Cleaveland penned a cautionary tract, *Attempt to Nip in the Bud, the Unscriptural Doctrine of Universal Salvation, and Some Other Dangerous Errors Connected with It, Which a Certain Stranger, Who Calls Himself John Murray Has, of Late, Been Endeavoring to Spread in the First Parish of Gloucester.*

Murray was called before Gloucester's Committee of Safety and warned out of town. He answered the charges with an eloquence that soared above theological prose with his new sense of pride as an American. He declared that "I am a staunch friend to liberty, genuine liberty. It is well known that I have labored to promote the cause of this country, and I rejoice that I have not labored in vain."

But antagonism toward Murray ran deep. From Gloucester's earliest days each family had been taxed for support of the Congregational church for the simple reason that Congregationalism, the heir to Puritanism, was the established religion. To be sure, that old faith was no longer commanding the loyalty in the community that it once enjoyed. The three meeting houses on Cape Ann away from the harbor were poorly attended and in disrepair, one even with its roof caving in. But the idea of admitting another version of Christianity was anathema to the faithful.

When the Universalists refused to pay the tithe, the First Church people sought to balance the ledger by selling at auction some of Epes Sargent's silver plate. Then they shamelessly offered for sale the anchor off a ship about to sail. John Murray and his fellow religionists took them to court, quoting the freedom of religion guaranteed in the new Bill of Rights in the Constitution of the Commonwealth of Massachusetts, the work of John Adams.

It was a landmark legal battle, with eminent Federalist lawyers taking up the case for the Universalists. Among them was Rufus King, later ambassador of the fledgling United States to the Court of St. James's. And William Tudor, Advocate General in Washington's army (and father of that most quixotic of Boston maritime traders, Frederic Tudor, who made millions peddling ice in the tropics). Murray and his group eventually were judged to be within their rights in refusing to pay a tithe to the Congregational church. A precedent for separation of church and state was established in America then and there – by some stubborn men and women of Gloucester who argued it made no sense for them to practice one faith but pay to support another.

So now the Universalists of Gloucester had a legal place of worship, a makeshift chapel which in 1805 was succeeded by the structure that soars today in a park-like setting off Middle Street. In the early days its facilities were sparse. Music for the psalm-singing was furnished by a barrel organ which, it was said, Captain John Somes had appropriated from an English merchant ship in his capacity as sometime privateer. Barrel organs were popular in the churches of England in that day because no musical skills were required – the organ was operated simply by turning a crank. The quality of the music so produced tended to outshine the efforts of amateur musicians of the congregation who played upon horns and pipes.

An initial difficulty was with the cylinders that arrived with Captain Somes's organ. They played not sacred but secular music, "inappropriate for religious service." Later a cylinder was contrived that played the basic chords for a number of psalms. That solution served until the flock was able to adapt a keyboard to the organ and thereafter broaden their musical horizons.

John Murray had sailed to England to await the legal decision on tithing. When he learned he had been personally vindicated and fully accredited as pastor of a church no longer beholden to First Parish Congregational, he caught the next boat back to marry Winthrop Sargent's daughter, who at last became Judith Sargent Murray.

Judith Sargent, said historian Babson, was "uncommonly attractive with a superior mind enriched by education." Much of this education was acquired when she studied alongside her brother Winthrop while he was boning up for admission to Harvard. Women were resoundingly not welcome at Harvard then, an injustice that very likely prompted Judith later to become an ardent advocate for women's rights.

Judith's father was a leading member of the merchant class that thrived when, beginning in the late 18th century, Gloucester was pursuing its maritime fortunes as a trading port. The wharves, stores and fish flakes of the overseas-venturing Sargents spread all the way from Duncan Street to Vinson's Cove, covering a good deal of the present downtown waterfront. Members of the Sargent family owned scores of merchant trading vessels.

At eighteen Judith had married John Stevens, also of a top-drawer Gloucester merchant trading family. On paper it was a dream union, linking two powerful clans. After the wedding Judith always referred to Stevens respectfully and loyally. But there was no talk of love, and no children in seventeen years of marriage. Winthrop Sargent built for his daughter what came to be the multi-hyphenated Sargent-Murray-Gilman-Hough house on Middle Street. He kept title to the house, though. As a savvy operator in foreign trade, Winthrop Sargent may have had doubts as to the business acumen of his son-in-law, young John Stevens.

Sargent-Murray-Gilman house, built for Judith Sargent and her first husband, John Stevens. *Author photo*

Then came John Murray to Gloucester and, in her father's parlor, Judith heard him speak the doctrine of universal salvation. The young woman, twenty-three and already trapped in a barren marriage for four years, met the thirty-three-year-old apostle of what seemed to her a liberating theology – and he was earnest and direct and inspired, yet had in his eyes tragic despair over his lost family.

Early Gloucester records speak little of romance. Most expressions of enduring affection are of a man talking about his boat. Thus the long-thwarted love of Judith and John Murray was something exceptional. Soon after Judith first heard John deliver a sermon, she wrote to him of how he had transformed her spiritual nature. She hoped that Murray would accept the friendship of one who wished to approach him "with the freedom of a sister" speaking to a highly esteemed brother.

Judith found in John Murray a correspondent she dared confide in, confessing her ambitions. For she yearned to write. She had read Samuel Richardson's English novels, *Pamela* and *Clarissa*, when she was in her teens, and she adopted the ornamented style of romantic novels. A grove was a "woody Vale," nature was frequently "clad in gay variety," and "Musick" was "wafted upon the kindly breeze." A poem was expected to express "sensibility," and Judith exerted considerable effort in that direction, her poems straying into the "haunts of memory," with thoughts recorded faithfully but "with humid eye."

Lucius Manley Sargent said of his Aunt Judith that "she wrote poetry by the acre," this "most kind, affectionate and excellent lady." But Lucius remembered that, as a boy, he was more impressed with Aunt Judith's cooking. "Her buckwheat cakes and symbals were incomparable." (In early New England a "symbal" was a spongy confection, a grade or two above a doughnut.) "While there was a symbal in the locker I got it."

Two years after her first letters to John Murray, Judith was hesitantly offering to send him her essays for his comments. The years went by, Judith bound in marriage to John Stevens but close to John Murray in the Universalist faith they shared. There was a suppressed urgency in her letters to him. After her feelings were wounded by a female friend, she wrote to John "I am passionately desirous to pour my complaints into the affectionate ear of sympathy."

While John Murray was in England awaiting the outcome of the litigation in Massachusetts, John Stevens failed in business. Judith's father spirited his son-in-law out of town in one of his ships, and John ended as a bankrupt exile on the tiny Dutch isle of Saint Eustatius in the Leeward Islands, halfway between Guadeloupe and Puerto Rico. Eustatius had been the busiest and richest port in the Western Hemisphere, but had gone into decline after it was taken by the British in 1781. John Stevens died there in 1786.

When John Murray returned to Gloucester in 1788, Judith was a widow. They were married the same year. By then she was thirty-seven, he forty-seven. But they were together. And Judith became joyously creative. She poured forth poems, plays, essays. As "Constantia" she published the romantic novel, *Margaretta.* Her poems were published under the pseudonym of "Honora Martesia" in the *Boston Weekly Magazine.* She wrote two plays, "The Traveller Returned" and "The Medium, or Virtue Triumphant." These were the first plays authored by an American woman to be performed on stage, in Boston. The reviews were not encouraging – especially that of Robert Treat Paine, namesake son of a signer of the Declaration of Independence. The younger Paine was repeatedly disowned by his scandalized father after he chose a life, and a wife, in the theatre. Paine wrote of "The Traveller Returned," "The traveller has gone to that bourne from which no traveller ever did return."

But if Judith's poems and plays are now historical curiosities, the essays she wrote between 1782 and 1794 are in a class with those of leading American essayists of the time, including that champion of American English, Noah Webster. They appeared first in the *Massachusetts Magazine*, the hopeful first Boston literary magazine (it was launched in 1789 and expired seven years later). *Massachusetts Magazine* featured fiction and poetry in the Richardson style, such as William Hill Brown's "The Power of Sympathy," and a piece of gothic fiction by Sarah Keating Wood with the mesmerizing title "Julia and the Illuminated Baron."

John Murray, proud of his wife's published works, also saw their practical value. They might help support her when he was no longer alive to earn his modest clergyman's salary. Despite the prosperity of the Sargents, Judith was not independently a woman of means. So with John's aid and encouragement she gathered together her pieces from the *Massachusetts Magazine.* They were published in three volumes in 1798 under the title *The Gleaner – A Miscellaneous Production*, by "Constantia."

The dedication was to President John Adams. John Murray had come to know John and Abigail Adams aboard ship when he returned from England in 1788. Adams was also listed as one of the 800 subscribers to *The Gleaner.* Another subscriber was George Washington,

Murray's old Commander-in-Chief. When Judith was later introduced to President Washington she saw remote Augustan grandeur, as in Gilbert Stuart's portrait of Washington, not suspecting the fires that burned within. Washington had fiercely disciplined himself in the restraint he had learned from studying the Greek Stoics.

The pieces in Judith's *The Gleaner* included instructive advice to young women, such as the virtues of cultivating natural beauty of person and spirit while, as she said, shunning the fripperies of fashion and cosmetic artifice. To support her arguments for female equality, Judith Murray cited examples throughout history proving that women were as brave and resourceful as men, and equally "susceptible of every literary acquirement."

In 1793 John Murray answered a call to the Universalist congregation in Boston, and he and Judith left Gloucester. They had their misfortunes. Their first child, a son, died in infancy. But Judith bore a daughter, Julia Maria, who lived, married and had children of her own. John died and Judith moved to Natchez, Mississippi to join her daughter's family. Judith died in 1820 and, in her will, left $200 to be distributed "for the benefit of the needy widows, and others who are poor, of my native place, who do not receive their chief support from the Town." In Gloucester ninety-six widows and sixty-one other needy citizens shared a final largesse from a woman they scarcely remembered – that spirited daughter of the Sargents, she who lived in the fine house on Middle Street.

Judith and the other heirs to Winthrop Sargent's estate had sold that house to Major Frederick Gilman. Originally from Exeter, New Hampshire, the Major was beguiled by Abigail Somes, daughter of a Front Street tavern-keeper in Gloucester. They married and their son Samuel, born in Judith's house, in due course became a Harvard man, Class of 1811. He is best known as the author of "Fair Harvard," crooned with emotional devotion by generations of sons, and perhaps even by some later daughters, of that pride of Massachusetts academia which, in her time, would never have considered admitting Judith Sargent.

A convinced Unitarian, the Reverend William Bentley dismissed John Murray's Universalism as "new vampt mysticisms." Bentley was, it must be admitted, not a Cape Ann man. He was pastor of Salem's East Church from 1783 until his death in 1819. However, much urbane and sprightly information on Cape Ann in the age of the Murrays is to be found in the voluminous *Diary* of the Reverend Bentley.

Behind Bentley's clerical collar was a Renaissance man. He was a dedicated bibliophile with a library of four thousand volumes on German romanticism, Classical drama, New England history, the civilizations of the Far East. It was said to be the best private library in the new nation, after that of Thomas Jefferson.

While some in Salem valued Bentley as a man of God, others prized him as a one-man world news agency. An accomplished linguist, he subscribed to journals from across Europe and the Middle East, scanning them for news items he translated and passed on to the Salem papers. His reputation for erudition spread as far as Boston where he was elected to membership in the Massachusetts Historical Society. Whether he was impressed with this honor is questionable – he later received a polite reminder from the Society that his dues were twelve years in arrears.

Bentley walked everywhere, when not hobbled by gout, and swam in the invigorating tides of Massachusetts Bay from March to October. Ecclesiastical duties frequently drew him to Gloucester, and in September of 1790 he arrived for a military review. "After the firings, a few bickerings happened but soon subsided, & the Regiment marched into the Harbour Streets and dismissed." And then the fun began. "There was a very genteel assembly of Ladies, &c., in the evening, the Boston Band, &c. I dined with Col. Pierce, Tea at D. Roger's, supped at Epes Sargeants, & Breakfasted at Captain D. Pierce's on Saturday morning."

The following spring he was again at Gloucester's harbor village. "In the evening we were conducted to a Mr. Sergeants at whose house music was prepared for the evening." (Like most writers of the 18th century before the tyranny of dictionaries, Reverend Bentley saw no virtue in spelling a word twice the same way.) Bentley continues, "There was a considerable number of gentlemen & Ladies & very handsome entertainment. The instrumental & vocal music were well performed. We have nothing like it in Essex." (The later town of Essex was always "Chebacco" in Bentley's *Diary*, so here he may mean the politer regions

Foster's wharf, Manchester. Chebacco boat at left with pinkeys behind and a flakeyard back on the shore.

of Essex *County*.) In any case, "The Conviviality is remarkable."

Bentley relished these innocent entertainments, as on that day when he "Rode with Miss N.B. into Danvers, where we spent an agreeable day with a pleasing company of Country Lasses. We walked, we sung, we played, & time never hung heavy upon our hands." All those picnics gave Dr. Bentley a rotund silhouette. He carried over two hundred pounds on a frame barely five foot in elevation. But Bentley had a hearty constitution. He needed it, when the business of the Lord called him to Cape Ann. The roads were terrible, the countryside so littered with boulders that Bentley declared the old meeting house by the Green to be in "the most rocky parish I ever beheld."

Ignoring discomforts, Bentley traveled everywhere on Cape Ann. And penned illuminating details of his adventures. At Halibut Point "We then put out into the bay among the wherries which are small flat bottom boats & are as numerous as the Jebacco [Chebacco] boats, & which in good weather make two fares a day & sometimes take as many as five hundred Cod & Haddock. They are rowed cross handed by one man & even by boys of 10 & 12 years." Alas, the day of his visit was not a good one for a landsman. "We succeeded in fishing & for the first time I caught several haddock, but the wind breezing, I was soon too sick to persevere."

Undaunted, Bentley was next on a fishing excursion off Eastern Point. "Our party consisted of above 60 persons of both sexes. With Col Pearce in a skif we caught several dozen of perch, & after two we dined in a friendly manner. Another party on a Sloop larger than our own furnished us with Cod from the Bay, & after dinner till Tea[,] parties were engaged in Walking, dancing, singing & Quoiting, & Swinging, & every amusement we could imagine. There was but one instrument of Music with us, which was a fiddle brought by its owner to pick up a few coppers. To see him play with it upon his head, under his arm, &c., furnished a pleasure which the happiness of ignorance may innocently occasion." In other words everybody was having a foolishly good time.

Everywhere Reverend Bentley ventured he squirreled away useful information. He collected tips on the local cuisine: "In Cape Ann they tell us that *Hog Island in Jebacco*, offers the *best Veal* in the Country, & that their own Springy tho' Rocky *Hills* afford the *best mutton* in America." An image to conjure with: fat sheep licking at cool springs on Dogtown Common.

One day Reverend Bentley sought out a professional to carve the stubble from his chin. "We stopped in [Gloucester] Harbour to be shaved by a woman, named Becky who in due form exercises all the functions of a *Barber*. She has her shop decorated with all the pictures which belong to such places of resort . . . with all the songs which are in the taste of the varied multitude of her customers . . . . She shaves well but has few attractions of her sex." A rare ungallant comment from the inquisitive, gregarious Reverend William Bentley. Becky was the daughter of James Broom, who operated his tavern and barber shop at the corner of Pleasant and Middle Streets. If Becky's charms went undetected by Bentley, such was not the case with Andrew Ingersol. Andrew was smitten either by Rebecca's attributes or her tonsorial skills, and they were wed.

Bentley's hosts, "Capt. D. Pierce" and "Col Pearce," were, like the principal figures of the Sargent and Stevens families, members of a prosperous new class in Gloucester – men quick to pounce upon opportunities in maritime commerce after the Revolution. The next epoch in the town's fortunes would belong to them.

CHAPTER 4

Shipmasters and Merchants

GLOUCESTER BECAME a deep-sea trading port toward the end of the 18th century. An "India Company" was formed by a group of merchants of the town. They fitted out a ship, the *Winthrop and Mary*, that entered the South Pacific trade, made two successful trips to Calcutta, then disappeared homeward-bound from Sumatra. There were at the time some forty ships, brigs, schooners and sloops engaged in trade with the Baltic, Bilbao and the West Indies, mostly with outbound cargoes of fish, then sometimes sailing on to Mediterranean ports for further trading, or returning direct to Gloucester with olives, wine and perhaps European manufactures as well. More than two dozen Gloucester skippers were also making regular voyages delivering fish and lumber to Surinam on the shoulder of South America.

In these vessels Gloucester's sons gained an intimate acquaintance with the sea, and the town contributed a sizeable number of ships' officers and seamen to merchant trading vessels making trips from other Atlantic ports, mainly Boston. One such sea dog was Captain Epes Sargent, born in Gloucester in 1784. This Epes belonged to a branch of the family that was respectable but of slender means. When his parents died he was raised by his grandfather until, at the age of fifteen, he went as cabin boy in the ship *Eliza* bound from Boston to the East Indies. Epes proved himself a reliable hand aloft, and decided to follow the sea. In Gloucester between voyages he studied navigation. He sailed before the mast to Tenerife in the Canary Islands on the *Astrea* out of Boston, officered by Gloucestermen: Solomon Stanwood, Captain; George Sawyer, First Mate; Eliphalet Davis, Second Mate. When Epes earned a berth as

Gloucester harbor in 1837, when the American merchant fleet counted many ships' officers and seamen from Gloucester.

an officer it was as second mate on the brig *Greyhound* under Captain Isaac Elwell of Gloucester.

After he became another of those Gloucester captains himself, Epes earned handsome returns for the owners of the vessels he commanded. In 1818 he retired from the sea, moved to Boston and decided to try his own hand as a merchant trader. After "many losses, crosses and disappointments" he returned to the vocation he knew best, that of ship's master. On one trip to Russia in the brig *Nectar* he took along his son, inevitably also named Epes, of whom we shall hear more. Captain Epes died in 1853.

Beginning with his first voyage, Captain Epes had recorded his adventures. "I commenced keeping a journal, or the 'ship's way,' as it is termed." This "ship's way" he culled for reminiscences he addressed to his grandson (another Epes). In the early paragraphs the reader can sense the apprehension of a fifteen-year-old leaving his familiar

Gloucester home for the first time to become a seaman.

> I well remember the first time I was ordered aloft, in a dark squally night, to furl the mizzen top gallant sail; it is true, I mounted aloft with fear that I should not succeed in what I was ordered to do, yet I was determined to try, and after struggling with the wind, that took the sail from me as fast as I rolled it up, by dint of perseverance, succeeded in rolling up, and making fast the sail, and having once succeeded, I was ever after, able to manage it, or any other light sail, that I was called upon to take care of.

Soon the mate was treating Epes as a sailor, not just cabin boy, and tutored him in navigation when they had reached China and were lying to in Whampoa waiting for cargo. Captain Epes's descriptions of the *Eliza* at anchor in the Pearl River roads rival the accounts of the Salem captains who visited that teeming entrepôt of the China trade. Despite the general exclusion of foreigners, Epes managed to enter the city of Canton itself where he bought parasols, silk handkerchiefs and a china tea set for his sisters back in Gloucester. But he did not venture into Canton again. Smallpox had broken out in the city.

Then the *Eliza* sailed south for the spice islands and was on course for "Sincapore" when the anchor parted in a gale. The vessel was adrift and helpless until the winds abated and they could sail back to Malacca for a new "hook." All was strange and exotic and colorful, the turbaned headgear of the Malaysian natives, their long robes, the uncomprehended chatter and tumult in the marketplace.

The musings at sea of another Gloucester square-rigger captain, Solomon H. Davis, were very different from those of Captain Sargent, at least in his early journal entries. Solomon was the son of Captain Elias Davis, whose home is today the core structure of the Cape Ann Historical Museum. Solomon was twenty-five when he sailed as master of the *Corporal Trim*, destination Valparaiso. From the first day at sea his journal effervesces with memorized verse and original poems. He is smitten by nature, effusing over the beauties of the ocean by day and the stars by night. He reads sentimental novels, such as *Hobomok* by Miss Francis of Duxbury, *Love Without a Doubt*, and *Emily; or A Wife's Affection*, which he finds "very interesting; but somewhat pathetic" (in the usage of the time that meant he found it dripping with emotion).

On the other hand he criticizes *The Three Perils of Woman* for being "not very sentimental." One day he recorded in his journal: "finished the love part – next comes deceit and falsehood." Upon finishing the novel he was chastened, but hopeful. "Undoubtedly very true, however – believe it relates to some of the sex – but not all."

What was provoking the captain's agitated emotions? Love, of course, as was evident from the verses Solomon Davis wrote after getting under way:

> The brown shore of Gloucester in distance grows blue;
> And that gem of earth's treasures -
> The scene of past pleasures,
> The land of my childhood – fades fast from my view;
> But I've 'scaped from the trammels – the word is – away -
> Then x_____x, my sweet one, look up, and be gay.

Far out on the ocean wastes, young Solomon was pining for his betrothed, "x_____x", who was none other than Mary Babson, sister of historian John Babson. Throughout his voyage along the coast of South America, Mary was constantly in Captain Davis' thoughts. And in this lovelorn condition he continued reading romantic novels. Off Tierra del Fuego not a word about the fierce challenges of rounding Cape Horn. Instead Solomon is caught up in *Flirtation*, another novel from his trove of shipboard reading. He is "much interested with Lord Mowbray's account of his flirtation with Rosalinda." He also judges Lord Mowbray's "opinion of Italian music, etc. very good."

Captain Davis's fidelity to Mary Babson is tested when, after three months at sea, he finds himself ashore among the señoritas of Buenos Aires. "The females of this country are very beautiful, very affable in conversation, and uncommonly polite. Their dress is very handsome, - gowns of silk, muslin, etc., coming up just high enough to display a beautiful alabaster neck, seen through a lace handkerchief . . . ." A

Señoritas of Buenos Aires. Young Capt. Solomon Davis found them especially attractive after he had spent long months at sea.

splash of sea water over the rail may have cooled Solomon's blood. "Perhaps I may conceive them handsome from the circumstance of the length of time since I saw any damsels."

Month after month went by without a letter from Mary, his own fairest damsel. "That is the hardest thing yet . . . to think my friends [i.e., Mary] have forgotten me, and [I] have made up my mind in return, to forget them – if possible." Of course it was not possible for

Solomon Davis to forget Mary Babson. They married the following year and in due course had four children.

Sixteen years later Solomon resumed his journal as master of the bark *Mindora*, sailing from Boston destination Oahu. Captain Davis is no longer awash with youthful passions. He is a solid, subdued middle-aged shipmaster weighted with responsibilities. There is no poetry. Little mental diversion, even: "I don't think I shall be able to read a great deal this passage owing to interruptions I constantly receive." His journal entries are now all business, recording the loading of cargo and the state of the sea. He frets about the skills of crewmen who cannot handle the sails properly.

The dangers of the sea are more foreboding than when he was young. He fears the "terrible ordeal" of rounding Cape Horn. There is much attention to religion, and endless gnawing worries about his wife and children thousands of miles away, months from any personal news. In frozen latitudes near the tip of South America he dreams of sharing springtime Gloucester with his family.

Solomon knew he had changed. But thought himself the better for it. More profound in his thoughts and emotions. "Talk of youthful love and happiness in the early part of marriage – I find my love and affection increases as I grow older." And all was not homesickness and gloom. Just as young Captain Epes Sargent had captured in his journals the color-drenched, chaotic trading at Canton, the middle-aged Captain Solomon Davis carefully recorded his impressions of the royal palace at Oahu, in the twilight of the last Hawaiian dynasty. He was presented to His Majesty, Kamehameha the Third, absolute monarch of what, in Captain Davis's time, were the Sandwich Islands. A tour of the royal palace included a view of the king's eight-by ten-foot bed, which must have seemed colossal indeed to a captain just ashore from his cramped cabin.

In the audience room he and other guests were formally introduced to the King and "the Chiefs, heads of the departments, and Ladies of the Court. They were all in their best attire. The King, etc. were in full uniform; the Chiefs were fine looking men" (one he judged to be six foot seven). "After the ceremony of presentation, we promenaded around the room, and talked with the ladies, Chiefs, etc. I was quite at home, as there was not a person there, with whom I had the least acquaintance; and I must say I received much attention . . . I am fond of attention – and, indeed, passed an hour and a half very pleasantly." He knew the reason for his popularity: "Stout men, here, are held in great esteem and veneration; and I, for the first time in my life, feel a sort of pride in my corpulency." It had come to that. The once dashing young Captain Solomon Davis now found that, with age, his great social advantage was his girth.

Captain Gorham P. Low was another of Cape Ann's trading ship captains who sailed out of Boston but returned home to Gloucester. He set down his recollections, drawn from logs and memory, long after he had prosperously retired from the sea at thirty-six.

Captain Low's beginnings were typical for a Cape Ann boy bred to the sea. He was born on a farm in Gloucester, but his father had been a sailor and all his brothers earned their living as seamen. He made his first trip to sea at sixteen, in 1822, on the brig *Falcon*, bound for Copenhagen and St. Petersburg. His brother David was master and part-owner. It was the first of a long series of voyages: to Charleston before the Civil War, to Pernambuco in Brazil, to Liverpool on packet ship runs, to Scandinavia and the Baltic, and around the world with stops at the Hawaiian Islands, Canton, the Philippines.

In 1826 Low shipped as chief mate aboard the brig *Cadet*. The master was a true Captain Queeg, a psychotic martinet of the quarter deck. But Gorham proved himself the tyrant's equal and in the process had a rip-roaring 'round-the-world cruise. Through the Caribbean and along the coast of Brazil they ran the gauntlet of pirate slave traders. Safe in Montevideo, Low chatted with Captain Eliphalet Davis of Gloucester and Captain Oliver G. Lane from Annisquam. The harbors of the world were thick with Cape Ann skippers.

Ashore in Chile, Low borrowed a fiery Andalusian horse and outgalloped the local caballeros along the beach, proud as they were of their horsemanship. Low was saddle-savvy from rounding up his father's cows on Dogtown Common. At Callao, the port of Lima, he was offering items of his cargo for sale to members of the foreign colony. One "rickety-built" customer tried on a dress coat and Low gave it a tug from behind, telling the man that it fit him perfectly –

Capt. Gorham Low spent a full career of adventure at sea before "swallowing the anchor" and retiring to Gloucester – at age 36.
Courtesy Cape Ann Historical Museum

"like a purser's shirt to a handspike," or like "a duck's foot in the mud." He made the sale, and said that was the first and last time he had ever tried his hand as a salesman of ready-made men's wear. The customer, he learned, was the United States Consul to Chile, William Tudor, namesake son of lawyer William Tudor who had defended John Murray's right to preach Universalism.

By 1830 Gorham Low was a trusted ship's captain and sailed several voyages to northern Europe as master of the bark *Garland*. In his new and elevated social position he was invited to dine with John Randolph, President Andrew Jackson's emissary to Copenhagen. Then off for a weekend in Sweden with the very best people. "Of course, they all came in carriages. Many of them were officers in the army who had the fiercest kind of whiskers, and they wore their buskins high. There were ladies of high rank and merchants of all countries, some with ladies and some, like myself, lone birds. I never saw so large a gathering for a private party." But then midnight struck and Low's carriage turned into a pumpkin. "Soon after, I returned to Gloucester, where I assisted my father in getting in the crops."

The people back in Gloucester did not read the journals of the likes of Captains Sargent, Davis and Low who regularly entered fabled ports in the course of their far voyages. These accounts were not seen by the public until many years later. But the neighbors had heard the exploits recounted first-hand, and visited the houses of the sea captains, supercargoes and merchants, the rooms furnished with export from the foreign trade. Porcelain mandarins and gold lacquer boxes and sandalwood and ivory fans lurked in the shadows. For parties a white Canton or rose porcelain serving set would be brought out.

How these families lived was recounted by Alfred Mansfield Brooks. When in his late eighties Brooks decided it was time to get down on paper his recollections of growing up in Gloucester in the company of a grandmother and great-aunts whose memories of Gloucester's merchant shipping aristocracy reached far back down the nineteenth century, and a great-great aunt who was a child when George Washington was President. Brooks never got around to finishing these memoirs, and they remained as disorganized fragments for a dozen years. Joseph E. Garland organized and edited Brooks's manuscript and saw it into print as *Gloucester Recollected – A Familiar History* (1974).

Professor Brooks was remembered by Joe Garland as someone perpetually active, interested and amused. Brooks belonged to, and wrote of, Gloucester's deepwater merchant trading elite. He is authority for the social gulf that existed between the families of cosmopolitan, world traveling square-rig captains, and those of fishing skippers whose farthest venturings were to the Newfoundland Banks.

There was no "codfish aristocracy" among the fishing captains. Only the families of the maritime merchants could, like his aunts, lay claim to a gentility buttressed by capital reserves.

Of course, as Brooks admits, the fisheries proved to have greater staying power than the "carrying trade." Commerce with Russia, Europe, Britain, the West Indies and Surinam came and went, but fishing endured. Still, few fishing families prospered. Many were left in poverty when a husband or father was lost at sea. Brooks says members of the prosperous old trading families lent a hand by hiring the fishermen's widows as housekeepers and washerwomen. Ladies from the merchant class volunteered for the Female Charitable Association that distributed yard goods to be sewn up as clothing, and they paid for coal deliveries to the needy. A certain noblesse oblige, but carried forward without airs and with good-hearted sympathy. Brooks might not have been aware that the proud fishermen themselves also contributed to the best of their ability to the support of families left behind by lost crewmen. Deductions from the shares of earnings paid to schooner hands were earmarked for the Fishermen's and Seamen's Widows' and Orphans' Aid Society that was organized in 1859.

Brooks's ancient female relatives and their friends populated ample West End houses with gardens that reached down to the wharves of Harbor Cove. They lived a hothouse existence, terribly proper but tut-tutting with amusement at the scandalous foreign exploits of their brothers and uncles.

The fact that Captains Solomon Davis and Gorham Low regularly sailed from Boston is significant. The ports along the coast east and north of that center – Salem, Gloucester, Newburyport and Portsmouth, New Hampshire – did not have the financial resources needed to finance long ocean voyages in trading vessels ever increasing in size and carrying capacity.

But Gloucester, for one, was determined to remain a maritime town. It did so by returning to the economic base upon which the port was founded: fishing. Casual in-shore day fishing gave way to dropping lines, and later trawls, from sleek vessels that could pursue halibut off the coast of Newfoundland, and later on Georges Bank.

And could follow the migrating mackerel from the St. Lawrence, off the shores of Prince Edward Island and Nova Scotia, and into southern waters. And reap great harvests of cod, long the mainstay of the fisheries, on the rich off-shore grounds. It was the mid-19th century, and the great age of the Gloucester fisheries was under way.

CHAPTER 5

Sagas of the Schoonermen

THE DEFINING SYMBOL of Gloucester is the clipper schooner, the classic configuration that dominated the harbor from the 1860s through to the close of the 19th century, and a bit beyond. The Gloucester schooner had perhaps the most satisfying profile of hull shape and sail plan ever devised for a wind-driven vessel, working or recreational. It was the pride of Cape Ann. And also its sorrow, for the terrible loss of life in these fast but storm-vulnerable thoroughbreds.

These were the vessels that evolved when Gloucester opted for fishing as its hope for economic survival. The right of Americans to fish the eastern shores of North America had been secured by John Adams. When Adams was in Paris in 1782 negotiating a peace treaty to end the Revolutionary War, the representatives on the British side of the table wanted to change the wording of an American "right of fishing" within three leagues of the Canadian coast to read as permission to do so. Adams said the United States would never consider begging by-your-leave from his Gracious Majesty. He asserted that New England had fought long and hard to claim domination of the fisheries over the French, and America's right to that industry should be beyond dispute.

The British negotiators conceded the point, and Adams's terms were written into the preliminary draft of the peace treaty. He did not celebrate his diplomatic successes, though. Thinking ruefully of all the juicy legal work he was passing up back in Boston, Adams wrote to his wife Abigail that the only legacy he would be able to bequeath to their children was freedom – and their right to catch fish on the Newfoundland Banks.

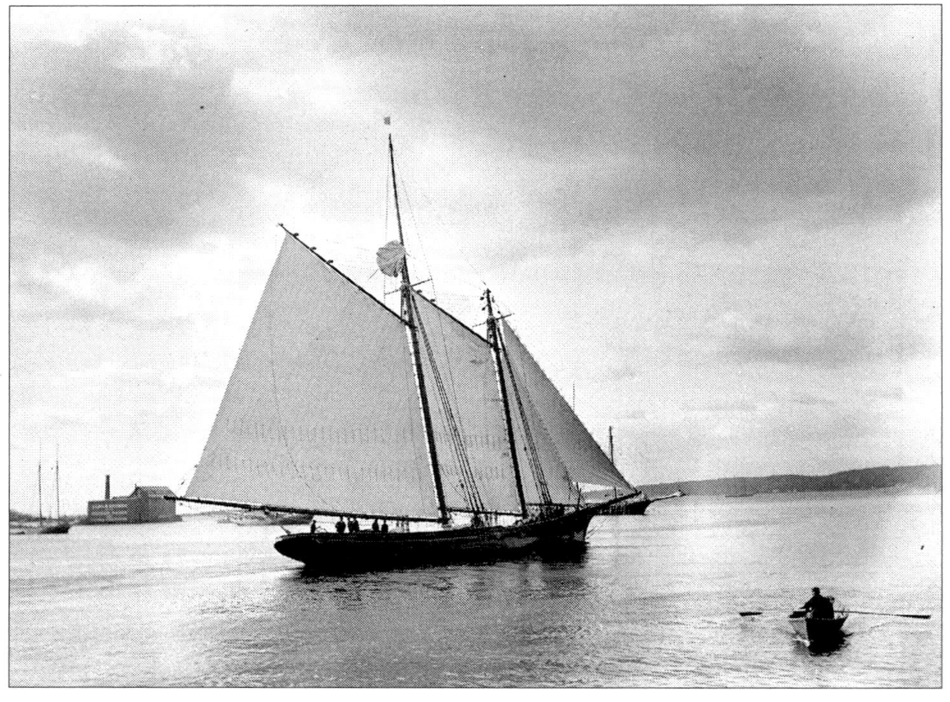

Schooner *Monitor* outward bound from Gloucester harbor, passing the Paint Manufactory. This was the classic configuration of the "fast and able" Gloucester schooners. *Courtesy Cape Ann Historical Museum*

Later American Presidents did not defend these fishing rights vigorously enough, and they were lost. What was needed was another John Adams, the strongest diplomatic champion the Gloucester fishermen ever had – before, during and after his Presidency. But that new champion did not appear. Still, American vessels had sufficient access to the rich Banks off the Maritimes shores when Gloucester committed to the fisheries in mid-19th century.

Gloucester did not rush into its new role without doubts. Fishing was deemed a somewhat demeaning occupation by deep-water sailors.

Even when Captain John Smith touted the lucrative promise of New England's fishing grounds, he had been almost apologetic in suggesting that gentlemen would do well to invest in pursuing this "base commoditie." Captain Sylvanus Smith, who had known the Gloucester waterfront from before 1850, said that, until the middle of the 19th century, Gloucester's young seamen would not sign on to go fishing when they could find a berth on a vessel engaged in the glamorous Canton trade. But as those opportunities dwindled, most accepted the inevitable and became fishermen. Even then, as Sylvanus noted, those recruits preferred inshore day fishing, by which they could sleep in their own beds at home each night.

But profitable pursuit of the fish required progressively longer trips at sea. As Gloucester took its fishing more seriously it built bigger vessels: the swift schooners, with crews of sixteen men or more, that carried profitable catches back from distant grounds. There were statistics enough. In 1847, 287 fishing vessels out of Gloucester (half of them of less than forty tons burthen) had landed 28,000 pounds of fish, mainly cod. There were fewer than 2,000 crewmen fishing from those boats, including 186 boys. The total value of the catch was under $600,000. In 1875 the catch was being measured in barrels and quintals (one quintal equaling 100 pounds), for a total value of close to $4 million. By 1886 there were 469 vessels in the fleet, owned by fifty-three firms.

The demand for fish was fueled by improved means of getting them to market. After the Civil War, when Gloucester schooners were bringing increasing quantities of cod, halibut, haddock and mackerel to port, much of the catch was packed in ice and shipped from the Eastern Railroad terminal. Ponds were dammed all over Cape Ann from which to saw ice in the winter, and huge ice houses were built. The Homans ice house on Fernwood Lake, for one, was the biggest building in Massachusetts when it was built, and held 10,000 tons of ice.

Despite all precautions, though, iced fish often spoiled on the long journey to neighborhood fish markets. Gloucester's Gorton-Pew Fisheries persevered in packing salt-cured cod in one-pound wooden boxes, and salt mackerel in wooden kegs. The wisdom of this seemingly antiquated marketing strategy was confirmed when the Gorton fleet grew to over fifty-five vessels, manned by a thousand fishermen. Then Clarence Birdseye moved to Gloucester and perfected his flash freezing technique, based on practices of the Inuits he had observed when posted as a naturalist to the Arctic. Gorton recognized the potential of Birdseye's innovations, began freezing its fish, and became a major player in the frozen food industry that transformed American eating habits.

Statistics about the development of the fisheries in Gloucester could be cited endlessly. But the era of schooner fishing in the 19th century was more than numbers. The beauty of the vessels and the perils and courage of the men who sailed them symbolized something fine in the human spirit. Someone, certainly, would rise to the challenge of capturing the fearsome adventures in words.

The first to make literature of the schooner epic was George H. Procter. He and his brother Francis were sons of a Gloucester shipmaster in the South American trade. But their own interests were in publishing. Francis was the businessman, two years older than George. It was George who edited their publications for nearly six decades. In 1853 the brothers launched their first newspaper, the monthly *Procter's Able Sheet*. This was a bulletin of fishing news that Francis printed and George hawked through the lanes and along the wharves of the waterfront. Business prospered and in 1856 the brothers launched the *Gloucester Advertiser*, later renamed the *Cape Ann Advertiser* which became a weekly. And for good measure, the Procters inaugurated the *Gloucester Daily Times* in 1888. The *Cape Ann Advertiser* continued under George's firm editorial hand until the company merged the *Advertiser* with the *Times* in 1901.

The Procter publishing enterprises mixed solid journalism with the extravagant promotion typical of periodicals in the mid-19th century. "The *Cape Ann Advertiser*," their notices trumpeted, was "a handsomely printed sheet of Thirty-Two Columns, issued every Friday morning . . . . Each issue has all the local news of Cape Ann, together with all the Fishing Items, a reliable Fish Market, Good Story, and choice Miscellaneous Reading Matter, making it emphatically The People's Paper!"

George Procter normally maintained an editor's anonymity in the

George and Francis Procter (left and right – man in center unidentified) outside their "Old Corner" stationery shop and newspaper printing plant in 1882. *Courtesy Cape Ann Historical Museum*

Procter Brothers' newspapers and books. His editorial utterances were "vigorous, logical, and strong . . . always clean and free from sensationalism." Occasionally he signed articles about Gloucester and the fisheries that appeared in *Scribner's Monthly* and *Lippincott's Magazine.*

In 1873, when George was thirty-eight and had been editor of the brothers' periodicals for twenty years, he compiled a volume, *The Fishermen's Memorial and Record Book*, which he described as "my first-born literary venture in book form." He hoped "the fishermen and their families may find [the book] of sufficient interest to insure . . . a welcome place on the home book-shelf, or a snug position among the

THE

Fishermen's Own Book,

COMPRISING

THE LIST OF MEN AND VESSELS LOST FROM THE PORT OF GLOUCESTER, MASS., FROM 1874 TO APRIL 1, 1882,

AND

A TABLE OF LOSSES FROM 1830,

TOGETHER WITH

VALUABLE STATISTICS OF THE FISHERIES,

ALSO

NOTABLE FARES, NARROW ESCAPES, STARTLING ADVENTURES, FISHERMEN'S OFF-HAND SKETCHES, BALLADS, DESCRIPTIONS OF FISHING TRIPS

AND

OTHER INTERESTING FACTS AND INCIDENTS CONNECTED WITH THIS BRANCH OF MARITIME INDUSTRY.

GLOUCESTER:
PROCTER BROTHERS, Publishers,
CAPE ANN ADVERTISER OFFICE.

Title page of George Procter's *Fishermen's Own Book*, a second sumptuous catch-all of schooner fishing losses, facts and lore, published nine years after *The Fishermen's Memorial and Record Book.*

reading matter on board the vessel." George Procter did not expect the book would interest anyone beyond the Gloucester fishing community. It was his tribute to the men engaged in that hazardous trade. "For some time past it has been my desire to prepare a Memorial Volume, which would contain, among other matters of interest to the fishermen, as well as to the large number of vessel owners and fitters, a record which should be as complete as could possibly be gathered, of that vast number who have been lost from the port of Gloucester, while toiling on the fishing grounds, in the arduous avocation of wresting from old ocean her finny treasures."

Listed are all the vessels and crews lost from the port of Gloucester from 1830 to 1873. There is grim poetry in the names of many of the doomed vessels catalogued by Procter: *Maid of the Mill, Only Daughter, Enchantress, Arbutus, Oolong, Young America, Neptune's Bride, Light of Home, Seaman's Pride.*

Besides memorializing the human losses, George Procter meant to entertain his fishermen readers, with "off-hand sketches, big trips, tales of narrow escapes, maritime poetry, and other matters of interest to these toilers of the sea." Plus engraved illustrations with explanatory captions. There were ads for products of interest to the fishermen, too, such as that placed by J. F. Carter who, "having devoted my whole time exclusively for years to the manufacture and improvement of oil clothing," modestly claimed "a superiority for my goods over all other manufacturers."

By gathering three-quarters of a century of Gloucester disaster, struggle and survival into *Fishermen's Memorial,* George Procter provided a mother lode of schooner fishing lore that was mined by later writers like Kipling, T. S. Eliot, James B. Connolly and Charles Olson.

Procter told the original incidents dramatically but with restraint and respect. As in his description of crewmen Marsh and Norwood on the mast of the shipwrecked Gloucester schooner *Neptune's Bride* at Malcomb's Ledge, Maine, in 1860. Their shipmates, swamped in the lifeboat, had climbed onto a ledge as the tide crept up. Marsh and Norwood, "holding on in the darkness, heard the men on the ledge talking of their chances for life, and earnestly wishing that they could only get on board the vessel." As the tide built over the ledge, "during the next hour, [Marsh and Norwood] could not avoid hearing their [shipmates'] struggles, as the sea rose, crested with raging foam, and claimed one after the other as its victim." There are no imaginings of the final agonies of the victims. Gloucester families could well be spared those details. Procter's understated account told his readers all they needed to know of the tragic end of the men on the ledge, and of Norwood who soon was swept from the mast. Marsh would be the sole survivor.

Sometimes the sea relented, though, and the men could save themselves. As when the schooner *Onward*, Captain Wilkes, "shipped a heavy sea, which capsized her and carried away both masts, bowsprit and the upper-works, even with the deck. The man who was keeping watch stood in the companion-way, and, seeing the sea coming, jumped below, pulling over the slide in season to keep the water from pouring into the cabin. It is supposed that she rolled completely over, as, when she righted, part of the shrouds were under the keel, and floated on the opposite side." The crew jury-rigged masts and improvised a set of sails from their bedclothes. With a half-broken compass "they shaped their course for home, the wind being fair."

On the passage they were spied by the schooner *Matchless*, of Boston. Appalled at the devastated condition of the *Onward*, the captain of the *Matchless* offered to take off the men. Captain Wilkes conveyed his respects, but said he and his crew were "getting along very comfortably," thank you, and were resolved to stick by their vessel. When the *Onward* eventually reached Rockport "hundreds of people visited her, and she was pronounced by all the most complete wreck that ever arrived at this port."

Then there was Procter's happy ending to the tale of a seaman given up for lost. When the schooner *Sevo* was run down by the steamer *Huntress* off Thacher's Island in 1839, twelve-year-old Winthrop Sargent caught hold of a splitting table as it floated by. He was taken aboard the steamer and, on its return trip, dropped off at Eastern Point. He walked home and, at four in the morning, tapped on his father's bedroom window. The sire was much put out to see Winthrop's pale spirit returned from the dead, as he supposed, and tapping on the pane. It took a good deal of convincing to get the father's head out from under the bedclothes, but Winthrop "gave evidence that he was alive and well, which caused great rejoicing in the family."

The most glorious tale in *The Fishermen's Memorial*, from Gloucester's point of view, was that of the recapture of the schooner *E. A. Horton* from the Canadian Dominion forces. Procter savors the sequence of events. In 1871 the *Horton*, accused of fishing in Canadian waters, was boarded and taken into Guysboro, Nova Scotia. Captain Harvey Knowlton, one of the owners, was determined to get his vessel back. He made his way Down East and through Nova Scotia, passing himself off as a prospector, showing off some quartz nuggets to anyone who doubted he was digging for gold. When he reached Canso he found some American fishermen, told them his story and they said there was nothing so low as to take a man's vessel from him. They joined up with Captain Knowlton, and the little party trekked eighteen miles through the woods to the outskirts of Guysboro harbor, taking care not to attract notice.

Knowlton's recruits holed up in a barn, while he marched into town cool as could be, telling his gold-digging story. He discovered that the *Horton*'s sails were stored in a shed, near where the *Horton* herself had been moored unguarded because her captors could not imagine that anybody would be crazy enough to try to steal her. Came a bright moonlit night and Captain Knowlton and his associates waited till the last dog had stopped barking and the last lantern had swung back from some outhouse. They crept down to the harbor, rigged the *Horton*, and pushed off in whispers. "Sail was put on . . . and with Captain Knowlton at the helm, the saucy little craft filled away, and showed a 'clean pair of heels' as she passed out of the harbor." Come morning, the Provincial in charge discovered that the *Horton* had been stolen right out from under his nose, and all hell broke loose in Guysboro.

The *Horton* was sailed home with the aid only of a compass, no charts, no nautical instruments, "the captain relying entirely on his own judgment in shaping his course." Word of the unsanctioned repossession of the *Horton* had reached Gloucester, along with a rumor that a British war steamer was in hot pursuit. The U. S. Navy responded by dispatching the supply steamer *Fortune*, bristling as menacingly as she could with two small howitzers. But the hearsay proved false and an international incident was averted. The embarrassed British Navy decided the less said the better, and dropped the matter.

When the eagerly awaited vessel sailed into Gloucester harbor, "the booming of cannon at Rocky Neck announced that the *Horton* had arrived. The news quickly spread through the town, and there was general rejoicing. Guns were fired, the bells were rung ...." Procter captures the fervor of the moment by including in his account a poem, "The *Horton's* In," by someone who signed himself "Old Locality," concluding with the verse:

> Boom! and a cannon's voice rang out;
> Boom! and a mingled cheer and shout,
> With drum and trumpet, swelled the din –
> 'The Horton's in! the Horton's in!'

More often than audacious exploits and brave survival, though, there was in *The Fishermen's Memorial* the helplessness of an unequal contest with the sea. A record of a haunting incident in the fleet appeared as "On Georges in the Terrible Gale of February 24th, 1862. The experience of one who was there for the first and last time." It was February when the fleet was sighted on the Banks: "Nearly a hundred sail, riding at their anchors, half a mile, and in some instances, a mile apart. It was a pretty sight ..." The young fisherman continues, "I began to think that the Georges fishery, after all, was not so bad as it had been represented, although it used to fret me exceedingly to see so many of the vessels lying so near together, knowing full well that, in case of a sudden storm and they dragged their anchors, chafed off their cables and went adrift, collision would be inevitable."

A fierce northeaster did come on, and the next morning ...

> .... the skipper sang out, 'There's a vessel adrift right ahead of us! stand by with your hatchet, but don't cut till you hear the word!' ... On she came! ... The drifting vessel was coming directly for us; a moment more, and the signal to cut must be given! With the swiftness of a gull she passed by, so near that I could have leaped aboard, just clearing us, and we were saved from that danger, thank God! The hopeless, terror-stricken faces of the crew we saw but a moment, as they went on to certain death. We watched the doomed craft, as she sped on her course. She struck one of the fleet, a short

distance astern, and we saw the waters close over both vessels, almost instantly, and as we gazed, they both disappeared. Then we knew that two vessels of the fleet would never again return to port.

The pitying witness, eyes meeting those of his fellow men who knew they were being swept to their deaths. It was an allegory of doom that later authors would summon up again and again.

George Procter included in his books first-hand accounts by fishing skippers. One of these was Captain Joseph Collins. Born in Islesboro, Maine, Collins had shipped in his first schooner at age ten, and at twenty-three was master of his own vessel. Somehow he had managed to educate himself and in 1879 came ashore to join the U.S. Fisheries Commission, where he wrote scores of professional articles, and ended up Chairman of the Massachusetts Fish & Game Commission.

The episodes he recalled were all in a day's fishing, however hallucinated they sound to a later age. As Captain Collins says, "On idle days, or when, late in the evening, the crew gather for their usual lunch before turning in, you will hear thrilling tales of . . . adventures, and escapes by only the breadth of a hair from boundless torture or sudden death. Nor are these 'yarns' – *they* are reserved for the gaping crowd around the store at the corner grocery ashore. When fo'c'sle men compare notes, each one knows the rest are critics, and does not draw the long bow – at least not beyond the limit of true dramatic effect. Yet whoever heard that these narrations of peril ever deterred a dory's crew from putting off when it deemed necessary?"

The most gripping tale was that of Howard Blackburn, and Captain Collins was the first to tell the full epic, after it had first been reported in the *Cape Ann Advertiser*. Collins's book, *The Fearful Experience of a Gloucester Halibut Fisherman, Astray in a Dory in a Gale off the Newfoundland Coast in Mid-Winter*, was illustrated by Captain Collins's brother Paul.

Captain Collins narrates the suffering of Howard Blackburn and Thomas Welch unflinchingly. How the two in their trawl dory set out from the *Grace L. Fears* in late January, 1883 and became separated from the schooner. How, after Welch froze to death, Blackburn rowed on and after five agonizing days made shore in Newfoundland, eventual-

It's an August day at "Fishermen's Corner," Main and Duncan Streets in Gloucester in 1875. Crewmen are gathered to catch up on the latest gossip of the fleet. *Courtesy Cape Ann Historical Museum*

ly finding shelter and aid, but over the ensuing weeks losing all his fingers and part of a foot to frostbite. The seaman Collins communicates Blackburn's hell starkly – as when he loses his mittens overboard: "Think of the presence of mind, the fortitude, the resolute determination, that are required for a man, under such fear inspiring circumstances, to calmly sit down and wait for his hands to freeze."

Who sent the fishermen out into these harsh and perilous conditions at sea? The easy assumption is that the fleet owners were portly plutocrats who had never been to sea. The reality is that many of them were products of the Gloucester waterfront themselves, men who had worked their way up as fearless skippers, then hired other captains who sold their catches at the highest prices by making the fastest trips, thereby attracting the best crews.

One of these owners was Captain Sylvanus Smith. Born in Sandy Bay in 1829, before it became Rockport, Smith made fishing trips with his father when he was eight. He dropped out of school early to fish full-time, and was a skipper by the time he was twenty. Sylvanus Smith owned his first schooner when he was twenty-two and was one of the first to enter the Newfoundland herring trade. He made freighting trips to the West Indies and carried matériel for the North during the Civil War. In 1864 he came ashore and went into partnership in a vessel-outfitting business. By the time James Pringle wrote his *History of Gloucester* in 1892, he could record that "the firm of SYLVANUS SMITH & CO. is known as one of the largest in the New England fisheries, employing a large fleet of first-class vessels."

In the late 19th century, Gloucester was spawning all the adjunct enterprises necessary to support a thriving fish industry, and Sylvanus Smith was a founder or officer of many of them: the Gloucester Salt Company, Gloucester Net & Twine, Cape Ann Anchor Works, Gloucester Safe Deposit & Trust Company. Along the way he found time to win election to the Massachusetts General Court and State Senate, and to testify as an expert on fishing issues before committees in Washington.

Sylvanus Smith summoned up his recollections of his career in a series of columns for the *Gloucester Daily Times*. His memory of the fleet of the 1830s was photographic, or perhaps daguerreotypic. He described fishermen attired in "satinet trousers, red flannel shirt, 'Guernsey' frock, a pea jacket, cow hide shoes and a tarpaulin hat." He remembered the big moments, like voting day when men (only) in the remote fishing villages along the Cape Ann shore marched in a body to vote, to the music of fife and drum, followed by a gaggle of small boys. And there were the parade drills of the Sandy Bay militia, the Sea Fencibles. Their hats bore the proud emblem "S.F." As they marched by, a cynical spectator downwind snickered that it stood for "Stinking Fishermen."

Captain Smith had, in his time, seen Gloucester shift from foreign trade to the fisheries, but said the influence of the old square-rigged fleet lingered in the local business world. The retired captains of the trading vessels ran the Marine Insurance Company merchant marine style, treating loan applicants as ordinary seamen who were expected to approach the quarter deck with hat in hand, and wait patiently to be called before the august officers. Sylvanus was not about to cool his heels in any outer office. He stomped out of the Marine Insurance Company and helped found the Gloucester Mutual Fishing Insurance Company. He and the other organizers assumed the risks of insuring the fishing fleet, even as the schooners ventured regularly onto the killer shoals of Georges Bank.

When he was eighty-six in 1915, Sylvanus Smith was persuaded to collect his *Gloucester Daily Times* articles into a little volume that was published by the paper under the title *Fisheries of Cape Ann.* The captain died the following year, having had his say.

Sylvanus Smith remembered fishermen locked into dependence on the merchant storekeepers, and this was the way of life Dr. Joseph D. Reynolds wrote about in his *Peter Gott, the Cape Ann Fisherman* (1856). After "reading Medicine" at Harvard, Dr. Reynolds launched his practice in Sandy Bay in 1833, where he and his wife Lucy settled in and began to raise their eight children. The young physician, making house calls to the fishing families along Sandy Bay and Pigeon Cove, heard their stories of struggle and survival – and creative reasons as to why he could not be paid right away.

In 1839 the doctor and his family moved around the cape to Gloucester and in 1846, when the Cape Ann Savings Bank was chartered, Dr. Reynolds was one of the incorporators, along with historian John J. Babson. Wide-ranging in curiosity and interests, doctor-author-banker Joseph Reynolds lectured regularly at the Gloucester Lyceum.

By the time he wrote *Peter Gott*, the first full-length work of fiction dealing with life in a Cape Ann fishing community, Dr. Reynolds had acquired a working knowledge of maritime Cape Ann. He knew the hard lives of his fishermen patients, and wrote of them with sympathy. With sympathy, but not sentimentality. Dr. Reynolds diagnosed the economic anemia of fishermen as being rooted in chronic improvidence. "The great evil in the life of the fisherman is, that he is idle through the winter, and eats up, during that portion of the year, what he had earned in the summer. This it is that keeps most of them poor all their lives." If worst came to worst, there was winter fishing. And as a very last resort, piecework like shoemaking for which fishermen had little skill and less patience. As Reverend John White had concluded similarly in the 1600s, Dr. Reynolds observed that "seamen have a sovereign contempt for all the occupations of landsmen." The prognosis for the economic health of the fishermen was, in Dr. Reynolds's opinion, not favorable.

By the middle of the 19th century a romanticized Cape Ann fisherman was becoming a figure of marketable myth. This icon caught the imagination of William T. Adams who, as "Oliver Optic," kept the presses humming with his facile juvenile novels, mainly with New England settings, all dedicated to fortifying the frail moral fiber of his young readers.

In 1869 Adams brought forth *The Starry Flag, or The Young Fisherman of Cape Ann*, an inspirational tale of humble fishing lad Levi Fairfield and perky young Bessie Watson. As to the settings in Pigeon Cove and Gloucester, "localities of the various incidents were fixed in the mind of the writer by a pleasant sojourn of a few weeks on Cape Ann during a summer vacation." The book was written with the hope that youthful readers "will also endeavor to be as noble and true, as void of offence before God and man, as [hero Levi Fairfield] labored to be."

The story begins when Levi pauses while hauling in dogfish (he sells their livers), to rescue Bessie Watson who is floundering in the waves. Bessie's father is, of course, wealthy and eternally grateful, and stakes Levi to the money to buy the boat he yearns for, *The Starry Flag*.

But there are complications, of course. When Bessie is kidnapped for ransom by a despicable bounder and carried out to sea, Levi sails after and rescues her. The entire population of Rockport is standing at the pier waving hats and kerchiefs and cheering when Levi sails in and delivers Bessie to the waiting arms of her father and mother. Levi, together with the adoring Bessie, will no doubt be heirs to the Watson

Fearless fisherman Levi Fairfield plucks Bessie Watson from the waves, and earns his just rewards in Oliver Optic's *The Starry Flag*.

fortune as soon as she is old enough to marry. Such were the rewards of dogfishing in old Rockport.

The Starry Flag was fashioned narrowly for the impressionable youth market. It was not in the same league as *Peter Gott*, which was written honestly of Cape Ann fishermen by a physician who treated their ills and understood their lives. But Dr. Reynolds was not a professional author, and his book attracted little attention beyond Cape Ann. It was not until later in the 19th, and early into the 20th century, that great fact-based fictions of life at sea on the fishing schooners thundered from the pens of Rudyard Kipling and James B. Connolly. Gloucester's maritime culture was beginning to stir major creative activity, and the output would swell to an efflorescence of writings and works of art.

In 1892 Rudyard Kipling, bard of the British raj in India, was living in, of all places, Vermont. He had married the sister of an American friend, and moved with his bride, Carrie, to her family's farm near Brattleboro. There would be media mockery when he impetuously sued a devious, threatening brother-in-law in defense of his wife. But in the beginning theirs was the bliss of newlyweds. Rudyard spoke of gathering wood and doing light carpentry in the blazing New England autumn and, when winter came down, feeling snug in their cottage as sleigh bells rang across the snowy meadows.

After three years in Vermont the Kiplings had their second daughter, Elsie. And when the family doctor visited Carrie and the baby, Kipling chatted with him: "the best friend I made in New England – Dr. Conland." James Conland, raised on Cape Cod, had gone to sea when Truro and Harwich still sent fleets to the Banks.

Kipling himself was familiar with the sea, if only from the deck of an ocean liner. He had crossed the Atlantic and Pacific to and from India, never the passive passenger, always the inquisitive newspaperman. John Hays Hammond, Sr., a fellow passenger with the Kiplings on a steamer bound for South Africa in 1897, spoke of Rudyard's insatiable curiosity, "prowling endlessly from engine room to bridge getting information which, as he said, he filed away in his memory for future use."

It was during the years in Vermont that Kipling probed Dr. Conland's knowledge of the fisheries. "Old tales too, he dug up, and the lists of dead and gone schooners whom he had loved, and I reveled in profligate abundance of detail – not necessarily for publication but for the joy of it."

When he closed the door to his study, Kipling shut out Vermont. He was back in India, writing about the life there. Writing *Kim*. But, for a time, he put both India and Vermont aside and turned to a totally different world: Gloucester. Loafing on a couch until the words came, smoking his thirty or forty cigarettes a day that kept the air thick, reciting aloud to his wife and their infants lines and whole paragraphs as he composed them, Kipling worked on a fishing story that would appear first in installments in *McClure's Magazine*. "I embarked on a little book which was called *Captains Courageous*. My part was the writing; his [Conland's] the details." Kipling dedicated the book to Dr. Conland. The title came from a line in "Mary Ambree" that was one of Kipling's favorite old English ballads.

Kipling was not entirely a stranger to Gloucester. He and his young family had twice taken lodgings at the Fairview Inn in East Gloucester for brief summer visits. Early in 1896, six months before Kipling fled America for good and all, he, with Dr. Conland, made two more trips to Gloucester to fill in the gaps in his knowledge of the fisheries.

Annisquam and other localities on Cape Ann treasured fond but faulty local recollections of the Kiplings as longtime summer residents. Even in *Pleasure Drives Around Cape Ann*, bearing the imprint of the Procter Brothers, it was reported that the Fairview Inn "has for two seasons past been the summer home of Rudyard Kipling and wife, and Mrs. Kipling's mother." However, David McAveeney demonstrates in his myth-shattering *Kipling in Gloucester* that none of Kipling's four visits to Gloucester lasted longer than three days.

It is tribute to Kipling's skill as a writer that he could absorb so much of the fishing life in such a short time. In his last visits to Gloucester with Conland, Kipling interviewed schoonermen when he could free himself from big city reporters hungry for a story. He visited the Procter Brothers' "Old Corner" shop and bought copies of *The Fishermen's Memorial and Record Book*, *The Fishermen's Own Book*, and *Fishermen's Ballads and Songs of the Sea*. Thus he had in hand the best possible sources for the lives the Gloucester fishermen led, at sea and ashore.

In *Captains Courageous* Kipling conjures up a rollicking, rousing, splendiferous cruise aboard the *We're Here*, one in which the vastness and rhythms and mysteries of the sea are evoked powerfully, inviting comparison with the darker voyage metaphors of Joseph Conrad. The reader is swept along from the opening pages when the self-important rich man's son Harvey Cheney, dizzied by a strong cigar, slips overboard from the rail of the ocean liner carrying him and his mother to Europe.

Kipling gets the character transformation out of the way almost impatiently. In his first interview with Captain Disko Troop, an insufferable Harvey so annoys the upright master of the *We're Here* with charges of thievery that Troop sends Harvey flying to the deck where he sits stunned with a bloody nose. Harvey is instantly transformed into a penitent, obedient lad, determined to become a credit to the vessel and earn the respect of his shipmates.

With Harvey thus therapeutically bruised and abruptly matured, we settle down to our trip aboard the *We're Here*. Kipling creates a crew remarkable in its variety. Dan Troop, Disko's son, is Harvey's age and they become fast friends, despite Dan's conviction that Harvey's tales of opulent privilege are either admirable inventions or delusions. There is Manuel, the Portuguese crewman who pulled Harvey from the waves into his dory. Manuel is good-natured, but essentially an ethnic archetype in the book (very different from the philosophizing mentor played by Spencer Tracy in the Hollywood version, with a swarthy complexion and greasy ringlets courtesy of a make-up department run amok). Long Jack is a Galway Irishman, Tom Platt a former Navy man from the square-rigger days, nostalgic for quarterdeck discipline with a cat o' nine tails. The black cook speaks Gaelic (Kipling had read of runaway slaves who, before and during the Civil War, had taken refuge among the Irish of Cape Breton). Salter Troop, Disko's farmer brother, has taken placid Penn under his wing. Penn had been a Moravian minister until seeing his wife and children swept away to their deaths in the Johnstown flood had "uncaulked his mind."

The crew members share life together amid the terrors, absurdities and lonely glories of life at sea. And occasionally Kipling will slip in a bit of description so true and visual that we are there, on deck, seeing. "The million wrinkles of the sea under moonlight, when the jibboom solemnly poked at the low stars ...."

In that unreal allegory ocean world occur encounters of the *We're Here* that linger dream-like in the mind. As when Captain Troop's vessel crosses courses with the ancient, disreputable heeltapper schooner of the outcast Abishai and his drunken crew. Abishai sails on, his curses fading in the distance, and then his shambles of a vessel dips into the trough of a wave and disappears. Disko and his crew judge that the tattered craft was leaking badly, and now she has "run under," without a sound, without a survivor. Kipling himself compares the doomed vessel to the sea-haunting *Flying Dutchman.*

When a crewman dies aboard a square-rigged French bark from St. Malo, and his personal gear is sold on board, the boy Dan Troop, casting superstition aside, buys the man's knife – rumored to have had a role in dispatching another man. Soon after, Dan and Harvey are in their dory, Harvey hauling in the line, when the corpse shoots to the surface. "He's come for it!" cries Dan, and the boys fall over each other jettisoning the knife overboard. It could be a Tom Sawyer-Huck Finn incident, but told under the vast skies of the Banks, waves lapping about the bobbing dory, sails catching light off on the horizon.

Harvey Cheyne's self-discovery unites *Captains Courageous* with other Kipling writings: courage and dignity of character transcend all rank and social privilege, whether embodied in a Hindu water-carrier, a British colonial foot soldier, or a boy becoming a man, a Gloucester fisherman, on the Banks. Kipling said he wrote *Captains Courageous* because "I wanted to see if I could catch and hold something of a rather beautiful localised American atmosphere that was already beginning to fade." He did capture the brotherhood of men pursuing fish across the sea's vastness, in ostensibly a boy's book that had much to say to adults.

Kipling did not live to see the movie version of *Captains Courageous.* Filming began in 1935 aboard a real Gloucester schooner, the *Oretha F. Spinney* that took the role of the *We're Here.* The director waited for a gale and finally got his wish. On a day when every sensible skipper in the Gloucester fleet remained inside the breakwater, he ordered the chartered *Spinney* out to battle monster waves off Thacher's Island. One of the crewmen was swept into the scuppers and almost overboard to likely death as the movie-makers tried again and again to force a jib to part so they could catch the mischance on film. Hollywood make-believe in the 1930s was often too close to the real thing.

The studio publicity department kept busy, of course. Photos were taken of the stars, including one of Spencer Tracy observing with unfeigned revulsion the splitting of a cod. Another photo showed Boston's Admiral Richard E. Byrd inviting Freddie Bartholomew to join him on his next expedition to the Antarctic (a generous offer the juvenile actor unaccountably declined).

In May 1937 "Captains Courageous," the movie, premiered at the Colonial Theatre in Boston, and a Gloucester contingent sailed across Massachusetts Bay to T-Wharf in the Gorton-Pew schooner *Corinthian* at the invitation of the studio. Aboard was maritime author James B. Connolly serving as technical consultant, together with as many old sailing skippers as could be rounded up from the smoking room at the Master Mariners Association hall in downtown Gloucester. "Captains Courageous" did not arrive at the North Shore Theatre in Gloucester until July, when it played at "popular prices" (evenings 35 cents, matinees a quarter, children a dime). The first 350 women attending the Saturday performance received a complimentary can of Gorton-Pew "Ready-to-Fry" fish cakes. The ad in the *Gloucester Daily Times* for the competing film playing at the Strand Theatre farther up Main Street carried the sly line, "Even Captain Courageous would laugh if he would see 'New Faces of 1937'."

Kipling's successor as celebrator of the Gloucester fishing fleet in fiction was James Brendan Connolly. Joseph Conrad called Connolly the best sea-story writer in America. Herbert Kenny said he "has preserved the age of sail in Gloucester for us as no one else has." Theodore Roosevelt said "If I were to pick one man for my sons to pattern their lives after, I would choose Jim Connolly." Roosevelt once invited Connolly to his estate at Oyster Bay on Long Island Sound to observe Naval target practice, and House Speaker "Uncle Joe" Cannon spoke of the incident as "the time the President had the fleet brought to Sagamore Hill so that his friend Jim Connolly could review it."

Connolly was a South Boston first-generation Irish-American, his parents having emigrated from Ireland's Aran Islands in Galway Bay. They arrived in Boston at a time when the collision between Irish and Yankee was most galling to both sides. The Irish Catholic refugees from the potato famine in Ireland had fled from British rule and found themselves in a city-state that had for two centuries been forging itself into a center of England-derived culture transformed into its own crusty, practical, salty, culturally and morally self-satisfied Yankeeness.

Boston was, to compound matters, chiefly inhabited by descendants of Englishmen who had separated from the Church of England because they believed it was going Papist, and to escape the persecution of Archbishop Laud who routinely called upon the Star Chamber for authority to lop off the ears of dissident Puritans. The Boston religion, harshly Calvinist in the 1600s, had mellowed into Unitarian equanimity, but many of its adherents continued to abhor Catholicism. Free spirits like Emerson rejected the idea of an anthropomorphic deity altogether and saw a universe infused with a benign Over-Soul. Others quietly ignored what they figured was unknowable.

Jim Connolly grew up within this clash of culture, race and religion, and he was deeply offended by the disdain of establishment Bostonians who had an Irish laborer joke for every occasion. Throughout his life he kept one foot in South Boston, so to speak, and the other in Erin. He reviled the British and made light of their Yankee descendants.

Nevertheless, in 1896 Connolly was a student at Harvard, which was then still bedrock Yankee and New England's seedbed of the intellect. He had qualified for an engineering program at the university by way of correspondence courses. Then he read that the Olympic Games were to be revived in Greece. Would Harvard grant him a leave of absence to compete? No, Harvard would not. As he recounted in *Sea-Borne: Thirty Years Avoyaging*, Connolly thereupon walked out of Cambridge, caught a steamer for Athens, arrived with almost no time to practice, yet won for America the first Olympic event held in 1,500 years, the hop, step and jump competition.

James B. Connolly was a born adventurer. After service in the Spanish-American War he spent much of his life at sea, in Gloucester schooners, in cattle boats; with English fishermen in the North Sea and German fishermen in the Baltic; aboard whalers, steel tankers, destroyers, airships, submarines. He was a war correspondent at the Mexican border uprising in 1914, in the Great War in Europe in 1917 and 1918, and at the Black and Tans dust-up in Ireland in 1921.

He first arrived in Gloucester around the turn of the 20th century when, as an ex-semi-professional football player, he was hired to be physical director of the Gloucester Athletic Club and halfback on the club's football team. Connolly came to know the fishermen who wandered over to watch the games, and he walked back with them to the wharves and the sea life he had known as a Boston boy. He remem-

James B. Connolly (left) at the wheel of the *Gertrude L. Thebaud*, with Ben Pine, who skippered the *Thebaud* in races against Nova Scotia's *Bluenose*. *Courtesy Cape Ann Historical Museum*

bered the time his uncle's boat shipped a sea and washed Connolly, age seven, out of his cabin bunk.

Strolling the Gloucester waterfront was for Connolly a feast for the senses: the sights and smells of vessels and spar yards and sail lofts, and the men "all alive and jumping to their work" fitting out the vessels and setting to sea.

Connolly's first trip in a Gloucester bottom was for mackerel, sailing in the *Monarch* under Captain Albert Rose. Later he happily recalled life in the mackerel fleet, as sixty or eighty seining schooners weaved among one another, men shouting gossip from boat to boat, others at the mastheads on the lookout for ripples that meant a school of fish.

Not content making summer mackerel seining trips, Connolly learned what Georges Bank could be like in January when *Scribner's* editor Edward Burlingame arranged for him to make a winter trip in the *Horace B. Parker*, Captain Bill McDonald. Back ashore, Connolly wrote the stories that appeared in *Scribner's* magazine and launched his writing career. In 1902 Rudyard Kipling was reading Connolly's early magazine stories and wrote to Dr. Conland in Brattleboro, asking, "Who is this J. B. Connolly who is working our lead about Gloucester and the fishing schooners in *Scribner's*? . . . It's ripping good work, and I am very pleased that corner of American life is being exploited at last."

Connolly's Gloucester fishermen's tales were collected in one volume after another, beginning with *Out of Gloucester* in 1902. These are brawny, brawling tales of men exhilarated by the challenges of fishing the treacherous shoal Banks, competitive beyond all reason in bending on sail, daring fate, giving no quarter to the demons of the sea and expecting none. Connolly was not sentimental about dangers. Some men were bred to the sea and destined to find their comforts or doom therein. And no one thought overmuch about the risks. "There are worse graves than the clean, green sea."

The facts in his stories, said Connolly, came from listening to shipmates and to legendary survivors like Howard Blackburn. One of his tales, "Dory-Mates," was based on his chats with Blackburn. Then Blackburn loaned him his diary, and Connolly loosely transcribed the frost-mutilated fisherman's recollections of his ordeal into "A Fresh Halibuter," which re-appeared in 1930 as a chapter in Connolly's *The Book of the Gloucester Fishermen*.

Many of the memorable characters that populate Connolly's fictions were based on men he had known at sea. Aboard one of the schooners Connolly sailed in was a Breton fisherman brimful of chatter and song. He became Connolly's model for "Frenchie" in "Between Shipmates."

Connolly knew and could speak for the crewmen, but his idols were the legendary schooner masters he sailed under, captains like Maurice Whalen and Tommie Bohlin. They were, he said, men who survived by brawn, balance and the instinct to instantly take the right course of action in any situation. But they had unexpected depths, too. Connolly remembered how quiet-spoken Captain George Peeples took him aside and asked his opinion on a book Peeples was reading. Connolly expected the captain had been dipping into a murder mystery but no, the grizzled skipper was asking what the young reporter thought of Herbert Spencer's *Synthetic Philosophy*.

Certain Connolly sea tales were unmistakably based on pieces in the Procter books. His "Georges Shoals" paralleled "On Georges in the Terrible Gale of February 14th, 1862" in *The Fishermen's Memorial and Record Book*. Here it is again – the schooner that has cut its cable and is drifting fatally toward a collision that will take two or more vessels and their crews to the bottom. In "Georges Shoals" the men on the drifting ship are not seen but heard. "If that ain't hell – talkin' to men you can't see and they driftin' away to be lost!" Inevitably that schooner collides fatally with another, timbers cracking and ice-stiffened canvass splitting in the gale.

"Price o' Fish," collected in *Gloucestermen: Stories of the Fishing Fleet*, draws from the account in Procter's *Fishermen's Memorial* of the schooner *Onward* that rolled over and was a complete wreck but, jury-rigged by Captain Wilkes and his crew, managed to sail back to Cape Ann while refusing all offers of assistance en route. For his version Connolly renames the *Onward* the *Mary Gurley* and installs Joe Gurley as master.

In "The Ice Dogs" Connolly borrows from Captain Joseph Collins's "Halibut Fishing Among the Ice Floes," which had appeared in the Procter volume *The Fishermen's Own Book*. Collins's description of a true escape from the grip of ice floes is exciting enough. But Connolly, in his version, heightens suspense in the dash of the *Arbiter*, the dauntless Clancy in command, to reach open water off the coast of Labrador, before winter ice closes in to crush the vessel.

Connolly's Irish-American enthusiasms sometimes distort a good story. As in "Echo o' the Morn," based on the account, in *The Fishermen's Memorial*, of the spiriting of the impounded schooner *E. A. Horton* back to Gloucester. In "Echo o' the Morn" the emphasis is not on the recapture of the *Horton*, but on the cleverness of the skipper, renamed Billie Simms, in outwitting the dastardly Brits. Simms tricks a British cruiser into aiming its big guns against an American dory, blowing it out of the water – an armed attack that, if it had actually happened, would have raised diplomatic eyebrows to say the least. The *Echo o' the Morn* manages to elude the entire British North Atlantic Squadron, comprised of warships manned by "their hereditary enemies." Connolly thus took the daring recapture of a Gloucester schooner from Canadian revenue officers and recast it as a feat of revenge against the British Empire.

Poet Charles Olson called Connolly "the greatest writer of Gloucester." But Olson complained that Connolly chose to write in "that goddam stage Irish, which ruins the thing." It went beyond language: Connolly's writing suffered from his scarcely concealed contempt for Yankees descended from the English. In "Americanization of Roll-Down Joe" he has a character say that the descendants of the old settlers were all "used up," and that "new blood" was manning the fleet.

Connolly did not live to see the roster of men lost at sea out of Gloucester that was engraved on a City Hall staircase wall in 1978, sponsored by City Councilor John "Gus" Foote. Nor the expanded version installed as a cenotaph beside the Fishermen's Memorial on Stacy Boulevard in 2000. He would have seen that the old blood was not entirely used up even in his day. In 1903, square in the middle of the period Connolly was writing about, the list of lost Gloucester fishermen does indeed include brave men with Irish names like O'Donnell, Hickey and Ryan. And Scandinavians Johnson, Stromberg, Hermstrom, Armburg. Portuguese with names like Lopez and Lewis. No Sicilians yet. But there are also names that had appeared on Gloucester crew lists for generations: Allen, Duncan, Hall, Merchant, Nelson, Parsons, Pierce, Stoddard, Strickland, Thomas. As James B. Connolly must have known, the brotherhood of death beyond the breakwater has no ethnic preferences.

Despite his bitterness toward the Yankees, no one paid more sincere and unstinting homage to the Gloucester schooner captains and crews. "The equal of that all-sail fleet of schooners and their hard-driving captains will never be seen again," he said. "And never shall we see the like again of those dory men, putting out from their vessels in tiny boats, to heave and haul their trawls." There was one other distinctive quality in Connolly: the ring of authenticity. He was the only major fiction writer who had been out there repeatedly, sharing the life under schooner sail, knowing the exhilaration salted with peril.

Many of the Gloucester fishermen of schooner times, especially the young and unattached, belonged to the breed of parched and randy crewmen who had heavy work making it to high ground beyond the booze parlors and brothels convenient to the wharves. Squarely in their path was the Fishermen's Institute, beckoning them to shun the shoals of gin and sin. The Reverend Emanuel Charlton had, in 1892, persuaded a benefactor to donate the funds required to purchase a former pool hall and barber shop on Duncan Street, in the middle of the red light district.

Fetching up at the building rebuilt as the Fishermen's Institute, a suspicious but curious fisherman would be lured inside by amenities that included a reading lounge and a "Friendly Room" stocked with coffee and donuts. In the basement were baths and hammock accommodations. On the upper floor the seaman would be welcomed into a chapel where he could tidy up his soul by attending non-denominational sermons and temperance lectures.

The Reverend Charlton was an inspired messenger of the Lord. He delivered sermons along the wharves, invited himself aboard ships to collar converts, visited the police lock-up Sunday mornings to "save" fishermen who had somehow lost their bearings the night before and awoke with a sketchy awareness as to their whereabouts. The charitable efforts of the Fishermen's Institute were broadly supported by the Gloucester community. Fund-raisers were held at George Stacy's Hawthorne Inn and other Gloucester hotels. On Eastern Point Cecilia Beaux rallied A. Piatt Andrew and Henry Davis Sleeper to contribute. The Institute was awash with donated books and magazines, handkerchiefs, soap, phonograph records, an upright piano.

One of Reverend Charlton's most enduring gestures of tribute to those fishermen, redeemed or not, who sailed out and never returned: he invited the widows and orphans to scatter flowers of remembrance onto the outgoing tide at the Cut Bridge – a ceremonial tradition that later fell into disuse, but was gracefully revived in 1998.

Gloucester's Fishermen's Institute offered crewmen an alternative to the saloons and brothels on Duncan Street.

Courtesy Cape Ann Historical Museum

The history of the Fishermen's Institute, compiled by Martha Oaks in *The Gloucester Fishermen's Institute, 1891–1991*, mirrored the fortunes of Gloucester's schooner fisheries. Around 1912, over 90,000 fishermen visited the Institute each year. But that was the high point. The sailing fleet declined thereafter, the waterfront became more morally salubrious, and the arriving Sicilian fishermen established the St. Peter's Club as a center for their own community. Despite outcries that another symbol of the old Gloucester was to be sacrificed, the Fishermen's Institute building was demolished in 1974.

The heroic age of the fleet was past. But new voices would be raised to sing its glories.

CHAPTER 6

Schooner Sails Dipping

WHEN THE 300TH anniversary of the founding of Gloucester rolled around in 1923, suitable celebrations were planned for the occasion, including historical tableaux and a parade of decorated autos. The "aeroplane carrier" *Langley* steamed into the harbor, and melodies rang from the new carillon bells at Our Lady of Good Voyage church. The cornerstone was laid on Stacy Boulevard for Leonard Craske's iconic Fishermen's Memorial statue, which may owe its inspiration to a painting that in 1905 had been adopted as the Gorton's Fisheries "Man at the Wheel" trademark. The hope was expressed that one day another memorial would be erected, to honor the fishermen's wives who endured the long anxious waiting when a vessel was overdue. Seventy-eight years would pass before this hope was fulfilled and a Fishermen's Wives Memorial, commissioned by the Fishermen's Wives Association and sculpted by Morgan Faulds Pike, was dedicated farther along Stacy Boulevard in the summer of 2001.

A Fishermen's Race had been scheduled for the opening day of the 300th observances, but the airs proved too light. Two days later it breezed up and the schooner *Henry Ford*, owned and sailed by legendary Captain Clayton Morrissey, won the trophy sponsored by Sir Thomas Lipton, plus $1,000 cash. Sir Thomas himself, the Scottish grocery magnate who made a fortune putting tea into little bags, chanced to be in Boston. He motored down to Gloucester with the trophy and, in an after-dinner address, regaled the assembled mariners with anecdotes that "gave him instantaneous grip on the risibilities and sympathies of his listeners."

There was a bittersweet sense to the events because Gloucester's fishing schooner era was clearly drawing to a close. Few new wooden schooners were being built, and internal combustion engines were sending out offensive puffs of smoke from an increasing number of vessels churning through the harbor.

Still, the anniversary was carried off bravely by James R. Pringle, Gloucester's unofficial historian of the period. He wrote a book commemorating the milestone, and a "pageant-drama" that was twice performed. Pringle had been on the scene a quarter-century earlier for a similar celebration, and had written a history of the city in which he dwelt upon Gloucester's role in the Civil War. Pringle wrote, for instance, of how the captain of the Confederate raider *Tacony* brought off the crews of New England fishing vessels near Portland before putting their schooners to the torch. The raider's captain invited the captured skippers to dinner in his cabin, and offered each a lieutenant's commission in the Confederate navy if he would defect. The Gloucester skippers declined. They were loyal Northerners and wanted no part of any other navy, least of all one offering such dim prospects for future advancement. The *Tacony*'s captain then agreed to put the skippers ashore if they would promise not to take up arms against the South. It was a gentlemen's agreement easy to accept. The Gloucestermen just wanted to get back to fishing.

Pringle told non-military maritime anecdotes, too. There was the crime of Gorham Parsons, whose haunted conscience is worthy of a tale by Hawthorne. While chopping wood, Parsons was annoyed by a boy who persisted in singing. No music lover, Gorham irritably split the boy's skull with the axe. He carried the remains to town, said the axe had slipped, and was acquitted by authorities who found it perfectly plausible that an axe could miss a chopping block and find a nearby juvenile cranium. Years later at sea Gorham unburdened himself of his crime to his crewmates and said he had carried the boy on his back long enough. He attached a millstone to his neck and jumped overboard, thus ensuring swift and certain release from his troubling thoughts.

Pringle reveled in military history, but he himself did not see service in uniform until, at age fifty-five, he was called up in the Naval Reserve in World War I. Pringle's service under the flag seems to have

Newsman-historian James R. Pringle stoutly claimed that Gloucester was the first permanent settlement in Massachusetts.

consisted largely of marshalling incontrovertible evidence to support the claim that Gloucester's was the first permanent settlement in Massachusetts, an assertion that had been challenged by certain parties in the miasmic bogs of Weymouth on the South Shore below Boston. They had demanded that the disputed language, penned by Pringle himself, be stricken from the memorial tablet in Fisherman's Field at

Stage Fort Park on Gloucester harbor. Buttressed by Pringle's research, Gloucester dismissed the Weymouth heresy as beneath contempt.

The forest of schooner masts in Gloucester's harbor continued to thin out after the brave festivities of 1923, and the cacophony of the working waterfront diminished by many decibels. Remembering the old days were the sailing captains who whiled away their later years at the Master Mariners' Association hall on the second floor of a building on Main Street. The walls were hung with photographs of famous schooners, and an oil painting of Howard Blackburn as a sort of patron saint in the secular theology of the fishermen. There were cards and a pool table, and comfortable chairs drawn up to give the old sea dogs a commanding view of the rigging of passersby on the street below. But there were fewer and fewer skippers of the old fleet to gaze out those windows, tap a pipe and stir up some glowing embers of memory.

Others in town remembered with wonder what had been lost. And summoned up their recollections of the age of sail that went so deep to all that was Gloucester. In 1972 William S. Webber, Jr.'s description of the Gloucester waterfront of pre-World War I days to the early 1920s appeared under the pseudonym of "Doc Walker" in a slim volume, *Waterfront – Around the Wharves of Gloucester in the Last Days of Sail.* Webber escorts the reader on a tour of the wharves in those twilight days of Gloucester's dominance in fishing, recalling all of the enterprises that supported the schooner fleet: sail lofts, fish packing plants, outfitters selling ship's stores and groceries, flake yards where the fish were cured in the sun, a marine salvage yard, a manufacturer of fog horns, horse-drawn drays that hauled the day's landings, teamsters who picked up a crewman's sea bag at the wharf to convey it to a boarding house. Blacksmiths. Seine boat builders. Freezers and ice plants.

Webber tells, too, how the latest fishing news was announced around the waterfront. How the secretary of the Board of Trade went by launch about the harbor, collecting the details of schooner arrivals with their "hail," the estimate of their catch. He would chalk these bulletins on a blackboard outside the Board of Trade office at Fishermen's Corner, at the corner of Main and Duncan Streets, as interested parties gathered around. This intelligence was updated a few hours later in a noon fishing edition of the *Gloucester Daily Times* that was peddled in the neighborhood of the wharves. Webber notes that several decades later, news of the fisheries was moving much faster – broadcast from atop a downtown Gloucester building by a tiny radio station, which later moved to Boston and up in the world as WHDH.

Waterfront concludes with an account of the departure of a schooner from the harbor in 1913, the tug giving a farewell blast after it drops its tow lines and the vessel's sails fill as she heels, picking up speed to tack around the breakwater and make for open sea. The scene is best imagined while studying one of the period harbor photos in the book from the glass negatives of Ernest Blatchford or Eben Parsons.

Men who had done some serious schooner fishing in their younger days also wrote down what it had really been like. Raymond McFarland, like Captain Joseph W. Collins, hailed from Down East Maine, his family's home perched over an inlet opening into Frenchman's Bay. He was born into a seagoing family but had his heart set on a career in education. In 1893 he taught for a winter term at a town farther along the Maine coast. Then, to earn the money to enter college, he made a trip in the *Yosemite* out of Gloucester under its high-line skipper, his uncle John McFarland.

Raymond McFarland did go on to an academic career in Vermont, but the sea was always tugging at his sleeve. In 1911 he wrote *A History of the New England Fisheries*, and fellow academics must have thought it an odd topic for someone teaching at far-inland Middlebury College. He authored sea novels, too, as a change of pace from his volumes about education. Late in life, as he looked from his study out over a Vermont mountainscape, McFarland wandered in thought back shoreward and he lived again the excitement of fishing under sail, and the trips he made with his uncle in the *Yosemite* forty years before. In 1937 he put it together in *The Masts of Gloucester – Recollections of a Fisherman*. The book is doubly interesting for the photos of work aboard a mackerel seiner in the 1890s, probably snapped by a young McFarland himself.

First arriving in Gloucester on a March day, McFarland was greeted by cold he found as penetrating as that in his native Maine. His spirits revived when he found his way through the narrow alleyways to the ships that seemed to him alive, sails fluttering from their spars.

McFarland boarded the *Yosemite*, found his bunk and stowed the contents of his sea bag. He had remembered to bring along some light reading: a history of Greece, Greenough's *Vergil*, Xenophon's *Anabasis*. He also had Le Conte's *Geology*, loaned to him by his mariner father to bone up on during quiet spells at sea. From his uncle's bookshelf aboard he would borrow Bowditch's *Practical Navigator*, and copies of the *Nautical Almanac*. In the musical tradition of the Gloucester fleet, Ray McFarland had also packed his cornet.

The crew was made up of Mainers, Newfoundlanders, Cape Breton Scots and Gloucester natives. Many, says McFarland, were family men, homeowners, proud of their children's grades at school. Not the sort to be tempted by the fleshpots along Duncan Street.

The culinary talents of cook John Mills were equal to the expectations of a Gloucester crew. The bill of fare for one meal: yeast bread and hardtack, potatoes and mashed turnip, canned corn and fried fresh codfish, corned beef, cornstarch pudding with egg sauce, apple and mince pies, sugar cookies, plum cake and molasses rolls, tea and coffee. All disappeared with dispatch when men returned from visiting their trawl, which did wonders for an appetite.

Came the moment McFarland had dreaded – climbing into the rigging for the first time. When he had actually done it, mounted to the crosstrees, the fear vanished and he loafed about for an hour getting familiar with this upper world, "confident that there was more to me than when I left the deck." He had, like Captain Epes Sargent, completed the rite of passage that came with talking himself into climbing to a dizzying height, swaying like an inverted pendulum over the deck.

When he got his sea legs, McFarland came to appreciate the functional grace of schooners like the *Yosemite*. As the vessel sliced through the seas day after day, and raced along with the lee rail under, his admiration grew for the Gloucester captains and crews, "always living on the very edge of the green ocean and glorying in the life."

W. Raymond McClure ranked McFarland's accounts of the Gloucester fleet with those of James B. Connolly. But there is no Anglophobia in McFarland's accounts. In fact, Connolly would be scandalized at the extent to which Gloucestermen fraternized with subjects of Queen Victoria, by McFarland's telling. There was the time when Liverpool, Nova Scotia was celebrating the Queen's birthday. The crowd spilling through the town was greatly augmented by hundreds of crewmen off schooners in the harbor, many of them from Gloucester. All were simply happy to be ashore, joining in the spirit of the day. As for the parade itself, one of McFarland's shipmates said it consisted of "an old man, a wheelbarrow, and a little yaller dog."

A decade after Raymond McFarland was remembering *Yosemite*, Gordon W. Thomas had just begun to compile his biographies of the Gloucester schooner fleet. Thomas was not a fisherman himself, although he grew up around the vessels, climbing in the rigging as a boy. His famous skipper father, Captain Jeff Thomas, would not allow the son to follow him into that hard life. Still, Gordon Thomas would not stray far from the fisheries. He worked for years in fish markets and at one time ran one of his own.

His recollections of the sailing fleet stayed with him. In 1948, when he was browsing through old newspaper files in Gloucester's Sawyer Free Library, he began to think about writing a book on the fishing schooners. For the next forty-five years Gordon Thomas was the Boswell of the schooner fleet, sifting out particulars on the "ablest" of the vessels from back issues of the *Gloucester Daily Times* and Boston newspapers, delving into U.S., Canadian and British archives, exchanging correspondence with government offices as far away as Lisbon.

Some of the old captains and crew members were still alive when Gordon began tracking down the fate of the vessels, and they would open up to any son of Jeff Thomas. Men like Christopher Neilsen. Neilsen had been weighted down with boots and gear when he was knocked overboard from the *Ingomar* on Quero Bank in 1923. He figured he was done for, but Captain Carl Olson dove in and pulled Neilsen back to safety. Neilsen's number was not up by a long shot; he lasted until he was 106 in 1972.

Gordon Thomas's profiles of the schooners went through several editions, finally called *Fast & Able: Life Stories of Great Gloucester Fishing Vessels*. It is not a book to rush through. Better to savor the biography of each of the schooners one at a time. Study the lines of the vessel in the photos that Gordon Thomas saved before the negatives disappeared. The captions tell much about each scene, because

Thomas had an eye for significant details. Here is the *Dauntless* slipping gracefully into the outer harbor, the *Clintonia* being launched with a great splash into Vincent Cove, the *Monitor* etched against the sky as it passes the Paint Manufactory, the *Cavalier* with her rigging in shreds and flag at half-mast mourning for two men gone astray, and the *Oriole*, magnificent with all sails set. Thomas thought *Oriole* the handsomest of them all.

At the back of *Fast & Able* are portraits that Gordon Thomas collected of some of the most famous of the schooner captains, men like Captains Joe Mesquita, Marty Welch and Sol Jacobs. James B. Connolly had admired Captain Solomon Jacobs, and Gordon Thomas added some particulars on that raw-boned "king of the mackerel catchers." Others have rounded up other details.

Born in Twillingate, Newfoundland, Jacobs was the most entrepreneurial of the Gloucester fishing skippers. He owned schooners and sent them to the Bering Sea after halibut and seals, until the British impounded his catches and threw him in jail. He found unsuspected halibut in the South Pacific, and outfished the Irish on their own mackerel grounds. He commissioned the first auxiliary schooner out of Gloucester, the *Helen M. Gould*, and the port's first fishing steamer, the *Ethel B. Jacobs*. Jacobs made and lost several fortunes, but never lost his nerve. When he died in 1922 the pall bearers for his funeral were other distinguished captains from the sailing fleet. There is a waterfront park named in his honor that adjoins the U.S. Coast Guard station on Gloucester's Harbor Loop, but the inscription does not do justice to colorful Sol Jacobs. And does not pay the respect due him as *Captain* Solomon Jacobs.

In addition to the Sol Jacobs and Gus Foote vest pocket parks on the Gloucester waterfront, there is another at the head of the harbor with a view toward open water framed by the Jodrey State Fish Pier on one side and wharves on the other. A plaque in this little green reads: "We pay tribute to Gordon W. Thomas ('Mr. Schooner') for his love, dedication and ability demonstrated in years of research and writing of the great schooners of the days of sail and the brave, hardy men who sailed them, the 'Gloucestermen.' Their fame and glory have been strengthened by his efforts."

As the years passed after Gordon Thomas's accounts of the schooners, the era of Gloucester fishing under sail might have faded into blurred, sepia nostalgia – had it not been for Joseph E. Garland.

Garland's passion for tracking down and bringing to life Gloucester's history ran deep. Joe had summered in Gloucester as a boy. In World War II he served as a combat infantryman in Europe, and after the war took a newspaper job in Minnesota. But his Gloucester ancestry reached out and pulled him back. He bought the Black Bess property on the Gloucester harbor shore at Eastern Point inside the Dog Bar Breakwater, and began to write. Over the next several decades he authored a good dozen books devoted to the many dimensions of Cape Ann, mostly Gloucester, mostly its fisheries. He also labored to great effect behind the scenes to recover and rekindle interest in the works of those who came onto the local scene before him, and to encourage his own contemporaries blessed with long memories to shape their narratives into print. Joe Garland's efforts have been of inestimable value in documenting the maritime heritage of Gloucester, and particularly that of its schooner fisheries.

Garland is one-half historian, relentless in his pursuit of a detail locked in some archive or log book, encyclopedic in his knowledge of the town his ancestors have inhabited as eminent citizens for generations. Garland's other half is literary evocateur. Herbert Kenny said Joe can make a page "ring with vitality." Garland splashes colors and voices and the cumulative sensory delights of Gloucester into paragraphs that are stylistically elegant. Elegant, but never precious. In the words of Bill Plante, long-time North Shore editor and columnist, "Garland sticks to fact, but he does it with language as colloquial to the setting of time and place as any fictional recounting, and with all the zest that one could ask of any literary work." Garland has chronicled the epic of Gloucester fishing with gusto, passion and grace out of print since Samuel Eliot Morison's *Maritime History of Massachusetts.* Garland and Sam Morison are two of a kind: scrupulous historians, exuberant story-tellers, and true amphibious spirits.

Garland's interest in the schooner fishermen began with a family connection. His grandfather doctor was the physician who cared for Howard Blackburn's frostbitten hands when Blackburn first returned to Gloucester. The original accounts of Blackburn's ordeal were long out of print, and Joe Garland felt the world should be reacquainted with the man.

For his telling of the Howard Blackburn epic, in *Lone Voyager*, Garland went back to original sources and followed the trail of Blackburn's life from his origins in Nova Scotia, his near death from exposure at sea off Newfoundland, his enterprise in making a go of it as a tobacconist and later a saloon-keeper in Gloucester despite his handicaps, a failed venture sailing around South America to the Klondike, and in later life twice crossing the Atlantic alone in small sailboats, somehow managing the sheets with his clubbed hands.

From Garland's account, Howard Blackburn emerges as a superb mariner, as well as a man of great appetites, with no small flair for self-promotion – but also of great charity and humanity. After he and his dorymate Tom Welch went astray from the *Grace L. Fears*, and Welch froze to death, Blackburn had been rowing day after day with frozen hands, thirsting and starving, before he made land and found a hut where he kept himself awake all night so as not to freeze to death. At daybreak his first act was to return to the dory to try to pull ashore Tom Welch's body. Blackburn did not have the strength, and the frozen corpse slipped into the water. Late in the day Blackburn finally met a group of men crossing the ice. Again, his first concern was for his dorymate, and he asked his rescuers to return with him to find Welch. They saw that Blackburn himself was in a bad way, but he would not accept attention until assured that his dorymate's body would be looked after. He believed Tom Welch would have done as much for him.

In his *Down to the Sea: The Fishing Schooners of Gloucester* (1983) Garland captured the glory of the era in words, complemented by photos the Cape Ann Historical Museum had acquired from Gordon Thomas. Garland said his research into the fishing schooners went slowly until in 1981 he was cruising on *Adventure*, when it was sailing out of Camden, Maine in the windjammer fleet. Garland found himself in the company of Captain Leo Hynes. Hynes had earlier been master of the vessel for almost twenty of her roughest years fishing under power but with her crew tub-trawling from dories, the old way that yielded sounder, more marketable fish. By the time they returned to port, Joe had absorbed from *Adventure* and Leo Hynes a final, fleeting sense of what it had been like to fish by hooks in an Essex-built Gloucester vessel. Garland caught the full flavor of that life in his *Down to the Sea.* He was also instrumental in bringing *Adventure* back to Gloucester, and stumping for preservation of this storied vessel. The ongoing restoration project is financed through contributions and grants raised by Schooner *Adventure*, Inc. under its president, Martin Krugman.

There were peripheral personalities attracted to the Gloucester waterfront in the latter days of fishing by sail-powered vessels. When the Gloucester schooner *Gertrude L. Thebaud* was preparing for a final series of International Fishermen's Races with Nova Scotia's *Bluenose* in 1938, a photogenic young Viking type was spotted high in the rigging. Somehow or other after the races, Sterling Hayden was recruited to take a film test and soon, to his surprise and amusement, he was on his way to Hollywood.

In his soul-baring autobiography, *Wanderer* (1963), Hayden wrote of his first winter dory-trawling trip aboard the *Thebaud* on the Grand Bank. On a dark night with the schooner pitching through the swells, Hayden was certain it was too rough to go out in the dories. But his dorymate Jack Hackett assured him that it was regular fishing weather, nothing out of the ordinary. Jack showed the new kid how to get their gear into the dory by torchlight, and to time a passing swell to drop into the black sea at the right moment. Hayden and Jack Hackett would sail together as mastheadmen on the *Thebaud* during races with the *Bluenose*.

Hayden had come to the *Thebaud* by a roundabout route. Years before, he had been moored in Smith's Cove in East Gloucester in his little Maine sloop *Horizon* when the wind came up and drove him toward a large white schooner. Many yachtsmen would have bawled out a young sailor in a leaky, drifting disgrace of a boat, but the owner of the schooner jumped aboard and he and Hayden had a glorious sail around Gloucester harbor in the gale. The owner-master of the schooner was Irving Johnson, who with his wife Electa was about to take *Yankee* on the first of year-and-a-half circumnavigations of the globe with complements of young college students, mostly boys plus a few girls, willing to pay for hard labor on sea treks to remote islands and forgotten ports.

In 1936 Johnson took on Hayden to be second in command for *Yankee's* second trip around the world. In *Sailing to See*, Johnson said Hayden was a natural-born sailor who, with calm assurance, issued orders that were executed without question by crewmembers sometimes decades older than this twenty-year-old mate.

"Sterling Hayden of Gloucester," Irving Johnson had called him. But it was when he was a boy stranded in Boothbay Harbor, Maine with his mother and con-man stepfather that Hayden first saw iced-up Gloucester schooners with tattered sails, their weary crewmen working with ripped hands and bandaged heads. Later the stepfather walked out and the mother and son took a slow, warm, friendly train from Boston to Gloucester. Young Hayden and his mother both felt they had found a snug harbor, even in the Depression, among fishing families who were no strangers to hard times.

After his subcommand of *Yankee*, and serving as navigator for one of the *Thebaud's* races with *Bluenose*, Hayden earned his papers as the youngest Master Mariner in Gloucester. But he was unable to escape the demons that followed him through his years in Hollywood (cast most memorably as General Jack D. Ripper in "Dr. Strangelove"), his wartime service attached to Tito's guerillas in Yugoslavia that earned him a Silver Star, and his self-disgust at having informed on Communist Party fellow-travelers to McCarthy-era committees. He sailed off into the Pacific, eluding judges and injunctions and divorce lawyers, his children smuggled aboard. His Hollywood agent said it best: "This man was born in the wrong century. He should have been a sea captain in the 1800's."

After their third cruise around an increasingly war-threatened world, Irving and Electa Johnson sailed their original *Yankee* into the shelter of Gloucester harbor in the spring of 1941. When the United States was finally plunged into WWII at the end of the year, Irving left to serve in the Pacific, and after it was over they wanted to replace their old vessel with a North Sea pilot schooner that would have plenty of beam with good space below, but not a tubby appearance. It was Sterling Hayden who discovered for them the *Duhnen*, the last sailing schooner the Germans had built for piloting. Irving Johnson had it converted to a brigantine at the old fishing port of Brixham on the south coast of

Capt. Irving Johnson and wife Electa sailed from Gloucester around the world three times in schooner *Yankee* before WWII, and four more times in a brigantine of the same name after the war.

Courtesy Cape Ann Historical Museum

England that reminded him of "our home port of Gloucester." When the Johnsons brought the new *Yankee* home, Ben Pine blew his whistle to alert the waterfront. Everybody gathered to watch the new big white ship tie up, with the familiar lettering: "*YANKEE* Gloucester."

The Johnsons' cruises around the world yielded a series of books: *Westward Bound in the Schooner Yankee*, *Yankee's Wander World*, *Yankee's People and Places*. Electa did most of the writing, Irving adding some words on ship design and handling. *Yankee's Wander World*, chronicling their 1947 trip, offered glimpses of remote Polynesian and Southeast Asian islands just recovering from wartime disorder, stirring to shake off the old colonialism. The South Pacific still retained, however briefly, a *National Geographic* romantic remoteness. *Yankee* showed its "Gloucester" nameboard in the lagoons and harbors of Moorea, Puka Puka, Tin Can Island, Amok, Tucopia, Wewak, Keeling Cocos.

Yankee was not the only vessel to sail from Gloucester for a trip around the globe. In 1895 Captain Joshua Slocum had set out in his 37-foot resurrected Delaware oyster sloop *Spray* on a voyage no one had ever dared before: a single-handed circumnavigation of the earth. Slocum was, like Sterling Hayden, a man more at ease with the tumults of nature at sea than with the shoals of ambition and false friendships ashore. Life was at its best cruising the South Pacific with his shipmate and soul-mate-wife Virginia who bore all their children aboard and once stood behind Joshua with a pair of cocked pistols to pacify a mutinous crew. But Virginia died and Slocum lost interest after that. He married again but remained mostly at sea, alone.

He started from Boston for his round-the-world cruise, then put into Gloucester for two weeks of fitting out. And to consider whether he was really serious with himself about making the trip. Many of the "old skippers" of the port came by to discuss his projected voyage, and did not come empty-handed. They heaped dried cod on board, and a barrel of oil to calm the waves, and a case of the local anti-fouling copper paint from Wonson's Paint Manufactory. And a "fisherman's own" lantern.

Finally Slocum cast off. Rounding a point in the harbor he saw "a flutter of handkerchiefs and caps" with pretty women at windows, hailing him. "When I made as if to stand in, a hundred pairs of arms reached out, and said come, but the shore was dangerous!" With some regret, Slocum turned from these alluring Loreleis and set his gaze upon the horizon. Half way around the globe, reaching Rodriguez Island after crossing the Indian Ocean, Slocum praised his Gloucester lantern for having shown him greater wonders than Aladdin's lamp ever revealed. Joshua Slocum completed his circumnavigation three years after he set out from Gloucester.

And so Cape Ann's era of sail drew to a close. Gloucester had established a connection with the sea as close as was possible for any shore community. Its people knew all about mythic connections with the omnipresent, surrounding ocean. Men overdue at sea were on the face of it statistics, but in another sense became one with a mysterious unknown. Had they joined the ranks of Billy Johnson overboard from the *Mary E.*, who would never find his way back to his wife on Cape Ann? Billy, as everyone knew, fell in love with a siren of the deep, and "Down among the mermaids / Underneath the sea, / Lives Billy Johnson / All so bold and free."

The fishing families of Gloucester could not have told you who Ulysses was, but the legends that reached back to the *Odyssey* and beyond lived in their folk memories. Had a lost fisherman been marooned seven years on the uncharted island of a Calypso-like sea-nymph? Had curious shipmates disobeyed orders and opened the bag loaned in trust by the Keeper of the Winds, unleashing a hurricane upon their vessel? Would there, after all, finally be a tearful reunion between a long-lost captain and his Gloucester Penelope? There was no telling what might become of a fisherman after his vessel departed upon the ocean highways.

CHAPTER 7

Myths and Music Under Sail

DESPITE THE all-too-frequent accounts of schooner wrecks and tragedies at sea, it would be a mistake to conclude that the life of a schooner fisherman was all work and terror. Those crewmen were a versatile lot. They entertained themselves with storytelling and singing, often accompanied by a fiddler or other musician who might possess unexpected talent.

The musicality of the Gloucester fleet is attested to in *A Summer Cruise on the Coast of New England* by *New York Tribune* correspondent Robert Carter. In the summer of 1858 Carter and some sailing chums aboard the sloop *Helen* found themselves moored in the midst of the mackerel fleet fogbound on Cape Ann in Pigeon Cove harbor. They heard the voices and laughter of hundreds of unseen fishermen in the vessels around them, all on deck like themselves in the warm summer evening. Then out of the fog came a ballad, sung beautifully and with feeling, and received with enthusiastic applause from the crews of the other vessels out there in the mist. Other songs followed from other vessels. A scholar member of Carter's party was reclining on deck, sipping his claret. These tunes, he said, came from the popular songbooks of the New England sailors.

Carter and three friends had chartered the thirty-three foot *Helen*, which came complete with the owner-captain and the steersman-cook who had sailed in a privateer in the War of 1812. Once under way the skipper occasionally treated those aboard to lemonade, made particularly refreshing by his practice of adding a dollop of whiskey to "correct the acidity."

One night the *Helen* put into Gloucester harbor. While waiting for dinner at the Gloucester House hotel, and looking forward to sleeping in real beds, Carter says they strolled through the streets that teemed with three thousand or more fishermen and sailors, out for an evening's diversion on the town. They would be humming along to the popular melodies of the day, sung to the accompaniment of strings and horns, issuing from taverns and other establishments that solicited the patronage of the seamen. Music got a man to dancing a jig, and helped him forget the ocean waiting out there in the dark.

In *The Fishermen's Memorial and Record Book* is the story of "A Musical Fisherman." This was John Jay Watson, son and brother of fishing skippers, who began as a young fiddler to the fleet. After being shipwrecked on Prince Edward Island, he played impromptu concerts to earn his way back to Gloucester, and determined to become a professional violinist. The present writer traced the career of this "fiddling fisherman" in *The Stream I Go A-Fishing In: Musical Adventures of Gloucester Schoonerman John J. Watson*. Watson became a concert-hall violinist acclaimed in his time, as well as an impresario on the New York entertainment scene, and a composer of parlor music that was the rage after the Civil War. At least one of his melodies, "Frolic of the Frogs," remained popular enough to be reissued a quarter century after it was first published. It is notable that a number of Watson's shipmates were also amateur musicians, playing before crewmate audiences who had little or no other entertainment.

The men on the boats sang the words to the songs of the day, and sea ballads and chanteys. But as to poetic verse, there was little worth reciting. The versifiers of Gloucester in the 19th century labored under the conventions of polite poesy of the period. Only when they escaped those trammels by venturing into the vernacular do they sound authentic. Hiram Rich was one who alternated between artificial and down-to-sea verse. Gloucester-born, he spent his days as a cashier in local banks. In spare moments between financial transactions he shaped stanzas in which he reveled in the dialect of the waterfront. In "The Skipper-Hermit" he speaks in the role of a harbor boatman who lives and fishes alone, his vessel *Wren* his only companion. Despite local references, the poem had broad enough appeal to be first published in *Scribner's Monthly*, then reprinted by George

Procter in *The Fishermen's Memorial and Record Book*. It ends with:

An' so we jog the hours away,
The gulls they coo an' tattle,
Till on the hill the sundown red
Starts up the drowsin' cattle.
The seiners row their jiggers by;
I pull the slide half over,
An' shet the shore out, an' the smell
Of sea-weed sweeter'n clover.

Rich's poems were printed in the *Atlantic Monthly*, too. Editor William Dean Howells accepted a dozen of them and printed them under the collective title "Leaves on the Tide."

Late in the century Clarence Manning Falt also attempted to make poetry of the life of the harbor. Falt described himself as "born in this seaport city, with blood of sea-faring people in my veins." He said "the grandeur and pathos of this variable life have ever enthralled me." In 1894 Falt published *Points of Interest of Gloucester in Song*, accompanying photos of Cape Ann landmarks with poesy larded with the conventional ornate verse of the period. But by 1902, when he produced *Wharf and Fleet – Ballads of the Fishermen of Gloucester*, Falt had fallen under the spell of Kipling's barracks ballads, as in "Th' Rigger":

Yer may blow erbout th' cirkis, th' man on th' trapeze,
Yer may pant yer breath erbout th' "Humin Fly,"
But if yer want th' dizzy that will infant-like yer knees,
Let yer opticks quizz th' rigger flyin' high…

This is dialect with a vengeance, difficult in spite of Falt's notes. (A rigger, he explained, is the man who climbs high in the rigging of ships in port to hang sails and scrape masts.) In later poems Charles Manning Falt returned to the adjective-heavy, allusion-encrusted poetical genre of the period. He would never surpass his honest experiments at capturing the rhythms of speech of the Gloucester waterfront.

In Henry Wadsworth Longfellow's journal of December 17, 1839 was the note, "News of shipwrecks horrible on the coast. Forty bodies washed ashore near Gloucester. One woman lashed to a piece of wreck. There is a reef called Norman's Woe where many of these took place." Two weeks later Longfellow was at his desk late into the night writing a "ballad of the *Hesperus*."

The "Wreck of the *Hesperus*" was published together with "The Village Blacksmith" in 1841, and these two poems established Longfellow as America's favorite fireside poet, his reputation then reinforced by "Evangeline," "The Song of Hiawatha" and "The Midnight Ride of Paul Revere." He was, after his death, the first American poet enshrined in the Poets' Corner in Westminster Abbey (many English still think Longfellow is one of theirs, of the ilk of Wordsworth and Tennyson). But it was treacherous popularity for this Harvard scholar of languages and translator of ancient sagas. Late in the century literary taste pivoted away from the romantic, conventional and decorous, and thereafter Longfellow was more parodied than praised.

Still, much can be said for "The Wreck of the *Hesperus*." It made palpable the hazards that crews of fishing schooners faced in winter storms along the Cape Ann shore. There is the all-too-typical overconfidence of the skipper-father, certain he can "weather the roughest gale / that ever wind did blow." There is language that races along with the *Hesperus* toward her doom: "And fast through the midnight dark and drear, / Through the whistling sleet and snow, / Like a sheeted ghost, the vessel swept / Tow'rds the reef of Norman's Woe." Many of the images are cruelly alive: "And a whooping billow swept the crew / Like icicles from her deck." Here, for the first time, a dramatic Gloucester sea incident was made known to a vast audience by a poet about to gain international stature.

In 1896, a sizeable new summer "cottage" was under construction up in back of Niles Beach. Henry Ware Eliot of the Hydraulic Brick Company of St. Louis and his wife Charlotte had been summering for several years at the Hawthorne Inn, and so enjoyed the ambience of East Gloucester they decided to build. The neighborhood, they decid-

Longfellow's "The Wreck of the Hesperus" made palpable to a broad audience the tragedy of a schooner foundering in a wintry gale.

ed, was just the place to vacation with their older children, and with eight-year-old Thomas Stearns who had been born when both parents were forty-four. He would become better known as T. S. Eliot.

The poet would spend all or parts of his young summers in East Gloucester: regularly as a young boy, then at intervals when he was a

T. S. Eliot, painted by his sister Charlotte about 1900. The poet vacationed in the family's East Gloucester summer home throughout his youth. *Courtesy Cape Ann Historical Museum*

student at Milton Academy and Harvard, and as a Harvard graduate student. When Eliot returned to Gloucester from England briefly in 1915 it was only to make some effort to explain to bewildered parents why he had abruptly married Vivien Haigh-Wood and given up an academic career. He did not return again until 1958 when he stopped by for a last visit to the fine big house on Edgemoor Road, by then sold out of the family.

In childhood photos taken by his brother, there he is, boy and book on the veranda of the family cottage. "Curl up the small soul in the window seat / Behind the *Encyclopœdia Britannica*" he said in his poem "Animula." This was the T. S. Eliot of intellect. The future candidate for a Ph. D. at Harvard who did all the spadework on the philosophy of F. H. Bradley but never returned to deliver his dissertation. Here was the later author of *The Waste Land*, the poetic work that spoke to the despondency of the post-World War I generation, and was richly annotated with references that sent critics scurrying to track down sources in Dante, Ovid and Baudelaire. Rose Macaulay said that in *The Waste Land* Eliot was heard as a new voice, "revealing ancient things in a new way."

This was the Eliot whose originality would establish him as the most solidly revolutionary American poet of the 20th century. He was, too, the respected literary critic. And the much-produced playwright, of *Murder in the Cathedral* and *The Cocktail Party*. His poetry sometimes had unexpected reverberations: from the litter of *Old Possum's Book of Practical Cats* came Andrew Lloyd Webber's long-running Broadway hit "Cats."

But there was another T. S. Eliot – the boy splashing on Niles Beach and exploring tide pools. Who learned to handle a sail in Gloucester harbor. Who, sailing with his brother in Henry's boat, the *Elsa*, became wind- and current-wise cruising down the back shore to Thacher's and Dry Salvages, coming about and making for the whistling buoy, the "groaner." Herbert Kenny was certain that the influence of those Gloucester boyhood summers persisted in Eliot's work: "One cannot read Eliot's poetry, and particularly *Four Quartets*, without sensing that the sea stirred in the depths of his being and stands as a major symbol in his work."

It was this T. S. Eliot who one time was sailing down Maine off Mount Desert Rock in a nineteen-foot knockabout with his Harvard classmate Harold Peters when gale winds and fog forced them to take shelter for the night at Duck Island. Next morning it was still rough weather, but late in the day they made it in to Somesville. Their log book showed a sketch of Eliot casting off, with the caption "heroic work by the swab." In 1964, writing to his distant cousin, historian

Samuel Eliot Morison, Eliot recalled those two days marooned at Duck Island when he and Peters "lived chiefly on lobster." He was writing in the last year before his death and he was still close to his other identity, the self-reliant sea-venturing T. S. Eliot.

He took an intense interest in what others, the best ones, had written about Gloucester and the fleet. As a boy Eliot had heard the schoonermen chuckle at the dialect Rudyard Kipling put in their mouths in *Captains Courageous*. Cape Cod talk, they said, and young Eliot took note that ways of speech could be so different from one cape to another across Massachusetts Bay. As a boy he had soaked up the rollicking Kipling ballads, and at ten recited *Danny Deever* for an audience of other children of the neighborhood. When Tom Eliot was older he read what that same Kipling was writing about the Gloucester fishermen, in *Captains Courageous*. Eliot said Kipling entered into his own verse.

Eliot admired the Gloucestermen stories of James B. Connolly, too. Connolly was little known in England (which probably did not distress that scorner of all things Britannic). But Eliot thought the oversight should be corrected and – in 1928, more than a dozen years after Eliot had emigrated to England – he persuaded his publisher employers, Faber & Gwyer (later Faber & Faber), to print *Fishermen of the Banks*, a collection of representative Connolly Gloucester fleet tales that included "A Fresh Halibuter," "The Lone Voyagers," "The Race it Blew" and "Driving Home from Georges." Eliot did not put his name to the Introduction, but these were without question his words as he looked from London back to the Gloucester of his young summers. Gloucester "has the most beautiful harbour for small ships on the whole of that coast" he said. But then the menace behind the beauty for the fishermen: "There is no harder life, no more uncertain livelihood, and few more dangerous occupations."

In his admiration of Connolly's tales of those fishermen, Eliot said they were written by "one who (with all respect) knows the subject much better than Mr. Kipling." These were true narratives, he said, that could "be learnt by word of mouth from the men between trips, as they lounged at the corner of Main Street and Duncan Street in Gloucester." That was Fishermen's Corner. Eliot remembered, then, himself venturing down Main Street as a boy, buying a notebook at the Procter Brothers' Old Corner shop. Eliot carried that notebook around for years, to Harvard and Paris and London, jotting down the lines of his early poems that shook the American poetic establishment.

The Gloucester fishermen would have figured prominently in Eliot's *The Waste Land* had it not been for Ezra Pound's red pencil. When Pound was done suggesting deletions from Part IV, "Death by Water," only ten lines remained. Purged was a long section that could have been spawned from tales Eliot overheard at Fishermen's Corner. It is a haunted passage in which a schooner scuds swiftly and fatally northward into a world of mist and myth, storm seas and final rush into the embrace of an iceberg. These lines are sea-aware and sea-rhythmed, distant from Eliot's deft sketches of the despair of hollow people in empty rooms. How did he learn to speak with such nautical familiarity of gaffjaws and gleet and garboard strakes and fore cross-trees and Marm Brown's house of ill repute on the Gloucester waterfront? Eliot himself is not helpful – he provided no notes for the "Death by Water" segment. He was probably right to take Pound's advice that *The Waste Land* would be tighter without these lines. But in themselves they are a masterly poetic telling of a fishing voyage to the winter Banks from Gloucester.

Gloucester surfaces elsewhere here and there throughout Eliot's poems. He titled one section of *Landscapes* "Cape Ann," and in it glories in songbirds, but concludes by conceding all to the seagull, "the tough one." There's nothing more to be said: "The palaver is finished." A sharp local touch – dismissing idle chatter as mere "palaver." Even in the religiously anguished "Ash Wednesday" there are brief images of Gloucester harbor, of a granite shore and of sails.

Four Quartets was T. S. Eliot's last major poetic work. The third section, "The Dry Salvages," distills finally the impressions the summer-sailing boy never forgot, storm seas bursting upon granite, and tossing upon the shore a "shattered lobsterpot" and "the gear of foreign dead men." Gear – the young sailor Eliot would speak of shipboard gear. And they were lobster "pots" to him, as they were to Winslow Homer. Lobster "traps," the modern term, had not yet taken hold.

There is much in the poem that speaks of Gloucester – but with

T. S. Eliot it is risky to jump to conclusions. For instance, the line "Lady, whose shrine stands on the promontory ..." Was Eliot talking about the Portuguese church on Prospect Street, Our Lady of Good Voyage? Poet Charles Olson thought so. In 1947 Olson was cultivating a friendship with Ezra Pound and sent a postcard to him that showed the façade of the church, and Olson in his note confidently identified it as the "shrine" in Eliot's poem. Pound sent the card to Eliot who replied frigidly to the effect that this Olson, whoever he might be, did not know what he was talking about. Eliot said he did not remember the church in the photo (it had been rebuilt in its present form in 1915, the year of Eliot's last previous visit to Gloucester). Eliot wrote to someone else that the shrine he really had in mind was the church of Notre Dame de la Gard, high up overlooking the Mediterranean at Marseilles.

But other elements in "The Dry Salvages" are unmistakably Cape Ann, as in the sense of some unknowable beyond speaking through the thundering waves: "The distant rote in the granite teeth." Eliot's use of the word "rote" fascinated his kinsman Samuel Eliot Morison. In an article, "The Dry Salvages and the Thacher Shipwreck," Admiral Morison said rote was an old English word, no longer heard much outside New England, used to describe the distant roar of waves along a rocky coast. But in New England speech, he said, it was heard often. In New England writing, too. In 1858, on the cruise that took him along the Cape Ann shore, Robert Carter spoke of a night on board "listening to the 'rote' of the sea." That was what his charter captain called the sound the waves made when breaking over ledges. Thoreau, too, quoted an old Wellfleet oysterman speaking of the "sea 'rut,' a peculiar roar of the sea before the wind changes." And George Wasson in *Sailing Days on the Penobscot* said the fishermen around Isle au Haut "found their way in a thick-o'-fog by listening for the distinctive rote of the surf on various ledges and islets." An old New England sea word was rote, and Eliot knew it, savored it, used it.

T. S. Eliot was everlastingly a study in contradictions. In Gloucester he was a Missourian, in St. Louis a New Englander. He was a Midwesterner in what was still Boston Brahmin Harvard. He returned to family roots in England because he could not tolerate what had become of American culture after 1830. In London he lived the roles of financial clerk in the City and later publishing house executive. He Anglicized his diction and nationality, and Anglicanized his religion. And suffered through marital mismatch across decades of his adult years until finally coming to a happy marriage. Here was the hypochondriac with polite, mannered reserve wending his way with rolled brolly toward his desk at Lloyds, more English than the English, writing fiercely erudite, wearily urbane poetry. Here was the Eliot described by literary critic Edmund Wilson as "a completely artificial, or, rather, self-invented character." Eliot was "the most highly refined and attuned and chiselled human being" Wilson had ever encountered.

Eliot became a British citizen, but the English never really accepted him as one of theirs (his poems contained odd Americanisms like "dory"). He became an Anglo-Catholic, but literary critics and friends sensed that deep down he was New England Calvinist. Wherever he was, he always felt himself an exile. He sometimes signed himself "metoikos," Greek for alien. But somehow he never escaped his Americanness, and admitted that he was a New England poet after all. "I speak as a New Englander." His creative daemon, like Hawthorne's, had been nourished by ancestral whispers north of Boston. "My country landscape . . . is that of New England, of coastal New England."

The cultural historians and analysts of poetic schools and influences have the T. S. Eliot of social decay, donnish wit and religion-drenched despair. Cape Ann has the Eliot of bright sailing days in Gloucester harbor, a boy's quick ear for palaver along by Fishermen's Corner, and that unfathomed metaphor the sea presents.

There is little record of what the "palaver" on the schooners actually sounded like. But in the early 1970s Peter Parsons and Peter Anastas recorded interviews with some elderly citizens for *When Gloucester Was Gloucester – Toward an Oral History of the City*, issued by the Gloucester 350th Anniversary Celebration. One of those taped was Charlie McPhee, who recalled an incident from his young days as a schoonerman fishing "down Labrador" among the icebergs. "And in them days the salt fishermen was getting a little shy on water, fresh water. And they'd go over to them bergs with barrels and get water, get their water right off the bergs." There on the ice was a black Newfoundland dog, almost starved to death. "So, geez," said Charlie, "they went, they got the dog. Brought him aboard and done everything they could for him, and he lived." By Charlie's telling, the dog was brought safely to Gloucester and became a popular fixture at Fishermen's Corner. "What a wonderful life that dog lived! After being picked up almost dead on an iceberg! Way the hell down in Labrador!"

Also in the early '70s, Linda Brayton and David Masters taped interviews with a number of local personalities for an oral history project, "Toward an Oral History of Cape Ann." Included were interviews with fishermen like Harry Eustis and Ken McCurdy whose recollections went back to schooner days, and to the changes in the waterfront during the transition to beam trawlers. The interviewers had some difficulty with the broad "a" that was once a hallmark of the fisherman's dialect, as heard in the speech of both Eustis and McCurdy. "'Course, them schooners was gahf-rigged." "Gahf? Could you spell that?" "Why, g-a-f-f." "Oh, 'gaff.'" "That's right, the mains'l and fores'l each hung from a gahf, which was a spah attached to the mahst."

Then there was the fleet as seen by the artists. Winslow Homer was the first major painter to portray the seductively sleek and fast schooners developed after the Civil War when hull and sail plan were refined to exploit the Banks fisheries on a large scale. (Other types of vessels predominate in Fitz Henry Lane's earlier paintings of Gloucester harbor, with only an occasional fishing schooner seen under way.) In 1873, when Homer stayed at the Atlantic Hotel in Gloucester, he was still doing wood engravings for *Harper's Weekly*. These were finely detailed sketches like the ones he had sent from the front during the Civil War. One of his Gloucester works of this period is "Gloucester Harbor," with boys in dories intent on something in the water, while younger ones loaf disinterested. Beyond them two schooners under full sail are catching the wind, heading out toward a horizon crowded with other vessels. On one level it is pure illustration. But you cannot ignore those boys. Homer knew that in a few years they would be manning other schooners sailing to uncertain fates.

Winslow Homer, "Gloucester Harbor." Harper's weekly, 1873.

Library of Congress collection

Homer was also painting watercolor versions of his subjects, exploring a separate form of artistic expression. His watercolors were freer, more spontaneous than the engravings. Here again many of his subjects are children inventing games on the shore with the schooner sails beyond in the harbor. The boys gaze out to the sea where a father might be alive or lost. They are boys growing up alongside girls in pinafores who would be their wives, and often their widows. In "Waiting for Dad" Homer makes the connection explicit: the confident but anxious son perched on a dory gazing seaward. Behind him is his mother, holding an infant, her expression and stance sad, stoic, resigned. She yearns for the return of her husband, to share the warmth of her bed briefly, perhaps leaving the seed of another infant before the cycle of parting, waiting and hoping repeats. In another of

Homer's Gloucester paintings, "Waiting for the Boats," one boy rests a reassuring hand on the shoulder of his chum as both study distant sail contours, hoping to make out a familiar shape.

In the summer of 1880 Homer was back in Gloucester, and this time he had talked Mrs. Octavius Merrill, wife of the lighthouse keeper on Ten Pound Island, into letting him stay in a spare house on the island. Mrs. Merrill was related to an old friend of Homer's who could vouch for the respectability of this boarder, even if he was an artist (the referral probably emphasized Homer's credentials as a successful magazine illustrator). Mrs. Merrill would be able to report that the boarder was well-behaved, although perhaps given to a sundowner or two, kept to himself, knew some uptown people ashore but reserved his limited store of sociability for a pair of fishermen who would stop by to see what he was painting.

Winslow Homer in that second Gloucester summer heeded a call from the sea. He renounced commercial illustration and began, with bold sunset watercolors of the harbor, the absorption with the ocean and its cryptic symbolism that would dominate his canvasses thereafter.

When the last fishing schooner sailed over the horizon, the fiddling tunes diminished in the distance with her, the accents of the talk of the sailing fleet became unintelligible over the waters, and the harbor was deprived of the visual excitement of hundreds of sail shapes against the sky. The fortunes of Cape Ann were on the verge of another sea change.

CHAPTER 8

Fishing by Dragger and Diesel

THE RAPID ACCEPTANCE into the world's fisheries of steam auxiliary engines, and later diesel power plants, sent Gloucester harbor into a slow spiral of decline. The port was reluctant to adapt to fishing with engine-driven vessels, and surrendered leadership in the industry to ports like Boston and New Bedford. As internal combustion engines gradually prevailed, the symbolism of the schooners was lost, that of vessels built from trees, catching the winds from the skies, to harvest creatures from the sea. James B. Connolly wrote that it was impossible to rhapsodize about the beauty of any vessel not propelled by wind in its sails. Fishing out of Gloucester became less a mythic challenge to the elements, and more a particularly hazardous maritime trade.

After the passing of the schooners, new people were making a living fishing out of Gloucester – Portuguese from the Azores and Sicilians – and they did not mix into the Gloucester cultural bouillabaisse at first. They kept their languages, their fishing methods, their lives to themselves.

There had been Portuguese in the Gloucester fleet as far back as the 1870s. Eventually more than 200 families settled a neighborhood that came to be known as "Portagee Hill," probably because it was easier for the other locals to say "Portagee" than wrap tongues around "port-u-guese." Disparaging? It could be, depending on how it was intoned. But so were the other ethnic terms uttered by members of every group except the one being referred to.

In 1893 the Portuguese community members built their own church, Our Lady of Good Voyage, overlooking the harbor. It later

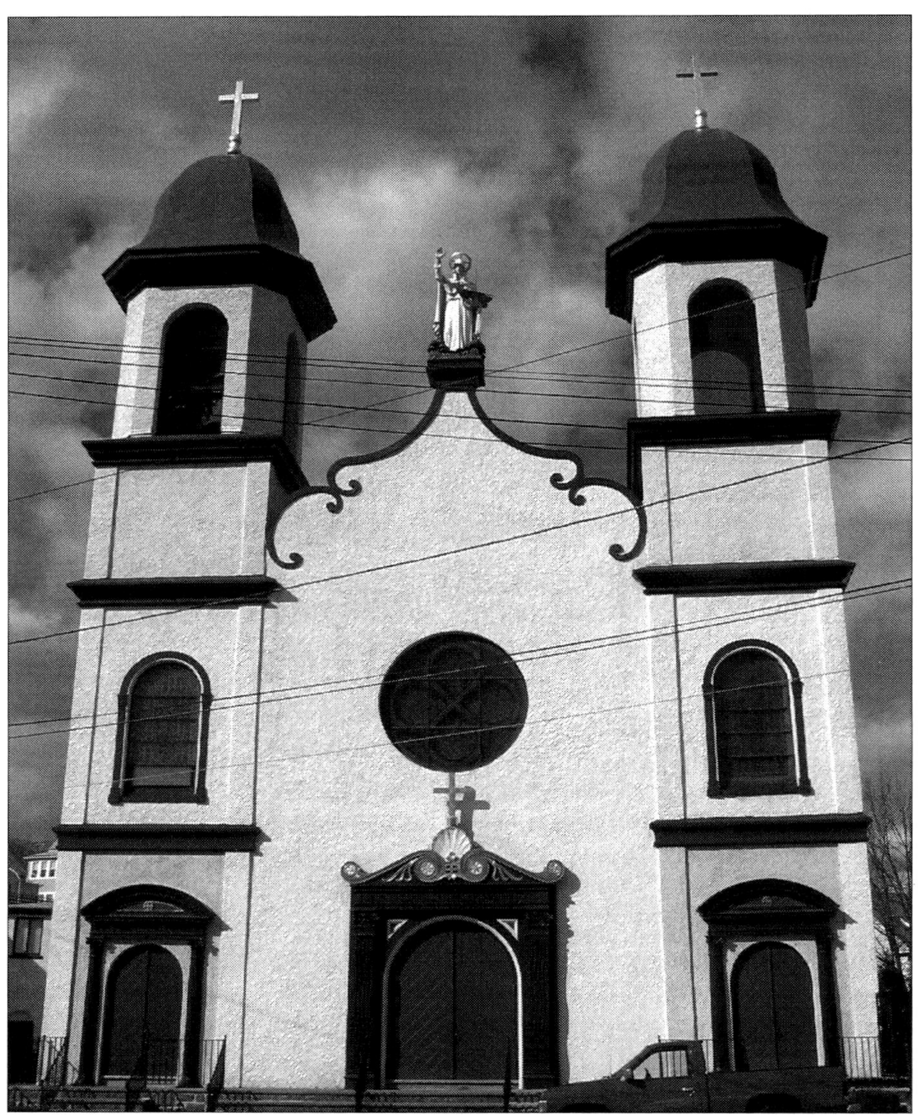

Gloucester's Portuguese Catholic church, Our Lady of Good Voyage. Ship models line the inside walls, and outside a ten-foot Madonna cradles, not the Christ child, but a schooner. *Author photo*

burned, but was rebuilt in 1915. It is a remarkable church by any standards, with ship models lining the inside walls, and outside a ten-foot Madonna cradling, not the Christ child, but a schooner. In 1922, twenty-three carillon bells were installed in one of the two stucco towers (later painted bright blue), and 5,000 people crowded in front of the church to hear the first properly tuned carillon in the United States.

When the Portuguese fishing vessels were still strong in numbers the Archbishop of Boston would visit in early summer to preside over the blessing of the fleet. On a bandstand in front of the church, decorated with banners and flags, a Portuguese band would play concerts for two nights before the ceremony. On the blessing day a High Mass was said for the fishermen, then they marched down the Jodrey State Fish Pier to their vessels that had been festooned with flags and flowers. After the blessing the boat horns would blast and the crowd cheer to propitiate the Lady of Good Voyage, asking her to give the fishermen good trips and safe voyages.

Typical of the early Portuguese families in Gloucester were the Da Cuhnas. After the first generation or so they began to spell the name Coney and Cooney, because that's the way people downtown were pronouncing it. And after they intermarried with families named Perry and Williams and Swarz, it became difficult to keep track of the family lines. By the 1920s and '30s there were Portuguese captains in Gloucester with the very un-Azorean-sounding names of Matthew Sears, Joe Lovett and Frank Brown.

Still, the Portuguese families retained a strong sense of community. When they organized a picnic on the Back Shore, they would chip in to rent a truck and pack washtubs full of vegetables from their gardens together with home-made wine. Arthur K. Rose wrote about it in his *Portagee Hill and a People* (1991). Arthur had played in a dance band in his early days, but then reality set in and he spent twenty years working at Gorton's fish company. Arthur said that on the beach the men would dig for mussels and pick periwinkles off the rocks to add a seafood course to the feast. Late into the night everybody would congregate around a fire built in the sand and sing Portuguese songs to the accompaniment of guitars, violas, mandolins.

At Christmas people from all over Gloucester would climb Portagee Hill and find a welcome at every door. They would come in, say hello, admire the tree and be fed – linguica, Portuguese sweetbread, fried eggs. The term "Portagee" came to be said with warmth and respect toward a people who knew how to fish and look after themselves and share the good things in life with their neighbors, Portuguese or not.

After a strike over declining redfish prices in the 1960s, many of the Portuguese left to go flounder fishing out of New Bedford, or shrimping in Texas or Louisiana. Others went into other lines of work. Today a declining number of people in Gloucester call themselves Portuguese-Americans. But in the veins of many runs the old maritime blood of the Azoreans.

The Sicilians populated the Fort district of town and spread grocerias, conversational barber shops and the St. Peter's Club along West Main Street. These were the immigrants from the Sicilian ports of Palermo, Messina, Marsala, Trapani, Sciacca. They were families with surnames like Nicastro, Randazza, Ciolino, Tarantino, Ciluffo, Ventimiglia, Agrusso, Scola, Parisi, Lavasco, Sinagra, Loiacano, Linquata, Palazzola.

In the early days the Sicilians had been wary of people outside their own community. Some they trusted, like Anthony Kyrouz, a Lebanese immigrant who sold meat and produce out of his truck. The Fort families called him "San Antonio" because he sold to them on credit when they were short of cash.

The Sicilian fleet was close-knit, with crews made up mostly of relatives and neighbors. At sea they entertained themselves playing mandolins, singing, swapping stories. Ashore in the Fort there was card playing, with all the families visiting back and forth among their crowded tenements, sharing the good times and hard times. During the Depression it was mostly hard times. Food was passed around, and nothing went to waste. Even the kids helped out. The boys found old torn seine nets along the docks, stitched them together, strung them between dories out in the harbor at night with torches lit to draw the fish. Slowly the boys rowed toward the eager neighbors shouting encouragement on Pavilion Beach, waiting with pans and buckets to scoop up the midnight catch.

It was rough going for the Sicilian fishermen at sea. In those days

"Eastern rig" beam trawlers in 1936. These were the workhorse draggers of the Portuguese and Italian fleets.
Courtesy Cape Ann Historical Museum

their boats were small and often unreliable, their navigation relying heavily upon memory and sea sense. The best account of the life is in *Memoirs of a Gloucester Fisherman* (1987). R. Salve Testaverde spoke of the struggles of a new nationality of fishermen to gain a footing in Gloucester. At first they fished trawling with baited hooks much as they had off Sicily, this "guinea fleet," as the locals called them. Salve Testaverde said they did not take offense to the expression. They just wanted to make a living and earn their place. They knew when they proved they could fish, they'd be respected.

Gradually trust developed between the Sicilians and fishermen of the old fleet. In the late '30s Salve was mackerel seining on the *Bethulia*, Captain Philip Curcuru, when one of the "American boats" made the rounds of the fleet to report a radio forecast warning of southeast gales. That was the first warning the Italian boats had of the monster hurricane of 1938.

Sometimes the treacherous sea offered an unexpected bounty. Like the time Salve and his crewmates found themselves steaming among crates of high-proof liquor jettisoned by a rumrunner fleeing the Coast Guard off Thacher's Island. Some of that catch of bootleg hooch was kept aboard, and during mug-ups the crew members reinforced their coffee with 200-proof alcohol. "We were the happiest boat in the tub trawling fleet." But they quietly brought most of the crates ashore. Salve's parents made whiskey anisetta from his share, and rossola, "a woman's drink." His father still had a bottle of anisetta left to toast Salve's marriage in 1940, and another for the birth of Salve's first son a year later.

Salve married old family style. He made the first move in his courtship of the beauteous Nina Randazza, but the engagement had to be approved by the families. When he took Nina out for a movie at the North Shore Theatre, her two married sisters came along as chaperones. Salve said it was like "having two seine boats alongside."

When the Sicilians migrated to Gloucester early in the 20th century, they brought with them their homage to St. Peter, patron saint of fishermen. In the 1920s one of the fishing captains had a statue of the saint carved, and a chosen few of the men of the Italian fleet carried it on their shoulders in a religious procession. Thus began the tradition of the St. Peter's Fiesta, which was long a neighborhood celebration, with families gathered on front stoops to celebrate among themselves and offer to passersby a glass of red wine blended from grapes that were stomped by the neighborhood kids. A makeshift altar was constructed near the entrance to the Fort neighborhood, and people pinned dollar bills to it.

In time, the events gained momentum. The area around the old Harbor Cove town landing became St. Peter's Square, and days were consumed each year constructing a giant altar. Today out-of-town Italian musical groups play there during the long weekend of Fiesta near the end of June. The Cape Ann Symphony Orchestra has played too, over a competing medley of sounds from the adjacent mini-amusement park constructed for the occasion.

In the backyards nearby, large numbers of the intricately interrelated families party together, feasting on Italian food. The daylight hours of the celebration are crowded with athletic events, most of them on the water. Three stout seine boats named after Columbus's vessels – the Nina, the Pinta and the Santa Maria – are rowed by eight husky oarsmen each. With a coxswain urging them on, they pull a half mile out into the harbor and a half mile back. The cheers go to the boat that touches the beach first.

A highlight of Fiesta weekend is the greasy pole race, a rite of manhood brought over from Italy, that is conducted over all three days of the celebration. Men, many of them in outrageous attire, run out, one after another, on a well-greased telephone pole fixed to a platform high above the water. The object is to keep their footing long enough to grab an American flag tied at the end of the pole.

Pleasure boats jockey about nearby in the harbor, video cameras from the local TV station capture the action for later re-broadcast. Spectators lined along Pavilion beach cheer as one after another of the contestants teeters, loses balance, falls flailing into the water. With the more awkward tumbles the crowd gasps, hoping no bones were broken or internal damage done. In the Sunday contest, when one of the challengers finally does capture the flag, he is met with the embraces due a conquering hero. In later years, they will make room for him on the benches in front of the St. Peter's Club on Rogers Street where the old Sicilians gather in the sun. Maybe he went on to become a respected fishing boat captain and paterfamilias. But his fame will be brightest for that day when he walked the greasy pole, caught the nation's flag and held it proudly as he took the long fall into the chilly June waters of Gloucester harbor.

World War II was a humiliating period for the Gloucester fishermen who hailed from Sicily. When America found itself at war, Washington feared attacks by "Fifth Column" agents planted on U.S. soil years in advance of a planned invasion. It was a tactic the Nazis had used all too effectively to undermine the defenses of countries in northern Europe and Scandinavia. Crewmen of Gloucester's Sicilian fleet were rounded up at the dock by the Coast Guard, questioned, required to account for their movements at sea.

A nervous wartime rule was imposed requiring that over half a fishing crew consist of American citizens. Many of the Italian fishermen had never bothered to take out citizenship papers. When these crewmen were not allowed to fish, Gloucester draggers were left at the dock. This at a time when the government was pleading with fishermen to increase fish landings to help compensate for a nationwide meat shortage. Also, many of the finest vessels in the Gloucester fleet had been requisitioned by the Navy. As a final impediment to bringing in the fish, the port of Gloucester was closed between sunset and dawn for a time in 1942. When the fishing boats did manage to put to sea, there was the danger of being run down by convoy ships not yet equipped with radar.

Despite all the problems the Gloucester fishermen had to deal with, they distinguished themselves in the Battle of the North Atlantic. When their vessels were commandeered by the Navy, many skippers volunteered for service, and their shiphandling savvy and general sea sense were put to good use. Captain Thomas Benham enlisted at sixty-three. Other Gloucester captains were indignant when they were rejected merely because they were over sixty-five.

Old Gloucester sailing schooners were pressed into service. They patrolled far off shore in antisubmarine service, giving the Germans fits because their U-boats could not detect a vessel that approached silently, with no vibrating propellers. But there was no doubt that Gloucester fishermen at war took their risks. After spotting a submarine, the *Helen M.* of Gloucester broke radio silence to alert the Navy. The crew of the *Helen M.* did not have to be told that if the U-boat heard their message and homed in on the signal, they would be an easy target. And the Germans did sink fishing vessels. The *Ben & Josephine* and the *Aeolus* were destroyed, their crews rowing for their lives through fog to reach the Nova Scotia shore. Pulling on their oars, the fishermen knew that Admiral Doenitz had ordered his submarine commanders to machine-gun survivors. Fortunately most of the German captains had the decency to ignore the order.

When the trawler *Lark* was attacked in 1944, Captain Abbott ordered the crew off and stayed aboard as the Germans emptied more than 2,000 rounds into the vessel. After the U-boat left, Captain Abbott surveyed the situation, confirmed that there were no holes in him personally, got the engine going, picked his crew out of the water and nursed the riddled *Lark* into port.

The war hit home on Cape Ann. The proportion of young men who volunteered for service from Gloucester was higher than in most towns, and there were many gold star and blue star emblems between the curtains in front windows, signifying a son who had died or been wounded. One way or another, the boats continued to bring in fish, and it was a vital commodity. When people used up their monthly quota of red ration stamps to buy meat, they could always fill up on fish that was off-ration.

Cape Ann was more an island than ever during the war. A non-essential automobile qualified for only an A-card on the windshield, and its limited gas allotment would not take the vehicle very far the other side of the Cut Bridge. The upper halves of the car headlights were painted black, as was done with the streetlights. Window shades were kept tightly drawn at night. Any glow in the sky could silhouette convoys in the crosshairs of prowling German submarines.

After the war the Sicilians took up fishing where they had left off. Thomas Piraino was one of them, a first-generation Sicilian born in Boston who came to know Gloucester during his young fishing days, as he tells in *The Sicilian Fisherman's Son* (1992). When Piraino was fifteen his uncle and his father bought the battered wooden hull of a World War I subchaser from the Navy and had it towed to Gloucester to be converted to a mackerel seiner.

Tom Piraino went along with his father and uncle to order a purse seine from the American Linen Thread Company. Then the net went to a shop on the waterfront where it was tarred. They trucked it out to the seine fields along Farrington Avenue in East Gloucester, and spread it on the grass to dry. A couple of days later the crew came back to the field, gathered up the net, took it aboard the subchaser, which by then had been fully converted and christened the *Santina D.*

Piraino made trips on the boat, often into Ipswich Bay, during his school vacations. Then he gave up fishing and became an engineer. But fishing was the only trade his father, Paul, knew. Paul told Tom what it had been like fishing in Sicily, rowing and sailing off the shores of Lipari Island near Spadafora. Lipari is one of the Aeolian Islands in the Tyrrhenian Sea off Sicily's north coast, and was mentioned by Homer in the *Odyssey*. So Tom's father, who had dipped nets into waters where Ulysses sailed, and who set his course back to port with the volcanic plume of Stromboli flashing lightnings in the dusk, was now fishing at the pleasure of whatever sea gods ruled Massachusetts bays. Paul Piraino was lost when, in 1940, the dragger *Frances* sank with all hands after an explosion off Provincetown.

Gloucester's stubby, chugging dragger fleet labored on in anonymity. When Kim Bartlett was waterfront reporter for the *Gloucester Daily Times* in the 1970s, this neglect was, he said, "an insult to the men who still go down to the sea in ships and still confront the treachery and the drudgery involved in hauling a living from the ocean." So Bartlett decided to tell the story of these forgotten men. He knew that, as a newspaperman and an "American," he would have trouble gaining the confidence of the Sicilian fishermen. So he shipped as a crewman on their boats for many months, getting to know the men and following their lives. He wrote about them in *The Finest Kind: The Fishermen of Gloucester* (1977).

On the Sicilian draggers the skipper was more of an autocrat than the old sailing schooner masters who slept and slogged with their crews. The dragger captain remained in the pilot house, a little world apart from that of the crew berthed up forward. No one dared to second-guess the skipper about the fishing, at sea or ashore, even if they were family. Kim Bartlett wrote of Captain Tommy Brancaleone of the *Joseph & Lucia III*, remote and unapproachable in his wheelhouse, playing opera recordings incessantly at full blast over the boat's loudspeakers. But Tommy had an instinct for finding fish, so there were no complaints from the crew.

There were those with cameras who saw that the wooden beam trawlers had a nobility of their own. And knew they would not be around forever. And decided to capture them on film. One avid marine photographer was William D. Hoyt, who compiled a photographic biography of the working fleet from 1927 to 1948. He began when, after classes in shorthand and typing at the Gloucester Business College conducted on Main Street by Mrs. Florence Martin, he prowled the docks of Duncan's Point taking photos. Later he took his Kodak to the Fort, along Rogers Street and down East Main. And over to Essex, where he photographed the building of draggers. His visual record of the transition from sail to power appeared in 1987 as *Hanging On: The Gloucester Waterfront in Change, 1927-1948.* Another documentary photo book was *Portrait of Gloucester – Charles A. Lowe Photos.* Lowe had been a photographer for the *Gloucester Daily Times* and roamed Cape Ann in a battered truck, stopping to capture, with a sure sense of the moment, compositions of waterfront fires, pretty girls, little league baseball, crewmen chopping ice from draggers back from winter seas.

Also in that era Peter Prybot was majoring in marine fisheries biology at the University of Massachusetts. Weekends home from college he earned a little extra working on boats making shrimping trips out of Pigeon Cove or Gloucester harbor. As his thesis for a fisheries biology course, Prybot wanted to do a photographic study of the Gloucester beam trawler fleet. He took photos of ninety-four of the draggers leaving or returning to port, and managed to line up most of their men on deck for crew photos.

Over the years that followed, Prybot lobstered year-round while also researching and writing articles for *National Fisherman* and *Commercial Fisheries News.* Always in the back of his mind was the notion of shaping a book around those photos he had taken of the draggers of the '70s and his interviews with their skippers and crews. Finally, with tough-love support from his wife Anne, he launched *White-Tipped Orange Masts* in time for Gloucester's 375th anniversary in 1998.

It was well worth the wait to get his photos of the fleet into print. Here are those trawlers, honest vessels built to bring back fish. And the men on deck, dressed for their trade. Self-conscious, kidding around, but happy in fact to "have their picture took." Here is the *Vincie N.*, then crewed by Captain Joe, Sam and Tony Novello, Louis Benson, Joe Orlando. One of the last of her breed, the *Vincie N.* fished until 2002.

And here, in Prybot's book, is a photo of the *Carolyn René*, Captain Winthrop "Bunt" Davis and crewman Frank Muise. The thirty-one-foot *Carolyn René*, one of the smallest vessels in the dragger fleet, was

Goose Cove fisherman Winthrop "Bunt" Davis. The likes of poet Robert Frost called him friend.
Photo courtesy Jean Davis Young

one of the vessels Prybot fished in back during the '70s. She was designed along classic lobster boat lines so Bunt could rig her for shrimping, dragging for groundfish, or harpooning for bluefin tuna, then known less appetizingly as "horse mackerel." Bunt built the vessel himself on his own shore behind his house on Goose Cove in 1957.

The present writer remembers Bunt. With a voice developed by years of bellowing over boat engines and water slosh in Ipswich Bay, Bunt was a model of rough dignity, sea-sense and selfless bravery to countless boys allowed to help crew his vessels. They learned honor from a man who would steam out into the bay into frothing combers in aid of pleasure boaters who did not have the sense to stay tied up in a storm. When, at the Annisquam fish market float, a summer boater's toddler fell overboard from the deck, Bunt plunged in without a moment's hesitation to pull the boy out, while the father considered whether first to secure his watch or wallet. Bunt said nothing when he pulled himself dripping onto the float. There was just a glance between Bunt and the father, who perhaps was haunted for life by the knowledge that he had failed his son when he should not have failed.

Bunt was not an isolated instance of an unspoken fishermen's code that calls for making every effort to rescue fellow humans in danger at sea, no matter by what idiocy they got themselves into a fix. In 2006, Brad "Dirt" Murray and his crewman Doug Ritchie were awarded the prestigious Mariners Medal (the first granted in fifteen years) after they raced out in a small boat into combing waves breaking over the sandbar at the mouth of the Annisquam River to rescue a pair of capsized kayakers. Thirty-three years before, Brad's father David Murray had, along with his friend Mark Standley and others aboard a vessel sailing toward Cape Ann, been awarded the medal after they pulled from the water survivors from a fishing party boat that had foundered. The Murrays were the only father and son ever to receive the medal. Posthumous Mariners Medals went to Frank Quirk and the other members of Gloucester's *Can Do* who responded without hesitation to the "Mayday" call of a Greek tanker off Salem, and went down after battling for hours the monstrous seas whipped up by the Blizzard of 1978.

Back to Peter Prybot. After publication of *White-Tipped Orange Masts*, he continued to appear in the *Gloucester Daily Times* with a weekly piece on Cape Ann fishing. At one point he said he was going to quit writing the articles and concentrate on fishing. But Peter Prybot seems born to write about Cape Ann's maritime life, and fortunately the articles keep coming. One told of the 50-foot *Lady Arlene* returning on autopilot after a day of gillnetting. Fishing alone, Captain Chris Brewer left the wheelhouse to move some gear on the deck. The next thing he knew he had rammed the 40-foot lobster boat *Graceann S.* Skipper Anthony Scola, alone on the *Graceann S.*, had just time to leap onto the *Lady Arlene* before his own vessel went to the bottom. Anthony Scola had lost everything, and Chris Brewer felt bad about it. Then Brewer remembered somebody who owned a lobster boat he wanted to sell that was similar to the *Graceann S.*. He told Anthony that if he liked the boat, Brewer would buy it for him. Scola said sure, but since it was a bigger boat than the *Graceann S.*, he would pay for rigging it. Chris Brewer would not take any credit for buying the boat for Anthony. He'd only done what was fair, he said. The important thing was that both men could get back to fishing. Prybot tells the story matter-of-factly, allowing the decency of the two men to speak for itself.

Another book that pictured the Gloucester fleet of the '70s was *Iron Men, Wooden Ships: Skippers of Gloucester, MA*, self-published in 1998 by Charles G. Nicastro, one-time fisherman and son and son-in-law of fishermen. The book had its genesis when Nicastro's wife bought him a darkroom setup so he could develop his own film. He took his camera all over the waterfront in the '70s, snapping shots of the wooden draggers and the men who fished aboard them. Then he talked Kay Rodolosi, owner of the old Captain Courageous restaurant, into hanging some of his photos on the restaurant walls. Other fishermen came in with their wives, liked the photos, asked Nicastro to come down to their boat and take some pictures. Sell them a couple of prints. That was in 1976, '78. In '96 Nicastro dug out the old photos, traced the history of the crews as best he could, and put together the book.

The sparse details alongside photos of skipper and vessel tell mainly the history of a boat, the skipper's marriage, how many children resulted. But Nicastro himself points out what makes the book special: "The important thing to me is the face on the page. That's what I would like you to focus on. The facts may be few and simply put but the faces of these men are the history and heritage of Gloucester."

The "face on the page" does say it all, paired with a portrait of each captain's vessel. At first glance some of these skippers have the style of a seagoing Casanova, sideburned, cap at a sassy angle, maybe a moustache. Others are no-nonsense elder statesmen of the fleet. Many have the look of forces of nature – massive, muscular, bred to a boat's deck. Each jaw has the set of resolution, each eye the glint of command.

These were masters of vessels who took their responsibility for boat and crew seriously.

Here is Busty Frontiero, captain of the *Cigar Joe II*, who after forty years of fishing retired to do wood-carving and make jewelry out of haddock nape bone. And Captain Thomas Parisi, skipper of the 97-foot *St. Nicholas*. His sons were often crewmembers, and son Nick was the skipper for twenty years after Captain Tom. Back when the Italian fleet brought Christmas to the waterfront, the *St. Nicholas* was the logical vessel to arrive from the North Pole with Santa Claus aboard. In 1973 in a fog off Maine's Matinicus Island, the ninety-seven-foot *St. Nicholas* collided with the 380-foot Nova Scotia ferry, *Prince of Fundy*. The bow of the *St. Nicholas* was crumpled, but luckily no one was up forward at the moment of impact, and she was towed afloat into Camden.

Nick Parisi later came ashore, became proprietor of the Savory Skillet restaurant in the old Brown's Mall building, where he made the transition from on-board banter to exchanging barbs with the regular counter crowd. And with friends from the dragger days remembering the things that used to happen. Nick works a long day and for a long time had to – he was putting a son through medical school. As he neared retirement, Nick Parisi turned to developing his latent talents as an artist. When he painted draggers at a wharf he did so in strong, vivid colors and with authority, drawing upon long acquaintance with fishing and the sea.

Among the riveting photos in Charles Nicastro's book is one of a grinning, husky, thirty-seven-year-old Captain Cosmo Marcantonio of the 86-foot dragger *Captain Cosmo*. The *Captain Cosmo* and her crew of six Gloucester fishermen disappeared without a trace on September 7, 1978 when a freak gale blew winds seventy miles an hour on Georges Bank. The men of the *Captain Cosmo* were on Peter Prybot's list of ninety-one Gloucester fishermen lost at sea between 1940 and 1995. Not on the gruesome scale of losses on the wind-driven schooners, but no less devastating for the family members left behind. On his roster of casualties Prybot also listed the three men with Gloucester addresses who were lost when the *Andrea Gail* disappeared in the No-Name storm of 1991: Captain William Tyne, Robert Shatford, David Sullivan.

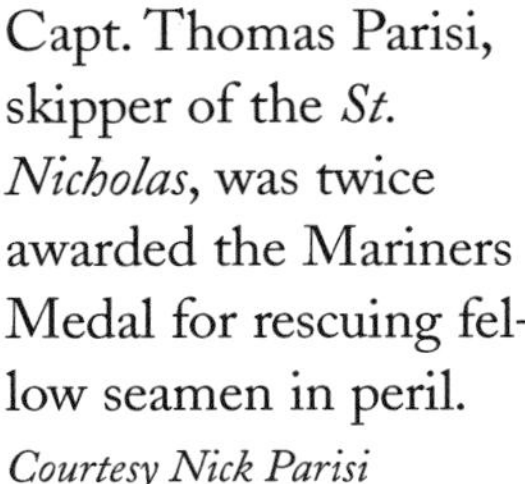

Capt. Thomas Parisi, skipper of the *St. Nicholas*, was twice awarded the Mariners Medal for rescuing fellow seamen in peril.
Courtesy Nick Parisi

The sinking of the *Andrea Gail* was the riveting subject of Sebastian Junger's best-selling book, *The Perfect Storm* (1997). Junger was a freelance journalist, writing pieces for men's action magazines. Then, as he told the story in a reading in Gloucester's City Hall, he was thinking about doing a book on dangerous occupations when the deadly storm hit in late October 1991. Junger read of the disappearance of the *Andrea Gail* and sent his literary agent an outline for a book idea. His agent was enthusiastic, but Junger had second thoughts. The story had no center because the fate of the *Andrea Gail* was not known for sure. Junger went off on assignment to Europe, hoping that would be the end of it.

But it was not. Junger's agent called him to say he had sold the proposal to a publisher, and Sebastian came back to research the book. He learned that the *Andrea Gail*'s crew members were habitués of the Crow's Nest, a barroom near the waterfront. Junger stopped by the Crow's Nest night after night, became acquainted with the regulars. Tending bar was Ethel, the mother of one of the lost crewmen, Bobby Shatford. The fishermen hunched over the bar grew comfortable with this writer from New York showing so much interest in the *Andrea Gail* (Junger had grown up in the Boston suburb of Belmont, so his accent was reasonably familiar). They told Junger what he wanted to know about swordfishing, taught him about the sea, invited him onto their boats.

He asked them about the lost crew of the *Andrea Gail.* He learned that they were not family fishermen like most in Gloucester. Aside from Captain Billy Tyne they were the itinerant laborers of the swordfish fishery. Typically young men with no fixed addresses, living high while they had a roll of bills in their pockets. They would say they were going to quit and stay ashore, then the cash ran out and they turned up for another three-month trip.

In what a NOAA meteorologist would call the "perfect storm" – ironically a storm in which the worst possible combination of factors was developing to produce destructive force seldom encountered even in the North Atlantic – the *Andrea Gail* was caught in an unlucky position too far from land to seek shelter. Just what happened to the vessel is anybody's guess. Only deck gear washed ashore. It is not mentioned in Junger's book, but a year earlier the *Italian Gold*, another steel vessel comparable in size to the *Andrea Gail*, went down and cameras lowered to the wreck showed it looking like a crushed beer can. Scientists familiar with wave dynamics speculated that a rogue wave had crested over that vessel and hit it from above. There was a very good chance something similar happened to the *Andrea Gail.*

The Perfect Storm promptly became a publishing sensation. As the book climbed the best-seller charts, the locals at the bar of the Crow's Nest accepted with dignity drinks offered by strangers in shorts and sandals crowding onto adjoining stools, asking Ethel Shatford questions about the *Andrea Gail* and maybe buying a souvenir T-shirt. Hollywood optioned the film rights. This would be the first movie about fishing vessels setting out from Gloucester since "Captains Courageous" of 1937.

(Well, the second. "Sealed Cargo," starring Dana Andrews, Claude Rains and a forgotten Carla Balenda, was confected in the 1940s from Edmund Gilligan's Gloucester-based romance, *Golden Hind.* Posters for that movie shouted "Cargo that blasts the sea wide open! Savage passions aflame in the North Atlantic . . . unleashed by treachery . . . hate . . . violence!" "A beautiful woman learns what it means to be held captive!" Gloucester movie-goers were stunned. They had never suspected that all this racy action was going on right under their noses.)

For the movie version of *The Perfect Storm*, Warner Brothers built its own version of the Crow's Nest close by the water on Harbor Loop and advertised for credible waterfront types to appear in scenes to be filmed in Gloucester. It was said that the studio pumped $10 million into Gloucester's economy in three weeks of shooting establishing shots in the summer of 1999, before moving on to the sound stages of Hollywood where most of the film was shot.

When the movie previewed in Gloucester in June of 2000, the local reception was politely favorable. Maybe there was not a whole lot of Gloucester in the final print, people said, and the real stars were computer-generated images of colossal waves and thrashing animatronic swordfish and sharks. But the film showed respect for the ship's crew, and the actors in the lead roles, George Clooney and Mark Wahlberg, had gone out of their way to demonstrate concern for the survivors of those doomed men. Fishermen in the audience said that at last somebody was showing what a tough life it was, fishing for a living.

Captain Billy Tyne, said Sebastian Junger, had a reputation for being able to smell fish. According to Junger only one captain could out-fish Tyne, and that was Captain Linda Greenlaw of the *Hannah Boden*, sister ship of the *Andrea Gail.* Junger's praises of Greenlaw as the only woman swordfish boat captain on the East Coast, and one of the best captains in the business, created another celebrity. Readers of *The Perfect Storm* wanted to know more about this woman college graduate who had succeeded so well in the man's world of commercial swordfishing.

Junger encouraged Captain Greenlaw to tell her own story, which she did in *The Hungry Ocean.* With its publication in 1999 she joined the select company of skipper authors who had sailed out of Gloucester: Epes Sargent, Solomon Davis, Gorham Low, Joseph Collins, Sylvanus Smith, Salve Testaverde. Greenlaw said she had been fishing for seventeen years and nobody had much noticed before. Now they asked her all kinds of questions. Mostly – to her annoyance – what it was like to be the only woman aboard a swordfishing boat, and the captain at that. She said she never expected any problems on that account, and never had any.

Greenlaw said a good captain had to be able to manage the boat, the men, and the fish. The men were often the most ornery piece of the equation. Her crew members called her "Ma," but they knew she could be a real terror. Like the time she put a fire axe through the TV set to get their attention. The other boat captains knew she would not put up with them intruding into her fishing space, in a business where success depended on a skipper's ability to read all the signs and be there first over the fish. "The meek may inherit the Earth," said Captain Greenlaw, "but they'll never get my piece of the ocean."

Fish stocks were low by the turn of the millennium, and technology is certainly partly to blame – all those electronic fish-finders tracking down everything with fins. There is not much of a Gloucester fishing fleet left, but the vessels that remain are a diverse lot, engaged variously in dragging, gillnetting, purse seining, long-lining, deep-water lobstering, and various permutations thereof.

The working technology of the fisheries is preserved at the Gloucester Maritime Heritage Center. This institution was nudged from dream to reality at the close of the 1990s by Geoffry Richon and others who felt it was important to keep the trades and traditions of the waterfront alive. A piece of harbor frontage was acquired that included a marine railway that had been in use for repairing vessels since 1849. Men who had the skills to build and repair wooden vessels pitched in, along with volunteers possessed of other skills, to create a busy maritime complex where historic vessels come to be worked on or tie up to be visited; dories and other small boats are built and launched; and children get to reach into salt-water tanks and touch real creatures of the deep. There is a pulse of excitement around the workshops and wharves of the Maritime Heritage Center not felt in museums consisting mainly of static exhibits. This is a working museum that not only preserves Gloucester's fishing heritage, but keeps it breathing.

Experts can always be found who confidently predict the demise of Gloucester fishing. But there are still young men (and some women) on Cape Ann who find the outdoor independence of commercial fishing more satisfying than any job ashore. Their goal always is to find the money to buy their own boat. As long as they can make a go of it, and the fish stocks can be brought into balance with the fishing technology, Gloucester will have its fisheries.

CHAPTER 9

Essex, Where They Built the Boats

GLOUCESTER BUILT many of its own schooners, in yards on Vincent's (or Vinson's) Cove and in East Gloucester. But by far the greatest number of vessels that sailed from Gloucester were towed around through Ipswich Bay from the adjacent town of Essex where they were built in shipyards lining the shore.

At first there were the little Chebacco boats, named after the Chebacco parish that once was Essex, and manned by two men and a boy. They were heavy for their size and had no standing rigging. But were they ever seaworthy! Judge Robert Hill, speaking before the Putnam Club in Salem in 1940, quoted an old skipper's testimony. If, when the wind got up, the foresail was reefed properly and the "hellum" lashed down, he said, those aboard could go below in perfect confidence, certain that the vessel would ride the waves "like a cork stopple" and take aboard "scursely a bucket of water."

The Chebacco boats were built in the back yards of Essex, hauled on two-wheeled rigs to the water, and sailed around to Gloucester. Some were later sailed down Maine for a summer's fishing, then sold or sailed back with a fare of fish. Double-ended pinkeys followed, then heeltappers high at the stern. Clipper and sharpshooter designs followed as the Gloucester schooner evolved into its classic configuration. In the 19th century, shipyards, the busiest of which were those of A. D. Story and Tarr & James, crowded the shore along the causeway that separates Essex Village from South Essex.

Each worker was a specialist in one of the shipbuilding trades. There was the loftsman who took a wooden model of the vessel-to-be, traced its lines, and enlarged the pattern into full-scale molds. Howard Chapelle, the dean of American watercraft historians, said that "The

March, 2006: Harold Burnham frames the 38-foot schooner *Isabella*, keeping alive the wooden boatbuilding skills of the Essex shipyards. *Author photo*

Essex modelers were rule-of-thumb designers, yet their work was on a par with that of contemporary yacht designers."

The hewers "beat out" the timbers and frames with broadaxes, and in later times with a pit saw. Dubbers trimmed off heavy frames with adzes, caulkers drove cotton and oakum into the seams. Joiners and trimmers followed. And the mast makers shaped perfectly straight and round masts from "sticks" eighty or ninety feet long that were delivered over the tracks of the Eastern Railroad to the terminal behind the Essex marshes, the logs spanning two or three flat cars. The masts-to-be were then hauled by oxen from the railroad terminal to the shipyard.

Each yard worker supplied his own tools and brought to work the tool box he depended on to make a living. It was all outdoor work, at the mercy of storms and deep snow. The shipyard owners kept the yards open in some ferocious weather, and with good reason – nobody got paid in full until a vessel was built and towed around to Gloucester. The output was prodigious. In 1901 alone, with only sixty men on the payroll, the Story yard launched eighteen vessels.

The patriarch of the Story yard was Arthur D. Story, whose career spanned the great age of the wooden schooners. Between 1872 and his death in 1932 at age seventy-eight, Story built well over 400 vessels, many of them among the most notable fishing schooners in the Gloucester fleet: *Lettie G. Howard* (reborn as *Caviare*), *Resolute*, *Yosemite*, *Rob Roy*, *Tattler*, *Effie M. Prior*, *L. A. Dunton*, *Columbia*, *Gertrude L. Thebaud*. Arthur D.'s life was his shipyard. He felt obligated to his men, to "keep the gang going," even when the work wasn't there. Sometimes he built boats he knew he would never be paid for, and ended up part-owner of many vessels he had built on speculation. The business never made him wealthy, but he had the respect of the town and the loyalty of the men who worked the yard.

Dana Story, a son born when Arthur D. was sixty-five, attempted to carry on the family tradition of shipbuilding. He went into business in 1945 and constructed several wooden fishing vessels for Gloucester captains. But in the late 1940s the demand for wooden commercial fishing vessels petered out, and there were not many men left with woodworking skills. In the end Dana was forced to lay off his crew and shut down.

Undaunted, Dana Story went on to a second notable career as the chronicler of shipbuilding in Essex, saying that "it begins to look as though nobody else will do it if I don't." His *Frame Up!, The Shipbuilders of Essex* appeared in 1976, and was the first in a series of volumes by Dana Story that defined shipbuilding in small-town Essex.

In his *Hail Columbia!* (1985), Story wrote a gem of a book on one of the most glorious schooners to slip down the ways from the Arthur D. Story yard. *Columbia*'s hour of fame came during the schooner races of 1926. The fishing schooner races had begun innocently enough as vessels sped back to port to be first in and thereby command top market price for their catch. But the competition was eventually corrupted by yachtsmen with committees and rules that bred arguments and ill feelings. By 1926, says Story, skippers were fed up with a lot of yachting rules and just wanted to get out there and prove who had the fastest schooner. It came down to a race between *Columbia* and *Henry Ford.* The captains of the two schooners agreed the racing would be to "fishermen's order" with no rule-book, no observers watching for some petty violation of protocol.

Dana Story's descriptions of the racing series are all happy sunshine and splash. *Columbia* was the winner, finishing well ahead in the first two races. There was pride in victory, but more important was the exhilaration everybody felt in putting two fine vessels to the test. Joshing prevailed at the awards banquet they held at Gloucester's City Hall. Then *Columbia* went back to dory trawling, with indifferent success. It was not easy any longer to find men who were willing to fish in an all-sail vessel. In a hurricane in August, 1927, just over four years after she was launched, *Columbia* disappeared off Sable Island with all twenty-two of her crew.

But that was not quite the end of *Columbia.* In an Epilogue Dana Story retells one of those episodes that explain why mariners are not easily disabused of belief in the supernatural. Dragging off Sable Island in 1928, the Canadian steam trawler *Venosta* snagged something massive in her gear. Hauled up, the catch proved to be *Columbia* herself, breaking the surface on a perfectly even keel, remaining on the surface for several minutes as the trawler's crew marveled at the sight. Then the *Venosta's* trawl cables snapped and *Columbia* slipped beneath the surface. Dana wrote that "In a sudden swirl of white water she was gone."

Dana Story wrote with first-hand knowledge of the shipbuilding in Essex, and of the language inherent in the culture. At a showing at the Essex Shipbuilding Museum in 2000 of a film about the Gloucester-Essex fishing connection, Story congratulated the filmmakers on a fine piece of work, but said he took exception on one small point. The narrator of the film had spoken repeatedly of the HAL-ibut fishery. Nobody in Essex or Gloucester, Story said, pronounced it HAL-ibut. "On Cape Ann it's HAUL-ibut!" (Hence the pronunciation of Halibut Point: Again HAUL-ibut because it was once Haul-About Point where sailing vessels tacked to run down east to Maine.)

In the final years of shipbuilding in Essex, the yards were constructing mostly wooden beam trawlers for the Portuguese and Italian fleets in

Gloucester. These were built to the same standards of seaworthiness that distinguished the Essex-built schooners. The white oak hull planks were massive, and still joined with trunnels ("tree nails," that is; wooden pegs that would contract and expand in concert with the wood parts they joined). "Not a nail in my boat," the dragger skippers would boast, and say in their elder years ashore that they'd had far greater faith in the seaworthiness of their Essex wooden vessels than in the riveted and welded steel boats that followed from yards elsewhere.

The Essex Historical Society and Shipbuilding Museum has taken up where Dana Story left off, acquainting new generations of visitors with the beauties of the Essex-built schooners. The museum keeps the craftsmanship alive, too, in conducting shipbuilding courses, and in building authentic replicas of Chebacco boats, pinkeys and small schooners. Another treasure trove in the museum is a rich collection of photos of the shipbuilding years in Essex, collected over the years by Dana Story. Courtney Ellis Peckham, museum curator, incorporated a number of them, along with text based on Story's notes, into her *Essex Shipbuilding* (2002). Courtney has carried on from her mentor, Dana, as maritime historian of Essex.

Small though the town of Essex may be, its fame has spread beyond shipbuilding interests. To many, from the 1920s forward, Essex has been synonymous with fried clams. Copeland and Rogers were the first to celebrate, in their *Saga of Cape Ann*, the contributions of the soft-shelled clam to the cuisine and coffers of Essex. According to the *Saga*, piles of shells attested to ancient clambakes organized by Indians visiting the seashore in the summer, presumably to get away from it all. Came the Europeans and a market developed for clams sold for bait, before the fleet turned to herring to tempt the fish. The clam industry then declined, but at least in the hardest of times no family in Essex was in danger of starving entirely. With a pail and a clam fork anyone could row over to the flats and come back with dinner on the half-shell.

Then came the clam revolution. Excursionists began to arrive in Essex by way of the spidery network of electric trolley lines spreading across the countryside, with local links provided by the Gloucester, Essex and Beverly Street Railway Company that went into business in

Daniel Chester French statue of Rufus Choate in the John Adams Court House, Boston. Generations of trial lawyers have kept the toe of Choate's left boot shiny by rubbing it for luck.

1895. But the private automobile was not far behind, and these little "electrics" on Cape Ann made their last runs back to the car barn a scant quarter century later in 1920. Summer restaurants had long since opened up to serve the trippers "shore dinners" compounded of Ipswich Bay cold-water lobsters, fresh-caught fish, and clams steamed or in thick chowders never sullied by tomatoes. After the fried clam was "invented" in Essex, what had been a causeway linking shipyards with South Essex became known as "Clam Alley," reeking of bivalves, French fries and onion rings all sizzling in fryer oil. A challenge to the gastric juices, but wicked delicious. Today antique shops jostle for position with seafood restaurants and marinas along the causeway.

Essex has also produced citizens whose renown has extended far beyond the causeway. There was the proto-Revolutionary Reverend John Wise, of course. And Rufus Choate, born on Hog Island out in the Essex marshes in 1799. Today the Trustees of Reservations runs summer boat tours out to visit the Choate homestead, built about 1730, that still stands on the island. Rufus went ashore and became a lawyer, then a U.S. Congressman. He moved on to the Senate to fill out Daniel Webster's term when Webster resigned to become Secretary of State. After Webster reclaimed his seat, Choate washed his hands of politics. This man from an Essex island became known as one of the most scholarly of American public men and – like William Bentley, a great collector of books – amassing a library of 8,000 volumes.

Essex remains Essex, welcoming those hungry for lobster-in-the-rough and an antique "find." But quietly engaged in its small-town pursuits amid proud family and civic mementoes of its shipbuilding past.

CHAPTER 10

The Quarry Coast

ALTHOUGH GRANITE quarrying may not sound like a maritime enterprise, on Cape Ann it was. In the 1830s and '40s, emulating the success of quarry operations south of Boston in Quincy, miners of rock began to attack the formidable resources of granite beneath the outer reaches of Cape Ann. Most of it they cut into paving stones that may still underlie some streets in New York and Philadelphia. Slabs were carved for post offices, monuments, bridges. In 1870, over a period of three weeks, fifteen yoke of oxen hauled an eighteen-by-seven-foot slab from Bay View to downtown Gloucester where it was installed as the front step of the First Baptist Church, then on Pleasant Street.

But what made the granite lode of the area particularly attractive was the proximity of all of Cape Ann to the sea. Quarries could be blasted out convenient to coves along the coast. At the outset, oxen hauled the great weights of stone to the harbors, where they were loaded onto sloops built for the purpose with enormous carrying capacity, and sailed off to markets along the Atlantic coast. Later, steam locomotives shifted the cut stone down to the docks: the *Nella* over the Bay State quarry railroad from Lanesville to Pigeon Cove, and the *Polyphemus* at Bay View. (Who was the classics scholar in the pits who had the wit to name a one-headlight steam engine after Polyphemus, the one-eyed Cyclops who held Ulysses and his followers captive in a cave, much as the immigrant stonecutters were herded into the quarries?)

The granite trade became so important to one of the outer villages, Sandy Bay, that it changed its name to Rockport. There were 400 to 500 men laboring in the Rockport and nearby Pigeon Cove quarries in the

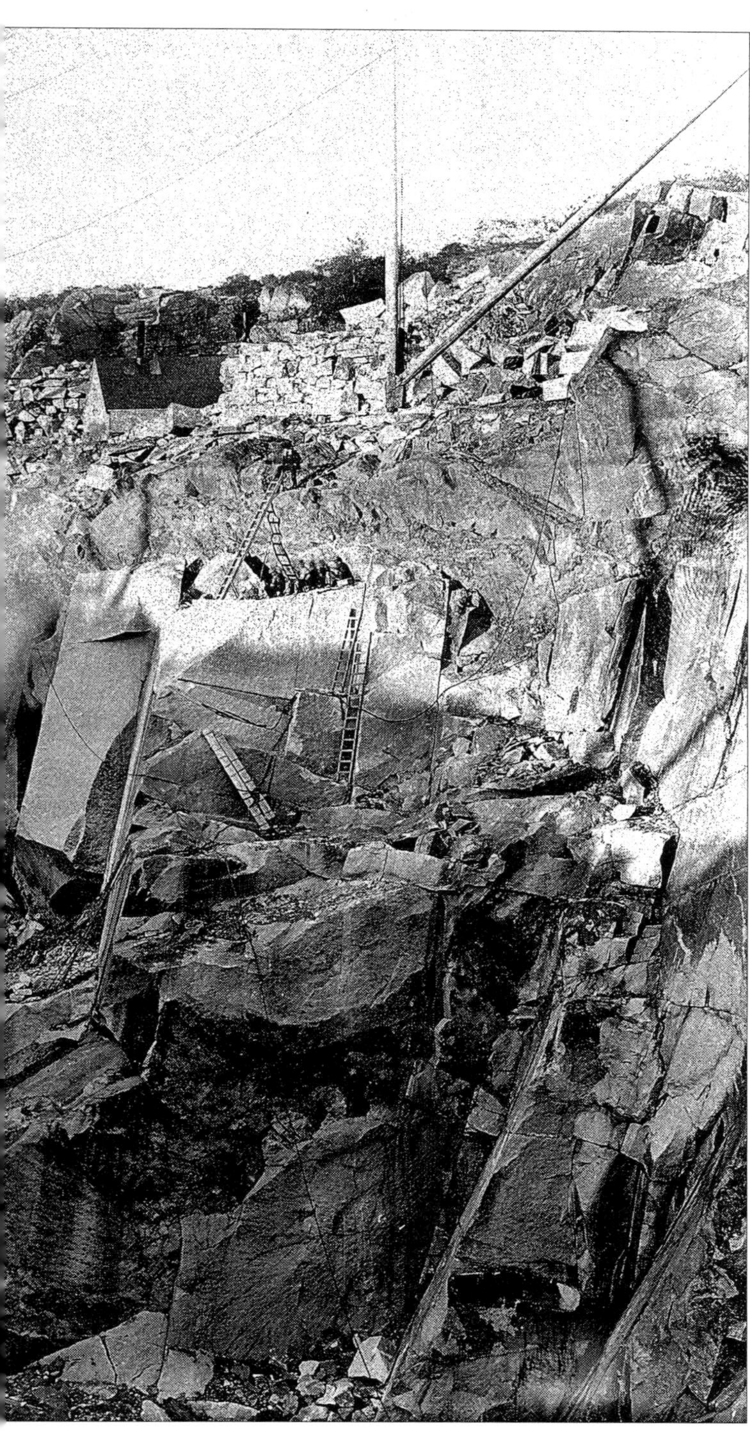

Dwarfed by the immensity of Rockport's Steel Derrick Quarry, stoneworkers drill blasting holes into a granite ledge in 1906. *Courtesy Cape Ann Historical Museum*

1880s, and a dozen vessels were in regular use carrying away the stone. Edmund Garrett visited the quarry "pits" of Rockport in the 1890s: "The air is filled with the tinkle of hammer and chisel, and the testy puff of steam-drills. Occasionally, comes the boom of an explosion, wresting the rocks from the hills. From the road itself, one may look down into a quarry, with its tracks and engines, its sheds and steam-drills, and its men, ant-like, beneath the high derricks." Garrett was awed by what he saw, but not pleased. "One cannot help wondering how the beauty of ledge and bowlder can be transformed into such ugliness."

Another important granite port on the outer cape was Lanesville. Its tiny harbor was protected by a high breakwater of granite blocks, inside which the sloops tied up, heeling over sharply when the stone was being loaded aboard them. Local Yankees could not be recruited to work the quarries inland behind Lanesville. It was, if possible, more dangerous than making trips in the fishing schooners. There were the constant perils of errant black powder blasts, rock slides, hundred-foot falls from a quarry ledge. And, over time, the high probability of contracting "stonecutter's consumption," silicosis of the lungs caused by prolonged exposure to stone dust. But it was a living for unskilled, unlettered immigrants who had known worse back the other side of the Atlantic.

Chief among those were Finns attracted by ads in the Boston papers for unskilled laborers. They came to work in the pits and sent word back to their relatives. The almost complete language barrier was bridged when the newcomers arrived with tags pinned to them directing that they be routed to the "Stone House, Rockport." The Finnish language is unlike any other. And to the other neighborhoods the customs of the Finns seemed as peculiar as their language. Steaming themselves in saunas, for example. Then rolling naked in the snow to cool off. *Sauna* worked its way into the Cape Ann lexicon, as did *sisu*, that special stamina the Finns believed was peculiar to their race. A "motion" had a local meaning as a shallow two-man quarrying operation. It came from the Finnish word *muusaria*.

The Finns in Lanesville were long a close-knit community until they began to blend in with those who had come before. Early in the 20th century the center of their local universe was Waino Hall, built by the Waino Temperance Society in 1897. The stonecutters and their

Granite from the quarries behind Lanesville being loaded aboard stone sloops in Lane's Cove.

families gathered there for tumbling and wrestling matches and folk dancing, amateur nights, Finnish movies. Then the hall burned in 1945. The community did fund-raising to build another hall. They held coffee socials, rummage sails, chowder fests and band concerts that featured famous local trumpeter Sylvester Ahola. But more and more the Lanesville Finns were thinking of themselves as belonging to Cape Ann rather than as immigrants, and it seemed less important to have their ethnic community center. Waino Hall has yet to be rebuilt.

The quarrymen were no more writers than were the fishermen, so there are few first-hand accounts of work in the pits. One eye-witness was Waino T. Ray who in 1997 saw into print his recollections of his youth as *A Young Finn on Cape Ann*. Waino remembered trudging over the paths with his older brother to see his father at work in a Bay View quarry. There was the tremendous sound of the drilling, and the sight

General Ben Butler, whose perceived insult to Southern womanhood earned him a reputation as "Beast of New Orleans."
Library of Congress, Prints and Photographs Division

of tiny figures working far down in the quarry. It was terrifying until he heard his father's welcoming shout. Father and uncles were sitting among a long row of men, all chipping stone.

A rich source of information on the quarrying century on Cape Ann is Barbara Erkkila's *Hammers on Stone: The History of Cape Ann Granite* (1980). Erkkila is to Cape Ann's granite industry what Gordon Thomas is to its fisheries and Dana Story to its shipbuilding. She is the historian of stonecutting on Cape Ann. She grew up in Lanesville when blasting still shook teacups in village parlors. Her grandfather was a quarry blacksmith and she married the son of a granite cutter, which led her to collect quarrying tools and write about the industry over her years as a freelance writer for the *Gloucester Daily Times*. Her husband died and twenty years later, when she was eighty-one, she married an eighty-six-year-old ex-granite company foreman who had started out in the same neighborhood as Barbara. Asked about their honeymoon plans, the bridegroom said "We'll probably go visit some quarries."

At Bay View a pier was built out into Ipswich Bay to provide access for the stone sloops. It was emblematic of the long reach of the local quarry developer, General Benjamin F. Butler. Controversial Civil War general and later member of Congress, Ben Butler had brass-knuckled his way up from poverty in Lowell to become a wealthy lawyer who won bankruptcy cases by impaling his adversaries upon obscure legalities. He became as prominent in Massachusetts legal circles as Rufus Choate, but there is no question but that Choate enjoyed greater esteem. Political clout propelled Butler to a general's star in the Massachusetts state militia, a rank which he parlayed into high but uneasy positions of command in the Civil War.

When he was Union commandant in New Orleans, Butler was accused of chicaneries on a grand scale, in which his relatives and friends always seemed to be in a position to profit. But whether through innocence or skill in covering his tracks, Butler could never personally be proved guilty.

Butler earned the sobriquet of "Beast" throughout the Confederacy from an act that was bruited about even in Europe as an insult to the flower of Southern womanhood. When the officers of his occupying Northern force in New Orleans were openly snubbed and derided by belles of the city, General Ben issued an order proclaiming that "hereafter when any female shall by word, gesture, or movement insult or show contempt for any officer or soldier of the United States she shall be regarded and held liable to be treated as a woman of the town plying her avocation." New Orleans women were indignant but chastened, and the Union officers found less cause to complain of insults. The cotton aristocrats of New Orleans never forgave Ben Butler.

Butler's association with Cape Ann came by way of a client's payment for legal services rendered, through which Ben acquired his property near Hodgkin's Cove (as Hog Skin Cove had been euphemized). Somehow, perhaps at the urging of the general, the area came to be known as Bay View. By establishing residence there – in a tent, he claimed, in his autobiography, *Butler's Book* – Butler won a seat in Congress from the Cape Ann district in 1866. Mark Twain saw Congressman Butler on the Capitol floor and described him as standing with his hands in his pockets, looking grimly at his opponents as if he had half a mind to crush them but it wasn't worth the trouble.

Twain said that when Butler smiled it was "like the breaking up of a hard winter."

Looking around his domain, Butler noticed that the neighborhood had boundless untapped resources of the granite that had proved profitable in Rockport and Lanesville. He brought along his former aide-de-camp, West Pointer Colonel Jonas R. French, whom he installed as the nominal head of the Cape Ann Granite Company. Art historian James F. O'Gorman is among those who have noted how mutually advantageous it was to have French at the helm of the granite business, while his old commander, now a Congressman, was able to exert persuasive influence over the awarding of contracts for federal buildings. By a wonderful coincidence, the Boston and Baltimore post offices came to be built of Cape Ann Granite Company stone.

Political opponents saw Butler's devious machinations at work when Colonel French became chairman of the then-minority Democratic party in Massachusetts, and began acquiring shares in the *Boston Globe*. The critics howled that Ben Butler was buying media influence, using Colonel French as a front man. French was embarrassed into selling the stock, but the *Globe* remained a loyal supporter of General Butler's political ambitions. Butler made it as far as the governorship of Massachusetts, to the consternation of the old establishment. He was pointedly *not* included on the Harvard honorary degree list, which heretofore had always included the governor of the commonwealth.

The populist Butler could shrug off these Brahmin snubs as he garnered the support of the Greenback and Anti-Monopoly parties for the Presidency in 1884. But he lost the Democratic nomination to Grover Cleveland, and faded from politics. Thereafter General Butler presided over his family and entourage from the strategic position of his porch overlooking Ipswich Bay, whose sunsets he pronounced to be "equal to those of the Bay of Naples."

Butler and French both built Italianate stone mansions above the shore near their granite works and shipping operations. The general named his manse "The Homestead." French called his, aptly, "Rock Lawn."

Concrete and macadam gradually shoved granite aside for construction and paving, and the big quarrying companies on Cape Ann closed down in the 1920s, with some stonecutting still being done into the '30s. Then silence returned to the outer reaches of the cape. Erkkila spoke, as did Waino Ray and Edmund Garrett, of what the quarrying did to the countryside, leaving it scarred with deep gashes. The denuded landscape was punctuated only by tall quarry derricks. Today even the derricks are gone and the scars on the landscape have healed, at least on the surface. The trees have grown back and the quarries that were gouged hundreds of feet down into the ledges have filled with water. They are now scenic ponds. The most visible reminders of the century of quarrying are the slabs making up causeways, piers, walls of houses and even of a barn or two. At the outermost point of Cape Ann, on Halibut Point, there is a high ridge of "grout," broken blocks that did not split properly. It serves mariners as an unmistakable sea mark.

And thus came to an end the most unusual of Cape Ann's maritime enterprises, by which the very granite underpinnings of the cape were chipped at and sent off to sea.

CHAPTER II

Dogtown Mystique

DOGTOWN COMMON, a deserted village in the wild commons land at the center of island Cape Ann, would seem on the face of it to have the least connection with the maritime compulsion that has ruled the cape since earliest colonial times.

Yet there was a direct connection, because those wild uplands were probably occupied by unfortunates unable to eke out a living on the populated coast. Not much can be said with certainty of those who did live there, whether they were stragglers from the original settlements, families that fled inland to escape pirate raids, war widows left with their barking dogs, or simply outcasts who scratched out a sparse living on the bare uplands. The archeological evidence shows that most of the structures were small, with shallow cellars. In any event, the area has not had a permanent resident, at least of the flesh-and-blood variety, since the early 1800s. Dogtown has persistently troubled Cape Ann as the dark mirror image of the viable villages along the shore.

Historian John Babson remembered seeing the poor widows who lived back there and survived by selling berries and herbs. The abandoned cellars and overgrown roads of Dogtown struck Babson as "melancholy." Later writers would wrestle again and again with unsettling presentiments in those abandoned uplands.

By late in the 19th century, Dogtown Common began to exert its fascination. Charles Edward Mann romanticized the rural ruins in his *In the Heart of Cape Ann, or The Story of Dogtown*. His account was serialized in the *Cape Ann Advertiser* in autumn of 1895, and the Procter Brothers published it in book form the following year. Mann had read Oliver Goldsmith's *Deserted Village* and was gripped by the "weird, poetic and sentimental charm [of] abandoned settlements." Dogtown was just what he was looking for, and he roamed its solitudes in the mid 1890s. By then "the only inhabitants . . . are lowing kine, [or] an occasional decrepit horse turned out to pasture as a pensioner." Mann chatted with old coastal villagers, they whose recollections stretched back to the 1830s when the last Dogtown dwellers were still tottering down the Commons Road.

The aged witnesses Mann spoke with told him about Luce George who lived on Fox Hill. She bewitched oxen so they would not climb the hill until she was given some of the grain or wood the team was carting. Luce's niece, Tammy Younger, born Thomazine, was known as the "Queen of the Witches." In this sense the term probably meant an aged female of disagreeable temperament. Pity the passing teamster who denied Tammy a mackerel or anything else she fancied from his wagon. Abuse would rain down Fox Hill from Tammy's window perch. They said she entertained disreputable men with fortune-telling and card games, but others said not. And she died in 1829, but maybe earlier, or later.

When they warmed up to the subject, Mann's informants told him of other scandalous goings-on in old Dogtown. After it had crumbled to ruins, James Witham's house in Stacy's Pines was "a great resort for young people for mirth and jollity." And then there was Esther Carter. "Easter," they called her. The young folks of Riverdale and Squam used to go up to her house in the Commons. She'd boil cabbage for them, tell their fortunes. One old gent said he had "often been up there with a parcel of girls." And oh, the walk home in the moonlight would be something, I tell you. But then maybe he was thinking of Rachel Smith's place. It was hard to recollect, it was so long ago.

This Rachel, or "Granny," or "Aunt" Smith was another of the peculiar personages up in Dogtown. She brewed a concoction out of foxberry leaves, spruce tops and other obscure botanicals. She would peddle it at villagers' doors, saying "Now, Ducky, I've come down to bring a dire drink, for I know you feel springish."

There were other legends of witchcraft loosely associated with Dogtown. Peg Wesson lived toward Fox Hill, on the lane that became Maplewood Avenue. Peg figured in the Cape Ann version of one of the most durable of darkside myths, that of the witch who takes the form

Peg Wesson. The Gloucester Colonial troops besieging Louisburg could certify that Peg was a bona fide witch.

of an animal, and is found to have the same wound when that animal is felled by an arrow, a bullet or whatever. In this version some of the volunteers in Captain Byles's company, on their way to attack the French bastion at Louisburg in 1745, so exasperated Peg she said she'd make them dance another tune at Cape Breton. Outside the fortifications of Louisburg the soldiers spotted a circling crow they decided must be Peg, and shot it with a silver sleeve button. Of course, at that very moment in Gloucester, Peg took a fall and the doctor extracted a silver button from the wound. Proof that would hold up in any court.

Superstitions still ran rife among Mann's informants, and it was easy to at least half-believe in witchcraft. But not all were so gullible. Snorted one, "In old times if somebody sawed a barrel in two, and made two tubs, they called him a witch."

If Charles Edward Mann saw Dogtown as enchanted ruins once peopled by eccentrics with peculiar powers, Percy MacKaye was fascinated by the place for its dramatic possibilities. A folklorist and author of pageants in which he massed together on stage assorted singers, musicians, dancers and other entertainers, MacKaye pounced upon Mann's work as authentic Cape Ann Americana. In it he found "many strange, half-forgotten facts concerning the old Puritan life of that region." In 1921 he worked Mann's legends and characters into a verse play, "Dogtown Common," a gothic fable flickering with anguished guilt, evil spells and suppressed passions. MacKaye was not native to Cape Ann, but his descriptions of the Commons world ring true to anyone who has ambled those paths, as he speaks of the fragrance of berry bushes and views of the sea from an upland among the granite boulders.

MacKaye mixes and matches the Dogtown legends at will, setting most of the action in Tammy Younger's shanty, where she lives with her niece Judy Rhines. From the opening verse we know we're in for shady doings in Dogtown's volatile spirit world. Granny Luce's voice is often heard from "beyond," and she sometimes knocks on the table. Youthful fishermen and their girls often visit for a lark, and Tammy has bewitched Judy into seducing the boys for a shilling or two. Judy evidently has also celebrated carnal communion with John Wharf, the minister of the haunted parish.

MacKaye clearly had read his Hawthorne. The Reverend Wharf's guilty association with Judy, whom deep down he loves, echoes that of the liaison between Reverend Arthur Dimmesdale and Hester Prynne in *The Scarlet Letter*. And when Judy picks flowers, they wither at her touch – an unsettling botanical defect she shares with the title character of Hawthorne's "Rappaccini's Daughter."

In a scene at Squam church, Judy is denounced as a witch by one Steven Lurvey, whose name was likely suggested to MacKaye by that of Peter Lurvey, the fallen Dogtown volunteer in the Battle of

Gloucester Harbor. Steven knows for sure that Judy is a sorceress. Did not fisherman Peter Bray cut Judy's arm, and out came a silver button? And had not Peter previously shot a crow with that very same button? (MacKaye could not resist hauling in the Peg Wesson legend.)

When another parishioner at Squam church accuses Judy in the suspicious demise of his sow, she can bear no more and rushes off through the woods. John Wharf pursues her and, to his dismay, finds the lovely Judy transformed into a deciduous tree. Despite the heavy rural dialect in the speaking parts, Percy MacKaye's "Dogtown Common" can be performed powerfully, given the proper setting. The meadows, woods and half-hidden cottages of Ina Hahn's Windhover Performing Arts Center at Pigeon Cove provided such when Nan Webber, of Theater in the Pines, directed a production of the work there in August 1999, staged and choreographed by Hahn.

Novelists have found Dogtown fact and legends suggestive for dark fictions. But that same material was given light-hearted verse treatment by Kitty Parsons Recchia. Kitty Parsons and her mother had bought a house in Rockport, and in 1927 Kitty married sculptor Richard Recchia, painted watercolors and became an active supporter of the Rockport Art Association. In 1936 she wrote her own "Dogtown Common." Dogtown characters brought to center stage by MacKaye and Charles Edward Mann – Tammy Younger, Becky Rich, martyred Peter Lurvey, and of course Peg Wesson – all trip through Kitty's lively stanzas. The artist-author captured the diminishing echoes of the abandoned settlement as credibly as any before her.

If many of the personages associated with the wilds of Dogtown are insubstantial and wraith-like, Roger Babson was, by contrast, a very solid citizen. Born in Gloucester in 1875, Babson counted himself fortunate to be of fine breeding stock that included his great-uncle, Captain Gorham P. Low, he who had alternated his sea duties with mixing in the diplomatic social whirl of Copenhagen.

Roger Babson proudly recalled the healthy life he had lived as a boy in Gloucester, when air conditioning was not needed, he said, because all the ventilation anybody could ask for was provided by air rushing through cracks around the windows and doors and up the chimney. In his opinion the introduction of steam heat and oil and gas stoves was

Roger Babson was the author of thirty-three books, countless articles – and slogans carved into the rocks of Dogtown Common.
Courtesy Cape Ann Historical Museum

responsible for the common cold. Babson had also grown up in an age of social purity, by his telling. When he was in Gloucester High School in the 1890s the boys had their girlfriends, but "there was no immorality whatsoever." If any of Roger's classmates remembered differently, no one stepped forward to contradict him.

Young Roger's moral probity was sorely tested on one of his first jobs, as bookkeeper in a Gloucester spar yard that supplied masts and booms for the fishing schooners. There were rum shops on every corner, he said, with liquor flowing in the streets. Many "houses of ill-fame" as well. When the police made a periodic sweep of the neighborhood, a "pretty little 'inmate'" of one of the brothels would run across the street and hide in a flour barrel in Roger's office. "I wonder what has become of her! They called her Gloria."

Whatever yearnings may have lingered for the Glorias of his youth,

(alias Judy Rhines), together with Molly Jacobs and Liz Tucker helped to account for that reputation. Copeland and Rogers, in *The Saga of Cape Ann*, are more circumspect in their assessment of Judy. By their account she made a precarious living by picking blueberries, telling fortunes and "by other unrecorded means." On the other hand, she "is said to have had many friends . . . attracted to her not by pity, but by her heartiness, her broad compassion, and perhaps by a freedom from conventional restraints."

Whatever her faults, Judy inspired admiration. Babson offered his opinion that so-called witches like Judy were in reality strong individualists with executive abilities. Which suggests that today's search firms are missing a good bet. They should consider recruiting in witch covens for charismatic corporate managers.

In his old age Babson became increasingly obsessed with his ancestry. While searching for family graves in a cemetery, he fell and broke a rib. When rescuers loaded him onto a stretcher, he quipped "better to be carried out than in." It was not until he was ninety-one that clean-living, high-thinking Roger W. Babson was finally carried in.

Roger Babson's interpretation of Dogtown had been no-nonsense, contrary to the impressions many visitors carry away from those spellbound uplands. Elliott Rogers and Melvin Copeland and their fellow ambulators of the paths of Cape Ann also were rational, clear-headed men of the world. Until they entered Dogtown. One time, when they were on the Commons Road, a disheveled old berry-picker came "stivering" [bristling] toward them, a piece of rope for a belt, carrying a pail of berries. She seemed to be there one moment and gone the next, and the detachment of ramblers wondered if they had met the spirit of an earlier resident, risen from her cellar hole to pick a few berries among the living.

The surprise here is that the witnesses admitted to a perhaps spectral encounter. Most who experience such meetings in Dogtown decide against mentioning the matter. The less said the better. Even today there are those who have ambled past the tumbled foundation stones on the Commons Road, or continued around Wharf Road onto the Dogtown Road, and been certain that, as shadows lengthened in the pale afternoon light, they were not alone. What was that rustle among the red cedars? Was that a figure down at the bend in the fieldstone wall? Where has it gone? Maybe they should pick up the pace. Whistling helps.

The hardest-headed realist has a sense from time to time of whispers from some haunting unknown. Seamen putting out from Gloucester, and from every other port for that matter, are aware of mysteries of the deep that defy any feeble human reasoning. Along the coast, the voices of the surf speak cryptically, thundering on the beaches. And inland, back along the rough tracks of Dogtown Common, the mystery is felt and, though rationally refuted, persists as a folk certainty.

Until the middle of the 20th century, there were long vistas across the treeless, boulder-strewn moors of Dogtown. After Dogtown's trees had all been cut, cows kept the pastures bare. Then the cows were called home for the last time and natural reforestation obscured the long views across the Commons. Dogtown was in peril by the 1980s. There were title disputes in the old shared grazing grounds, and uncertain jurisdictions left the area vulnerable to dumping, casual hunting and wild parties. In 1984 a coalition of conservation groups, coordinated by a Dogtown Steering Committee under former Gloucester mayor Robert L. French, filed for grants and raised money for deed searches. The Gloucester City Council voted to take title to disputed lands by eminent domain. Abandoned cars and trash were carted out, reasonable rules for public access were written and enforced. Cape Ann's interior semi-wilderness will be preserved for generations to come, so long as the surrounding communities take care to exercise prudent vigilance.

CHAPTER 12

Seaways, Flyways and Byways

The natural world of the maritime coast is ever-present in the lives of the people along its margin. Herbert A. Kenny said, in his *Cape Ann: Cape America*, that a five-minute walk anywhere on Cape Ann would take you to woods, marsh or ocean. In these surroundings, he said, it was almost impossible to avoid becoming a "naturist," which he defined as an amateur naturalist.

This cape is sea-bound at every turn. The ocean presence from Essex to Manchester intrudes on every conversation, gently or imperiously. The waves rise, peak and fall, with an insistence dismissive of human concerns. Walk on Good Harbor Beach on some "perishin' cold" day when wind whips the tops off the breakers and blows ankle-high streamers of sand from the dunes to the water. In a warm season drift in a boat through channels among the high grasses of the Great Marsh in West Gloucester and Essex as a red-shinned hawk settles on an island branch, Bonaparte gulls splash down upon the waves, quick silver glints of fish flash deep in the unclouded water, the marshscape meandering to the horizon. Or step outside in deep night amid an excess of stars, an echo of light from the moon across the water, the sky-outlined darkness of the opposite shore more mysterious than total blackness. Only an icy soul can ignore such largesse, which permeates the senses of the beholder.

The wild shore of Cape Ann attracted two of the most ardent worshipers of nature of the 19th century, Ralph Waldo Emerson and Henry David Thoreau. Each had delivered talks sponsored by the Gloucester Lyceum, then later returned to Cape Ann at private expense (although Thoreau's spending habits would scarcely have caused a ripple in the local economy). Emerson was well-pleased with Pigeon Cove when he first visited in 1855 with the Reverend Cyrus Bartol. A year later the Bard of Concord brought his whole family down for a week. The sea spoke to Emerson at Pigeon Cove, and Emerson answered back with exhilarated lines in his journal:

> Returned from Pigeon Cove, where we have made acquaintance with the sea, for seven days . . . And behold the sea, the opaline, plentiful and strong, yet beautiful as the rose or the rainbow, full of food, nourisher of men, purger of the world, creating a sweet climate, and, in its unchangeable ebb and flow, and in its beauty at a few furlongs, giving a hint of that which changes not, and is perfect.

Henry David Thoreau's experience with Cape Ann was very different. When Thoreau took a two-day walking tour of the island cape he was visiting not only to commune with nature but to study the cogs of the universe. He jotted down his observations in the *Journal* he had come to regard as his life work, and for which he adopted the informal title "Says I to Myself." Where Emerson found sermons in stone, Thoreau closely studied each bud and leaf through the seasons, alert for clues to unifying principles. Edwin Whipple knew Thoreau well and said he "seemed to me a man who had experienced Nature as other men are said to have experienced religion." (Whipple, like other New Englanders of the time, would pronounce Thoreau's surname to rhyme with "borrow.")

It was late in September of 1858 when Thoreau and a walking companion strode along from Manchester – where he thought his footsteps scuffing on Singing Beach sounded more like "the sound made in waxing a table" than in vocalizing. Thoreau and his companion put up in Gloucester for the night, and next day ambled around the shore until they stood facing out to sea from Good Harbor Beach. "Having reached the shore, we sat under the lee of the rock on the beach, opposite Salt Island. A man was carting seaweed along the shore between us and the water, the leather-apron kind, which trailed from his cart like the tails of oxen, and, when it came between us and the sun, was of a warm purple-brown glow." Thoreau, the first American master of simple English honed to great clarity, capturing the quiet image of a seaweed-gatherer and his cart against the long curve of sand, sunlight

tainment [lodging].” But a hiking companion was waiting for him up the trail, and somehow Thoreau never did get back to the mountain girl combing out her long black hair.

Thoreau attracted devoted followers. One was Thomas Wentworth Higginson who regularly brought literary enthusiasts together in Worcester to read letters from Thoreau. When Higginson was minister of the Unitarian church in Newburyport (before, as he said, he preached himself out of the job), Henry David arrived as a house guest when on a speaking tour. Another time Higginson made arrangements for Thoreau to speak in Boston. And in 1861 when Thoreau was nearing death from tuberculosis, Higginson visited him in Concord and they talked about birds.

Throughout a long activist career Higginson supported women's suffrage, the temperance movement, and during the Civil War was colonel of a regiment of freed slaves. An essayist and popular speaker on the Lyceum circuit, Colonel Higginson championed promising authors, and for years carried on a correspondence with Emily Dickinson, discreetly encouraging that reclusive poet.

Higginson, like Thoreau, had once tramped the paths and lanes of Cape Ann, after his brother bought the “Garrison House” in Rockport (known as the “Witch House” after 1890). His recollections of those walks appeared in *The Atlantic Monthly*, and in 1877 were reprinted in *Oldport Days* (“Oldport” was Newport, Rhode Island, where Higginson had moved for the sake of his ailing wife). He remembered the interior of Cape Ann as “a continuous woodland, with granite ledges everywhere cropping out, around which the high-road winds, following the curving and indented line of the sea, and dotted here and there with fishing hamlets. This whole interior is traversed by a network of footpaths, rarely passable for a wagon, and not always for a horse, but enabling the pedestrian to go from any one of these villages to any other, in a line almost direct, and always under an agreeable shade.”

The Cape Ann he remembered was essentially wild.

> Often we stepped from the edge of the sea into some gap in the woods . . . . A piny dell gave some vista of the broad sea we were leaving, and a clearing in the woods displayed another blue sea-line

> before; the encountering breezes interchanged odor of berry-bush and scent of brine.

Newport was fine, of course, but it was Cape Ann Higginson saw in his reveries. "I used to wander in these woods, summer after summer, till I had made my own chart of their devious tracks, and now when I close my eyes . . . I long for those promontories of granite where the fresh water is nectar and the salt sea is a regal blue."

Fifteen years after Thoreau's visit to Cape Ann, Reverend Henry C. Leonard included in the nature chapters of his *Pigeon Cove and Vicinity* lists of fifty varieties of birds on Cape Ann, twenty-nine trees, forty shrubs and well over a hundred flowers and herbs. In his time all of the birds were fair prey. Once Reverend Leonard was listening as General Ben Butler delivered a speech on the shore, his "husky voice sending forth sentences like rattling shot." It was one of those moments suspended in time:

> The picture of the quiet crowd listening to the orator, the many-colored costumes, the surrounding tall trees and the thick underbrush, the shining waves of Ipswich Bay discerned through a rift of the wood, and the wild pigeons, some with reddish, and some with pale-blue breasts, distributed throughout the cherry-tree's top, is a novel and exceedingly pleasant one in the memory.

He adds, without comment: "On the day following that of the gathering, from a cover of oaks and pines near the cherry-tree, a young sportsman shot fifteen of this flock of pigeons."

Reverend Leonard was intentionally haphazard in his walks to the interior of Cape Ann.

> Sometimes ramblers, who know the highest and purest enjoyment of rambling, spend day after day in the woods, purposely losing themselves in the complexity of intersecting paths to get the surprises here and there of new views of the sea, and of old views too, frequently not recognized as familiar till the maze of the forest is left behind.

Mason Walton's insistence that animals thought much like humans earned him a listing in *Who's Who in America*, and the faithful beat a path to his forest cabin.

By this method he discovered that "one may go from Pigeon Cove to Gloucester without seeing a public road." The wonder is that, at the dawning of the twenty-first century, "ramblers" can still pursue these meandering paths for hours in undisturbed deep woods. There is no risk of becoming dangerously lost: a walker anywhere on island Cape Ann will sooner or later stumble upon the ocean.

One dedicated "naturist" of Cape Ann was Mason A. Walton, self-described "hermit of Gloucester." Walton was born in Maine in 1838 and was living there in 1877 when his married life ended tragically with the death of his wife in childbirth. He became a political activist for the Greenback Party and worked for Ben Butler's successful gubernatorial campaign. In 1884 General Butler made his run for the presidency and

Walton came to Gloucester to join what proved to be a futile cause. At loose ends he thought he'd try life aboard a fishing vessel, but the schooner captains looked him over and said he was too lame and ailing.

So Walton took to the woods. In his *A Hermit's Wild Friends, or Eighteen Years in the Woods* he tells how he first pitched a tent on Bond's Hill and called the camp his "Eyrie," his eagle's nest. In the 1880s he still had unobstructed views in all directions: "Day after day I watched the vessels of the fishing fleet as they rounded Eastern Point, bound outward or inward. These vessels were models of beauty, and looked as if they were built for racing instead of fishing. I often compared them with the clumsy coasters that rode at anchor in the Outer Harbor. Now and then a vessel, homeward bound, rounded Eastern Point with her flag half-mast. Mute reminder of the hardships and perils of a fisherman's life."

Looking down on Essex Avenue, Walton could see "a constant stream of travel over this highway, divided among farmers, icemen and pleasure-seekers." And he had an equally good view along the southern rim of the harbor: "The travel on Western Avenue is . . . made up largely from the summer colonies at Magnolia and Manchester. Showy turnouts passed and repassed, so that I had enough to attract my attention from sunrise to sunset."

But the Eyrie was too exposed to the weather, and after that first year Walton built a cabin for himself on the Old Salem Road, untraveled since Colonial times. There is a plaque in Ravenswood Park that marks the spot. He reveled in the botanical wonders he saw in his strolls: "The silvery cinquefoil grows all along the roadsides of Western Avenue, from the Cut to the drawbridge. In late spring and early summer the viburnums afford a mass of bloom that makes the old road look like a cultivated shrub garden."

While still at the Eyrie, Walton had made his breakfast by a fire outside his camp. Then his gregarious instincts got the better of him.

> One morning I dropped into the little store at the head of Pavilion Beach, and the proprietor asked me to have a cup of coffee. He piloted me into a back shop, where he told me that he served a light lunch with coffee, to the farmers. The coffee was just to my taste, and for twelve years I patronized the coffee trade in that little back

> shop . . . I would leave my cabin, summer or winter, at half-past five o'clock, so I could sit down to breakfast in the back shop about six.

Walton was thus the first documented convert to what, for many, is the social event of the day in Gloucester: a hearty breakfast washed down with mugs of honest coffee, in the company of regulars exchanging late-breaking local news.

Mason Walton was described in those days as "a familiar personage on our streets, usually attired in the conventional deep black, large slouched hat, under which rests a head well covered with sandy hair, and being lame, is always accompanied by a heavy walking stick."

Back at his woods cabin Walton got to know the animals, although modern ornithologists would regard his birding observations as largely fanciful. He said he was visited by the same chestnut-sided warbler from 1886 to 1897. "Deeper wrinkles and gray hair told the story, but the little bird . . . was apparently as blithe and young as . . . eleven years before." There was Wabbles, the song sparrow, with his "shy, demure little wife." Other animal acquaintances included Satan the raccoon, Bismarck the squirrel, Triplefoot the fox. Walton described how he tracked Triplefoot in the snow through Magnolia Swamp, over the ice on Wallace's Pond, across Magnolia Avenue below the lily pond, all the way to Coffin's Beach and back – territory that is now all houses, roads and fences but that then was still open and free for the roaming.

Walton was convinced that his furry and feathered neighbors on the Old Salem Road acted on emotions, memories and logical decisions that were very close to the human, and he stoutly defended his convictions against scoffers. "In all my life I have never found the birds stupid. They are as intelligent as to the requirements of bird life, as man is as to the requirements of human life. The theory of instinct is only a dream of the uninitiated. Nature's children are never troubled by such nightmares."

The behavioral scientists might shake their heads, but Walton had popular sentiment behind him. His fame was spread by newspaper stories and picture postcards. His theories on animal intelligence earned him a listing in *Who's Who in America*. And the faithful beat a path to his forest cabin. Walton entertained the children with his animal tales, or took them and their parents on nature expeditions. "Bee hunting," he said, "is a sport that can be followed by any number of persons, without regard to sex. For pure enjoyment it is far ahead of golf. It can be followed without fatigue, and it allows plenty of time for social chats."

In 1917 no one had seen seventy-nine-year-old Mason Walton having breakfast down at the Pavilion Beach coffee shop lately. They went up to the cabin and found he had died. The guest book in the cabin showed that, over thirty-three years, he had averaged four thousand visitors a year, often two hundred on a single Sunday. It worked out to an average of almost eleven visitors a day, winter and summer, stopping by to share the wildlife musings of the very unhermetic hermit of the Gloucester woods.

While Walton was studying the animal life of Cape Ann, Nathaniel Southgate Shaler was reporting on the underpinnings of the cape. Shaler's "The Geology of Cape Ann" was published as part of the U.S. Geological Survey's *Ninth Report*, that for 1887-88. Shaler had been trained by Louis Agassiz, the Swiss-born geologist who revolutionized the teaching of natural science at Harvard by emphasizing observations in the field, rather than by the book. Agassiz's scientific triumph was to prove that Europe and North America had once been buried under glaciers in an Ice Age. (Agassiz's memorial on Cape Ann is Agassiz Rock, reached by a short climb up a steep path from School Street in the Essex woods.)

Shaler himself was an inspiring teacher of geology at Harvard for nearly forty years, and Dean of the school's Lawrence Scientific School. Psychologist William James called him, in tectonic prose, the "myriad-minded and multiple-personalitied embodiment of academic and extra-academic matters." As chief of the Atlantic Coast Division of the U.S. Geological Survey, Shaler walked most of the Atlantic Coast from Maine to Florida. In his "Geology of Cape Ann" Shaler reinforced Agassiz's theories by charting glacial movement across the cape.

Island Cape Ann was still largely deforested when Shaler made his study, and this he said made it easier to study the glacial deposits. His report is illustrated with sketches of stone walls snaking over a moonscape of bare pastures cluttered with glacial erratics, the boulders Thoreau had said looked as if they had "rained down." It was terrain Marsden Hartley would later interpret on canvass.

Another Harvard student persuaded by Agassiz to observe nature closely in the wild was Alpheus Hyatt, a colleague of Shaler's. However, both broke with Agassiz after their mentor refused to accept the theory of evolution, newly expounded in James Darwin's *The Origin of Species*. Agassiz, a devout Christian, believed that new species were introduced periodically by the Creator, after periodic cataclysms such as the Biblical flood.

Still, eager investigators like Shaler and Hyatt had been introduced to a liberating scientific method by Agassiz. Hyatt helped form the Peabody Academy of Science in Salem, and began publication of *American Naturalist*. He was curator of the Boston Society of Natural History, and professor of zoology and paleontology at MIT.

In 1880 Hyatt set up a modestly equipped marine laboratory in two rooms of his 17th century house on "Seven Acres," a property on the shore just west of the Goose Cove causeway in Annisquam. Hyatt would take his daughters, Harriet and Anna, on expeditions at low tide to collect starfish. Harriet remembered in the '80s when a schooner would be tied up alongside the tidal mill at the far end of the causeway, its bowsprit telescoped so as not to block the occasional passing wagon. If the mill operated into the night, she would see a pale light in one of its windows, reflecting eerily upon the current rushing through the sluiceway.

Hyatt tied up to the wharf his expedition schooner *Arethusa* that he equipped for sub-arctic expeditions. (There was a sly scholarly allusion in the title: in Greek mythology, the nymph Arethusa was pursued by the passionate river god Alpheus until he was thwarted by Artemis who transformed Arethusa into a woodland spring.) Alpheus Hyatt expanded the scope of his marine researches when he became one of the founders of the Marine Biological Laboratory at Woods Hole, Massachusetts.

In 1923, the same year that Gloucester was celebrating its tercentenary at the harbor with schooner races and processions of flower-bedecked auto floats, a gentle book of nature walks was published. No author was listed for *Along the Old Roads of Cape Ann*, but everyone knew it was Susan Babson, drawing upon the work of her good friend amateur botanist Mrs. Charles Rogers. Sarah Rogers had long been a student of the flora of Cape Ann and from 1894 to 1920 led nature walks to share her discoveries of plant life in the wild.

Along the Old Roads speaks of leisurely treks through the back country of Cape Ann, the author pointing out elusive wildflowers but easily distracted into local history and anecdote. Susan Babson's writing style is at times old-fashioned, quoting often from the New England household poets. But there is a crisp, no-nonsense tone in her writing, too, as in her front matter: "No liberty of trespassing on another's property is here encouraged, and it is hoped that an earnest desire to conserve our native flowers has been engendered." This was the crisp Gloucester personage who startled Ruth Steele Brooks, the Midwestern bride of Alfred Mansfield Brooks, with the high compliment that "you look as clean as a smelt, my dear!"

Along the Old Roads sets off down the Magnolia shore in early spring where arbutus might still be found in certain undisclosed locations near Rafe's Chasm. In April the excursion is to Salt Island, catching dead low tide to make a sortie from Good Harbor Beach to the island in quest of Dutchman's breeches and dogtooth violets. The party would have to be quick about it though, and be back before the rising waters covered the spit of sand that links the beach to the island when the tide is out. Later in the season they would make the same scramble in search of columbines and anemones.

Other walks took Miss Babson, and anyone who wished to tail along, to the woods near Cape Pond in pursuit of mountain laurel. Or along the Old Rockport Road, nostrils alert for the first whiffs of skunk cabbage in March. Then returning each month through the growing season with high expectations of new glories: "If this walk is taken in April, Hobble-bush and Spice-bush buds may be found; in May, Robin's Plantain, Wild Roses and Lady Slippers in Babson's pasture; in June, Mountain Laurel; and in July, in Curtis' pasture, Red Lilies and Polygala."

Along the Old Roads of Cape Ann is by a writer at ease in the Cape Ann countryside, familiar with and considerate of its plant life, confident in her knowledge of local history. And paying tribute in this way to her flower-wise friend, Mrs. Rogers.

Sarah Rogers had educated her son Elliott in the plant lore of Cape

those who wish to familiarize themselves with the seashore populations and the general ecology around Cape Ann . . . . This is the best handbook that I have yet seen for the serious student or the enthusiastic amateur."

Merrill F. McLane celebrated the pursuit of the wild blueberry in his *The Adventure of Blueberrying on Cape Ann, Massachusetts.* Career U. S. Marines officer McLane spoke as an authority on trail skills: earlier in his career he had co-authored *Mountain Climbing Guide to the Grand Tetons.*

These guides speak of nature mostly in its benign moods. But Peter Prybot has seen wind and wave in a temper. Prybot hauls his string of lobster traps year-round, and consequently has more than a casual interest in nature along the coast. It can nuzzle him affectionately. Or it can put him in deep trouble. In a chapter of his *Lobstering off Cape Ann* (2006), Prybot compiles an almanac of the serene wonders and ornery furies of wind and sea that he has encountered during his forty-six years in the trade. Autumn, says Prybot, brings relief from waters crowded with summer traffic, and the sky becomes interesting with migrating loons, harlequin ducks and gannets. But changes in weather patterns also spawn the "mountainous waves and swells of northeasters and southeasters." Winter can be a profitable time for the lobsterman if he can force himself to bundle up and head out in the dark into sullen, threatening seas. There is always the risk of frostbite. Or worse. In spring the shoreline explodes into color and the ocean teams with new life. But the barometer goes skittish again, too, and storms can rake the coast and tear up lobstering gear. Until the brief hiatus of summer again.

The naturist on Cape Ann can revel in the beauties of landscape and seascape. But will be well advised to stay alert to omens of change, in cloud shapes or wind direction or the smell of the air. Nature at the margin of the sea can never be entirely trusted.

CHAPTER 13

The Rediscovery of Cape Ann

CAPE ANN had gone about its maritime occupations in more or less happy obscurity for its first two centuries. Travel by water to Gloucester was possible for the curious, but the harbor was much preoccupied with fish. Anyone approaching by land had to negotiate rough roads and then cross a drawbridge, the sole link between the island cape and the mainland. The railroad arrived in 1847, but did not initially tempt great numbers of visitors to book stays at the few no-frills hostelries.

However, the shores of Cape Ann did attract a few summer vacationers even before there was a rail line, decent local stagecoach service, or the forty-cent steamboat ride from Boston. Edward Everett Hale, one of the exalted breed of Boston Unitarian clergymen and author of "The Man Without a Country," remembered, in his *A New England Boyhood*, the time in the late 1820s when his parents arranged themselves in the family barouche with maps and hand baggage. Hale and his brothers climbed up on the box beside the man of all chores who flicked the reins and away they all went clattering down Boston's Tremont Street. It was a two-day trip. The first night they put up in Lynn, then finally arrived at a "great tavern" on Cape Ann (taverns would later be called "inns" because it sounded more genteel).

Whatever the attractions of the hostelry to the adults, the Hale youngsters busied themselves on the shore getting acquainted with sand dollars and sea urchins and horseshoe crabs. When they all went out in the big open carriage, fishermen's children lined up and bowed as the carriage passed. Said Hale, "It was done good-naturedly, with no sign of deference, but rather, I should say, as a pleasant recognition of human brotherhood ...." For many of the local children it was their first sight of a fashionable barouche. "What is it?" they wondered aloud. "It ain't the mail, and it ain't a shay." A generation later Hale's daughter, Ellen Day Hale, identified with what became known as the Boston School of painting, would be a perennial summer resident at Folly Cove.

In 1873 that naturist, the Reverend Henry C. Leonard, described in *Pigeon Cove and Vicinity* his summer visits to the Ocean View House and the Pigeon Cove House. At the time Reverend Leonard was writing, he could speed to Cape Ann in comfort on the "cars" of the Eastern Railway. But he had a sense that something of the old summer adventure had been lost. He remembered what it had been like to arrive at Pigeon Cove by stagecoach: "The memory goes back to the stage-times of Addison Center, Joseph B. Winchester and Edward H. Shaw. They had strong, well-upholstered stages, and good horses; and they were careful, skilful drivers. Mr. Center and Mr. Winchester drove between Salem and Gloucester; Mr. Shaw, between Gloucester and the end of the Cape. It was a favor to have a seat on the box with either of these gentlemen of the whip."

The coach swayed along late in the day. As Reverend Leonard remembered:

> From Gloucester to Rockport and Pigeon Cove in the twilight or early evening, fanned by the sea-breeze, and smiled on by the stars, was a natural and agreeable ending of the journey.... At the base of [Great Hill] the village lights were a sign of welcome; lanterns, swung in the rigging of vessels on the ocean, rose and sank.... The stage ascended the hill [above Pigeon Cove harbor], passing the few dwellings with lighted halls and parlors, and stopped at the gate of the Pigeon Cove House. From the door of the inn came forth the earlier comers to welcome the later.

Here are stagecoach days recreated as fondly as in Charles Dickens's *Pickwick Papers*. Once set down in Pigeon Cove, the seasonal boarders could settle in to the recreations and delights of the area "to be kept in memory as better than wealth, or all that one might gather and hoard in a lifetime of unbroken, avaricious toil."

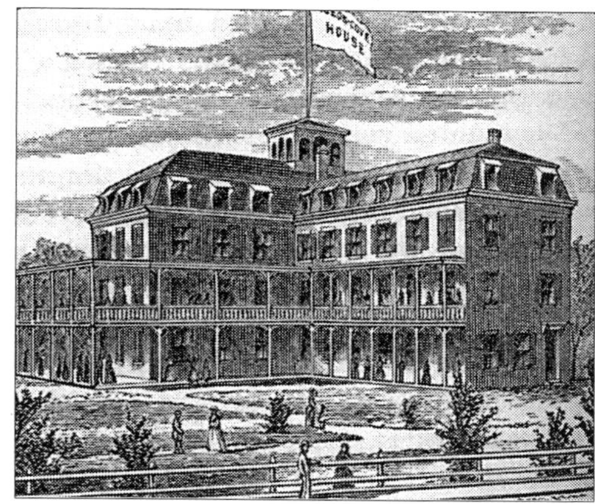

The original Pigeon Cove House of the 1850s was replaced by a rambling resort hotel by the 1870s, as Cape Ann became an increasingly popular summer destination during the 19th century.

Those who came to board at a hotel, whether taking a breather from avaricious toil or not, seldom ventured far from the inn's grounds. The first visitors intent upon actually *traveling* Cape Ann arrived with two wheels under them. These were the "wheelmen" of the 1880s – the debonair young sports who bounced over the countryside atop high-wheeled bicycles. As the recreation of bicycle touring wobbled into a craze across Europe and America, devotees of the sport were banding together into fraternal cycling orders that provided the latest intelligence on routes and accommodations for their members eager for new experiences.

The leading U.S. club was the League of American Wheelmen (L.A.W.), whose members were heartily welcomed by Cape Ann hotelkeepers always on the lookout for new sources of custom. An international club was headquartered in Gloucester, England, and its representative in Gloucester, Massachusetts was John S. Webber, Jr., son of the collector of the port and uncle of the William Webber who would author *Waterfront – Around the Wharves of Gloucester*.

In 1885 John Webber wrote *In and Around Cape Ann: A Hand-Book of Gloucester, Mass., and Its Immediate Vicinity, for the Wheelman Tourist and the Summer Visitor*. It was an invaluable volume for Webber's fellow cyclists bent on negotiating Cape Ann's rutted routes. Imagine an eager band of enthusiasts with Webber's guide at the ready, sallying forth from the Gloucester Hotel at the corner of Main and Washington Streets, "the headquarters of all visiting wheelmen in this city." Proprietor George L. Smith was described as "a warm friend of the touring 'cyclist and a genial and painstaking host." Terms \$1.50 to \$2.00 per day, with a 25% discount for wheelmen.

The intrepid cyclists venture off toward East Gloucester via "the rather uneven surface of Main Street." The easiest going is over slabs of granite from Porter to Hancock streets. Dismounting at the entrance to Niles Beach, they "watch the merry throng of bathers in their sportive antics in the cooling sea, and inwardly wish that we were among them in the refreshing exercise."

A spin to Magnolia meant first pedaling up a gravelly road near the west shore of the harbor to Fishermen's Field. Then it was "legs over!" – feet up and over the handlebars – for a "charming little coast" down to Cressy Beach. It may sound counter-intuitive to loop legs over the handlebars of a high-wheeled contraption gathering speed down a steep slope, but that was the recommended practice. The reasoning was that in case you were shot forward, better to land on your feet than on your head.

Webber guessed that "a wheel around Cape Ann" could be accomplished in two hours, which might have been optimistic considering the state of the lanes, and the likelihood of having to detour around hay wagons and livestock. But the efforts were rewarded. From the top of Great Hill above Rockport the view was unobstructed in a day when the summits had long since been deforested. "As the 'cyclist wheels along, the picture is truly grand." The steeples of Rockport and Pigeon Cove ahead, Thacher's Island to the right, to the left a vista all the way to the Annisquam River and the Fernwood Lake ice houses beyond.

After a good dinner at the Gloucester Hotel the touring wheelmen could amble down to the harbor where "on a dusky night, the spectacle is most magnificent, when perhaps half a thousand sail of vessels are riding calmly at anchor with lights sparkling brightly from their positions on board." John Webber's cycling comrades might perch on bollards, lighting up cheroots, debating which routes to essay and what enchanting destinations to strike out for on the morrow. They would have been objects of curiosity to fishermen wandering by, struck in wonderment at the notion of young men traveling on Cape Ann simply to amuse themselves, not on any legitimate errands of business.

By the 1890s the roads had been much improved, as reported in *Romance & Reality of the Puritan Coast* by Edmund H. Garrett (1897). Garrett was, like John Webber, a cyclist. "How often, when the winter days lengthen and drag, the wheelman sighs for springtime and the road!" But for Garrett the important thing was not to get somewhere in a hurry, but to appreciate what you saw along the way. "Surely the riding is only a part! – for what of all this does the 'scorcher' see? . . . Most people ride too fast. The art of strolling a-wheel should be cultivated. The best way to do this is to take the mind off the cyclometer and the clock, and put it on the landscape and its life."

As he "strolled a-wheel" through Gloucester of the 1890s, Garrett was swept up in the tumult of the waterfront. "One is continually reminded of [Gloucester's] chief occupation, for the signs read of ships and their stores, of boats and seines, of nets and fish, and up the side-streets, from the yards and wharves, steal fine marine odors.... The fleet crowds the harbor; and through the maze of shrouds and masts are seen the towers and steeples of the city."

If the cyclist could pass unstained and unchanged through the uproar of the waterfront, he would emerge safely on the eastern arm of the harbor. "Here one enters the land of rackets [racquets] and golf clubs, summer girls, novels, and hammocks, water-color kits and white umbrellas." The East Gloucester shore was as seductive to Edmund Garrett as it had been to John Webber's wheelmen a few years earlier.

Also in the 1890s, visitors could tour Cape Ann in comfortable carriages, armed with a copy of *Pleasure Drives Around Cape Ann* (1896). Its

By the 1890s, parties of both sexes were touring Cape Ann on the new, safer bicycles.

promise was to describe "the most popular drives . . . to intensify the interest of tourists in Gloucester and introduce to them the places they should surely visit by carriage, and . . . lend color to their anticipations of the charms old Cape Ann can throw about them."

Pleasure Drives drew the reader's attention to local banks and businesses. To places of worship, as well, although here, the visitor needed to exercise some caution. According to the guide, the Methodist-Episcopal and Baptist churches were "situated within rifle shot of one another." Had some fierce doctrinal dispute escalated into an actual state of hostilities between the two? *Pleasure Drives* says no more.

Niles Beach was described as "the main plaisance of the whole summer colony, for here we meet the bicyclists, the promenaders, the bathers, the yachters, the driving parties and the artists." Perhaps John Webber's wheelmen were there, back for an excursion eleven years later. Or Edmund Garrett resting beside his wheels, taking in the panorama.

There would be greater variety among the bicycles now. The sport had gained wide popularity among wheelpersons of both sexes, with the introduction of the chain-and-sprocket Rovers with low wheels of equal size, reducing the distance to the pavement if you took a tumble.

According to *Pleasure Drives* the visitor would share the ride to Magnolia with "fine equipages and equestrians, which are proofs of the fashionable resort which we soon are to have the pleasure of visiting." And while in Magnolia, why not push on to Manchester-by-the-Sea? There "the tennis tournaments of the [Essex County] Club, their dinner parties and balls are of the 'swellest' type, and thus the 'smart' set from all the neighboring resorts all flock to Manchester and revel in this club's social generosity."

When touring by automobile became the rage in the 1920s, guidebooks were rushed into print to help the new trippers-on-wheels find their way around. *The Gloucester Book* by Frank L. Cox (1921) served to showcase the author's "artistic photographs." These included finely detailed views of the waterfront, especially of the Italian fleet at Harbor Cove. And of old houses, Dogtown boulders, and scenic attractions such as Half Moon Beach.

Travel on the roads of Cape Ann was intimidating into the 1920s.
Courtesy Cape Ann Historical Museum

Cox mentions historic houses and taverns, the Fishermen's Institute, Dogtown. And the two banks that stood solid and seemingly as timeless as the pyramids on either side of Fishermen's Corner: the Gloucester National Bank, "Gloucester's most historical banking institution," and the Gloucester Safe Deposit & Trust Company which Cox, with some partiality, urges visitors "to make . . . their banking home during their stay."

The ads in *The Gloucester Book* give the flavor of downtown Gloucester in the '20s. Car trouble? Roll the Ford into the Perkins & Corliss garage for authorized service. And while waiting, stroll for refreshments up to Ye Judith Sargent Tea Rooms and Gift Shop located in the Sargent-Murray-Gilman House. Exclusive distributor for the guide was F. M. Shurtleff at the Waiting Station on Main Street, where the important little buses pulled up to load passengers for travel along roads that by then had been for the most part paved, to romantic distant destinations: Long Beach, Folly Cove, Rocky Neck. A bonus of *The Gloucester Book* was its 1920s map called "The Cape Ann Trail" that evokes a summertime of gentlemen in plus fours on the golf links, and flappers in the shocking new bare-legged bathing costumes.

In 1931 came *Know Cape Ann: The Garden Spot of the Atlantic* by Edward Vassar Ambler. Ambler commented on the scenic attractions, but reserved his highest admiration for men of the four Coast Guard stations then operating on Cape Ann. At Fresh Water Cove or Straitsmouth, he said, you could see the surf boats at the ready, the lookouts on patrol along the shore. At the Coast Guard air station on Ten Pound Island were based the seaplanes that might be called upon to search for fishing vessels in distress, or spot the fast boats of rumrunners. The Coast Guard says that the first Vought seaplane at the station, borrowed from the Navy, had a crude battery-powered radio on board. According to Ambler, back-up communications gear consisted of homing pigeons that could wing their way back to the station carrying urgent messages.

Ambler's tribute to the daring Coast Guard pilots is seconded by a stone monument at the eastern end of Stacy Boulevard, near the Fishermen's Monument. Its bronze plaque depicts a bi-winged seaplane swooping down to rescue a fisherman overboard and clinging to wreckage. The inscription reads, in part: "In honor of the men who established Coast Guard Aviation in May of 1925 on Ten Pound Island in Gloucester Harbor. Home of the first continuously operating Coast Guard Air Station."

F. J. G. Robinson, like Ambler, was fascinated with the new technologies that were revolutionizing navigation and bringing new safety to the high seas. The visitor gazing out to Thacher's twin lights was assured by Robinson, in his *Tragabigzanda, or Cape Ann* (1935), that a Radio Compass Station was in action on the island, with operators patrolling the "ether waves" to communicate with ocean liners arriving off the coast from Europe.

Always popular with visitors was the view of those twin lighthouses of Thacher's Island (originally Isle of Thacher's Woe, named for the Reverend Anthony Thacher who, with his wife, were the sole survivors of a shipwreck on the island in 1635 that took the lives of their children and all others aboard). Guy Currier surely included a stop to gaze at those towers in his tours of the Rockport shore in the 1950s. Currier, then in his late sixties, had been driving a taxi for a year or so and realized he did not know as much about his home town as he thought he did. So he boned up to the point where he felt he could discourse knowledgeably when he took visitors out on tours. He wrote about his experiences in *Cape of Islands – Cape Ann*.

The reader imagines Currier, at the wheel of some vintage pre-World War II vehicle, pointing out Rockport landmarks and quoting statistics to his passengers. Sooner or later, though, Guy Currier would slip in a few of the anecdotes he relished. Like the exploits of the Patches Corner gang in Dock Square. How they would spend Saturday evening in the barrooms of Gloucester, then return singing and carousing on a streetcar. The motorman would clang for the Dock Square stop, and that's where most of the fishermen would tumble out, all in noisy hilarity.

Currier might grin into the mirror and tell the tourists there was one fellow in the gang who played a cornet, and another a fiddle. And an old Civil War veteran who would warm up on Medford rum and burst into some favorite song or other, maybe "The City of Baltimore," so loud he'd be heard a mile away. By this time Guy Currier's tour party might complain that this was not the sort of antiquarian lore they had

Loening OL-5 takes off, in 1929, from Ten Pound Island, "home of the first continuously operating Coast Guard Air Station."
U.S. Coast Guard photo

signed up for. Well, all right. He would give a shrug and drive them to Little Cape Hedge, and show them where the Commercial Cable Company built a shore station for the telegraph cable they had laid all the way from Canso, Nova Scotia. If that's what those customers wanted to hear, so be it. He would save for more discriminating audiences his select tales of the Patches Corner gang, and perhaps anecdotes of Bearskin Neck before the artists took over the fish shacks.

The most historically informed guidebook to Gloucester is Joseph E. Garland's *The Gloucester Guide*. It is an indispensable companion for anyone spending serious time in Gloucester, from the visitor on some personal pursuit, to the devotee of the locality who has come by that interest through bloodlines or by conviction. The revised edition of

1990 Garland subtitled "A Stroll through Place and Time." He draws upon his reservoir of local knowledge as he escorts the reader around Gloucester's portion of Cape Ann, through the villages, down old roads and along beaches, finishing downtown with condensed background information on every neighborhood from Main Street to the waterfront and the Fort district.

In the sections on the fisheries, *The Gloucester Guide* takes on the thoroughness of a Michelin Green Guide describing a cathedral city in Europe. Garland digs down through the historical strata, unearthing shards of anecdote as he goes. At Fisherman's Wharf, for example. In the 1930s, Garland says, this was known as "Piney's Wharf" where racing schooners were tied up at the Atlantic Supply Company, managed by Fishermen's Races enthusiast Ben Pine. But Garland does not stop there. He says that before it was Ben Pine's Wharf it was Boynton's, and before that Central Wharf, and before that the wharf of William Pearce and Sons. Pearce had shipped fish to Surinam, and brought back sugar and molasses that served as the prime ingredients for his rum distillery.

When he was researching his first edition in the early 1970s, Joe Garland could still find sources whose memories reached deep into the past. Lyman F. Allen had worked at the Riverdale tide mills as a boy in 1904 and said he earned ten cents for every wagon load of corn he shoveled onto the grain mill's conveyor belt. Lyman really earned those dimes: Garland says each wagon held two to three tons of grain.

The language of the *Guide* sometimes soars into the poetic. Garland speaks of Lane's Cove in Lanesville where stone schooners once put in to take on cargos of granite and "the heavy rusted rings and chains, and the cylindrical granite bollards for springlining the vessels to the piers, are still here, and vestiges of the derricks. Small boats have hauled up since colonial times at the end of the marsh where the stream meets the sea and the purple loosestrife grows."

For those interested enough to delve into the deeper waters of Gloucester lore, Garland concludes the book with a select list of sources for further reading. *The Gloucester Guide* is the one best field guide to Gloucester past and present, distilled from Garland's store of lore into a volume slim enough to slip into a jacket pocket or a glove compartment for an outing down some wandering lane or up some lookout hill just for the view.

If, beginning in the late 19th century, tourists were discovering Cape Ann, drawn by the tall masts of the fish-busy harbor and the scenic attractions of the rugged coast, could extended-stay vacationers be far behind? No, they were not. They began to arrive by stagecoach, and by ferry boat from Boston, and by the trains of the Boston & Maine Railroad (which had absorbed the Eastern Railroad). A seasonal population was laying its claim to July and August on Cape Ann.

CHAPTER 14

Summer Romance

GLOUCESTER TOOK its summer vacationers on its own terms, and any who did not wish to abide by those terms were welcome to vacation elsewhere. Those who returned regularly knew that they were expected to stand a safe distance from the edge of the dock, not venture opinions on maritime subjects of which they knew not, and keep to themselves any observations as to the smells and usages peculiar to the waterfront. Gloucester would then be hospitable to its summer visitors, whether they were a family roughing it in a plank-floor camp up a dirt lane in Bay View with a long walk to Plum Cove beach, or the latest in a dynasty to occupy the old house on the shore with antlers over the great hearth.

Writer Elizabeth Stuart Phelps had come to understand, if not accept, the sufferance with which the locals put up with summer people:

> The result of my own observation has been that Gloucester, in her heart of hearts, regards her large summer population with a certain contempt. We are weak on the topics of main-sheets, and job-hanks, of blocks and 'popple-ballast,' and seines . . . . Our incomes, if we have any, are drawn from invisible sources looked upon with instinctive suspicion. They are neither caught with a hook nor salted in a box . . . . We are artists, whose crop of white umbrellas sprouts everywhere . . . and whose brushes do not know a back-stay from corn-silk. We are boarders who capsize the cat-boats, or pay by the hour to sail in a calm and don't know any better.

Many of the early "summer boarders" stayed at the Fairview Inn, in Phelps's summer neighborhood of East Gloucester. One such was

The Fairview Inn, East Gloucester, 1870s. Louisa May Alcott, William Vaughan Moody and Rudyard Kipling and family signed the register. *Courtesy Cape Ann Historical Museum*

Louisa May Alcott who boarded at the Fairview in 1868 when her *Little Women* was just being published, and again in 1871 when it was bringing her fame and, at last, some comfort and security. Kipling also put up at the Fairview with his family twice in the 1890s before he set to work on *Captains Courageous*, and incorporated into that work his haughty impressions of the American guests at a provincial hotel.

William Vaughn Moody was another literary bird of passage who signed the register at the Fairview, he in 1900 when he was just over thirty. Moody wrote the original pencil draft of his poem, "Gloucester Moors," on Fairview stationery (preserved in the library of the Cape Ann Historical Museum). Initially the poem rollicks along in a Kipling-esque canter. Reformist zeal takes over in the later verses, though, as Moody targets unequal distribution of wealth. This was, after all, an era when muckrakers were pinioning malefactors of great wealth. Moody named no names, though; chastised no specific robber barons on Eastern Point.

William Vaughn Moody also wrote for the stage, his first plays based on Greek myths. Then he began to explore North American mythology, and, in *The Great Divide*, fused Greek tragedy with the rites and dances of the Hopi Indians. He was a close friend of Percy MacKaye, another playwright who was crafting American folk themes for the stage – one of which was his drama "Dogtown Common." MacKaye edited *Letters to Harriet*, which Moody wrote to his wife-to-be, who would see him through his final illness to his death at forty-one.

Well-known (in their time) Gothamites and Philadelphians and Buffalonians graced the guest lists of the other East Gloucester hotels. Among the Washingtonians at the Harbor View was "Major Powell, of the Bureau of Psychology, Etymology and Analogy, author of great philosophic and scientific works." Judge Bumpus, Charles Dodge of Washington's Department of Fibre and Invention, and Lucy Cannon, the Baltimore artist, were installed at George Stacy's Hawthorne Inn. Stacy's slogan for his establishment was "the place where you see the right side of life."

Magnolia was another prime destination for summer sojourners. For a hundred years its granite shore, westerly from Gloucester harbor, was built up with enormous summer hotels, and an arcaded Lexington Avenue hosted branches of so many fashionable Boston and New York shops it came to be known as "Robbers Row."

Families "of means" booked year after year at hotels like the Oceanside and the Hesperus. (Hildegard Hartt confides in her *Magnolia, Once Kettle Cove* that "the quieter well-bred Bostonians and many others preferred the Hesperus.") The social event of the season was the magnificent annual ball at the Oceanside, where Mrs. John Hays Hammond, Sr. was the reigning queen, holding court in splendid gown and jewels topped off with a diamond tiara. John Philip Sousa played band concerts in the Oceanside, demanding absolute silence during each number. Cars would park along the roads near the hotel, full of locals listening for free.

In 1912 the Oceanside, by then a resort behemoth of 750 rooms plus cottages, vacuumed up the genteel but anemic Hesperus. The Oceanside itself had been long out of fashion when it burned in 1958, in a decade which saw abandoned old hotels combusting spontaneously, and mysteriously, all over the North Shore.

Manchester, just over the Gloucester line on the coast toward Boston, became populated in the summer more by wealthy property owners than by hotel guests. In the 1890s the Reverend D. F. Lamson lamented that Manchester was losing its individuality as a small town of lobstermen, fishermen and cabinet-makers now that outsiders were buying up property to build summer homes on a grand scale. Still, Lamson could look on the bright side and point to how Manchester had benefited from the new squirearchy: "Acres once covered with a tangled growth of wildwood, and considered too valueless for taxation, have been threaded by romantic avenues, and beautified by lawns and gardens."

Reverend Lamson also took heart by reflecting that summer was brief and the locals could look forward to their return to Elysium after Labor Day. "The most beautiful months, September and October, with their bright skies, crisp and bracing air, and 'softly pictured woods,' witness the departure of the summer crowd, and Manchester is left to its own quiet loveliness."

As to Manchester's full nomenclature as "Manchester-by-the-Sea," Lamson credited publisher James T. Fields for suggesting the three-word tag, although others have suggested that Fields's wife Annie was the responsible party. Reverend Lamson stoutly defended the elongated name, saying that, inasmuch as there were Manchesters all over New England, "the name Manchester-by-the-Sea serves often as a useful differentiation, preventing mail matter from going astray, not to speak of freight and passengers even." Good point. A gentleman entrusting his fate to the rails in Boston's North Station could be certain of stepping down at his North Shore retreat, and not at Manchester-by-the-Merrimack in the savage wilds of New

Hampshire. In 1990 the town voted to officially incorporate "By-The-Sea" into its title. Another Fields – W. C. – might have felicitated the municipality upon its choice of this euphonious appellation.

Robert Grant reported on the recreations of the youth of that "summer crowd" referred to by Reverend Lamson. "Occasionally small parties drive through the woods to Chebacco Lake to sup on broiled chickens, thin fried potatoes and champagne, to dance a gay waltz or polka or two, and drive home by moonlight; but apart from occasional dinner-parities, this is the limit of the social gayety."

Manchester's Essex County Club was the site of more exclusive social gayety. It was patronized occasionally by Presidents Taft and Wilson and General John J. Pershing. Members included some of the *really* important people, like the Boston financiers Augustus Hemenway and Thomas Jefferson Coolidge who acquired great swaths of prime ocean frontage and built their imposing cottages.

In the midst of all this giddy wealth and social distinction, village life carried on, as reported in the pages of Manchester's durable newspaper, the *Cricket*. As when, in 1913, Chief of Police Sullivan quashed the nearest thing to a pop concert riot in Manchester with the decree that "'bunny hugs,' 'turkey trots,' and similar modern fancy dancing that is popular in some places at this time, will not be tolerated in Manchester." Those with a yen for fancy dancing would have to indulge their depraved inclinations elsewhere.

Over at Floyd's paper store, the gleaming equipage of the Argentine ambassador pulled up, and the ambassador's son entered, loudly calling for his father's newspaper. The proprietor was unmoved as the boy, assuming diplomatic impunity, continued to demand the ambassador's paper. Finally Floyd said, in so many words, that he did not particularly care who the boy's father was, and to sit on that stool and shut up until it was his turn to be waited on. The boy sat.

One of the more impressive summer estates along the shore was not at Magnolia or Manchester but on the western shore of Gloucester harbor. It was hidden from Western Avenue by a high wall reminiscent of those surrounding Mexican estancias. Which was a clue to the identity of the owner.

John Hays Hammond, Sr. was born in San Francisco as the Gold Rush was tailing off in 1855. Hammond grew up tall in the saddle on the family ranch. His father sent him across the country to get polished up at Yale, then he moved on to Germany to study engineering before he headed back to the California mining camps. He was still young but knew how to wield the rough justice of the West. He hired Wyatt Earp to discourage claim jumpers. Could Hammond be certain Earp would shoot only in self-defense? Why of course, Wyatt assured him. His attacker was always allowed to draw first – before Earp dropped him with a single shot.

Hammond's ability to sniff out rich ore became legendary, and he was hired to oversee a mine down in Mexico. This was the age of the swashbuckling civil engineer, and Hammond lived on horseback, his revolver at the ready, the landscape thick with "marauding Indians," rebellious miners and assorted revolutionaries. After Mexico, Hammond traveled to South Africa. Cecil Rhodes had hired him on as his field man to scout out and develop diamond mines.

Rhodes was a man with an uncomplicated vision: to extend the advantages of British rule, culture and commercial dominance across the globe. In fact the original purpose of Rhodes scholarships was to recruit young fellows from English-speaking countries who would implement this Pax Britannica. Of course, before general bliss under the Union Jack could be realized, the United States would have to forswear its silly detour into independence and rejoin the Empire. Mad? Maybe. But Rhodes had a charismatic aura and, despite his harsh treatment of workers in his mines, the native blacks preferred him (according to Hammond) over the even more severe Dutch Afrikaners under "Om" (Uncle) Paul Kruger.

The job paid handsomely, but got Hammond into trouble with the Afrikaners who charged him with sedition and sentenced him to death. International diplomacy was put to the test as Hammond languished for months in the Johannesburg lockup before he was finally spared the hangman's cravat. He decided a career with Cecil Rhodes was a trifle too exciting, so he returned to America for less hazardous duty as a highly paid mining consultant and appointee to international commissions.

He also decided it was time to enjoy the rewards of a vigorous life. In the summer of 1903 Hammond and his wife Natalie cruised along the New England coast in search of a likely retreat, "always anxious to avoid such enervating routine as one finds in Newport and other fashionable resorts." "Finally, we decided on Gloucester, Massachusetts, because it was a town of fishermen – men whose rugged character reminded us of communities we had known and loved in the Far West." There they built their walled compound and called it "Lookout Hill." (After Hammond's time the estate would shelter nuns of a Catholic order, and after that adherents of the Reverend Sun Yung Moon.)

Hammond's fortress on the ledges was strategically situated between the tumult of Gloucester's fishing harbor on one side, and the haunts of world movers and shakers along the North Shore toward Boston. In time his friend William Howard Taft was elected President of the United States and began summering on the Beverly shore, where he and Hammond and their wives got together. Another neighbor was steel tycoon Henry Clay Frick.

One day Henry Frick rang up from behind the great iron palisades of his estate at Prides Crossing, said he had E. H. Harriman to visit and would Hammond care to join them for a spin around Cape Ann in an automobile? Frick's chauffeur took the curves on the winding, unpaved roads on two wheels, scattering hens, horses and bystanders, the rattle and roar of their vehicle drowning out the curses that followed in their wake. There they were: Hammond, the highest-paid man in America; Frick, the founder of U. S. Steel; and Harriman, multi-millionaire railroad magnate, hot-rodding around Cape Ann like a trio of teenagers.

Hammond enjoyed the company of the mighty but was equally happy consorting with the schooner fishermen who, like him, had faced danger for a living. He particularly liked to drop in on the cigar store Howard Blackburn was running at the time, and listen to the extraordinary tales of the man he called "one of the most undaunted sailors America ever had." When Blackburn died Hammond was an honorary pallbearer at his funeral, along with Arctic explorers Commander Donald B. MacMillan and Sir Wilfred Grenfell.

Hammond took to heart the dread he heard from many old fishermen of dying broke and being tipped into a pauper's grave. He set up a fund that eventually purchased over three hundred plots for a Fishermen's Cemetery in the Beechbrook burial ground near Little

River. Howard Blackburn is buried in lot No. 2, grave No. 1.

In his late years John Hays, Sr. could take satisfaction in the achievements – if not the peccadilloes – of his playboy-inventor son John Hays, Jr. who, farther along the western shore of Gloucester harbor, put up a medieval castle of his own. The English butler discreetly ushered through the gates of "Abbadia Mare" the likes of Igor Stravinsky, Admiral Byrd, Greta Garbo, Noel Coward, Ethel Barrymore, George Gershwin – and, in the wee hours, an occasional Hollywood starlet.

While his father was still alive the younger Hammond had already patented radio-controlled remote guidance devices. He invested considerable effort and expense in developing for the Vatican a secure radio system that broadcast on a dedicated frequency. The Holy See cancelled the deal and Hammond, in pique, offered the system instead to Benito Mussolini. FBI suspicions about Hammond, Jr. were mollified when, during World War II, the laboratory at Abbadia Mare performed useful military research. After the war young Hammond's inventions served the U.S. space program. His father would have been proud that, just as he himself had spurred a swayback cayuse over rough trails in Old Mexico, his son's guidance systems were nudging new rigs into outer space.

Other favored areas of the Cape Ann shore offered summer residents anonymity with no need for high walls. One was Annisquam at the mouth of the Annisquam River. The village core of the Annisquam section nestles on the sheltered side of a neck of land that provides the privacy almost of an island within an island. Annisquam had enjoyed a brief epoch as a fishing center, resulting from a happy congruence of granite and fish. As Copeland and Rogers recorded in their *Saga of Cape Ann*, stone piers were built out into Lobster Cove with rock from quarries above the village. At one point, seventy-five ocean-going vessels made Annisquam their port, most small but of a size to trade fish and wares to New Orleans, Western Europe and South America. During the decades after the wars with England until the Panic of 1837, merchants and masters built houses that were substantial but never ostentatious. Then credit collapsed and the Port of Annisquam relinquished its trading ambitions, and ceded to

Gloucester harbor dominance in the fisheries.

But the village remained self-sufficient. The inhabitants had scarcely any need to go beyond the confines of the locality, having at hand by the 1860s a fish market, a grocery store, the Deluge Fire Engine in its firehouse, a "mutton shop," a cooper shop which made their mackerel barrels, the stagecoach-line stable, and two blacksmith shops.

The elders of the village church at the head of Lobster Cove always had difficulty luring pastors to their obscure parish. They were delighted when they secured the services of the Reverend Ezra Leonard in 1805. The new minister more than lived up to his promise. First, Annisquam had no schoolteacher, so Reverend Leonard set up a school. The young men of the village had no way to prepare for a career at sea, so he taught them navigation. To provide practical guidance to his flock on matters of vital interest such as tides, weather, and the growing season, he authored a Farmer's and Mariners' Almanac, one of the many forerunners of the *Old Farmer's Almanac.*

There was only one disturbing element in Ezra Leonard's makeup. He was something of a free-thinker. He came to espouse John Murray's Universalism, believing that many seafaring men of his congregation, sorely tried by assorted temptations, deserved a kind and forgiving God. Leonard announced from the pulpit his decision to resign from the pastorate, and the church elders said they'd think it over. In the end the congregation joined Reverend Leonard in embracing his all-forgiving faith, and he served as their minister until his death in 1832. He was so well regarded that the main road in the village still bears his name, as does the men's club which was organized to balance the matriarchal influence of the sewing circle. In 1957 the church joined the International Council of Community Churches, in effect opting out of dogmatic disputes.

Late in the 19th century, the majesty of the views and charm of the locale became whispered about in the right circles, and people well known in commerce and the professions put up large, rambling summer homes adequate to the needs of their extended families and their large rosters of weekend guests. In time a yacht club was financed by a few property owners well able to indulge their whims. Perched on pilings just offshore, it burned, was promptly replaced, and became the

By the 1890s, Annisquam's maritime activity was diminished, but active. *Martha Hale Harvey photo*

center of activity for a summer set obsessed with sailing and tennis, followed by a sociable pick-me-up as the sun lowered over the Wingaersheek dunes.

The summer residents shared the Annisquam peninsula with a local population that exhibited all of the ornery independence of every other Cape Ann community. And that caused trouble. There had been tensions when the proud locals suspected that the newcomers privately regarded them as little more than a convenient labor pool. Sometime after World War II, though, the Annisquam winter and summer populations came to a joining that was more than accommodation. The natives were confident in the virtues of their world, and could afford to be patient with the Independence-Day-to-Labor-Day residents until they too, or their children, or their grandchildren, learned to relax into the rhythm of the tides.

Or until they returned to settle late in life and stood above Cambridge Beach, seeing sea smoke rising behind the sandbar, and a penetratingly blue sky over the "castles" at the end of Wingaersheek Beach, and beyond that Crane's, and Plum Island, to indistinct mirage-suspended shores toward New Hampshire, Maine, into infinity. Recognizing that this had always been home, that here was a splendor sufficient unto itself, which was religion enough for some of them.

The blended populations of Annisquam have come to share in all that makes it a congenial village. They pitch in to put on an August Sea Fair, then on winter Monday afternoons sip tea by the fire in the village library. They volunteer for a Good Neighbors Program that runs errands for ailing members of the community. In large numbers they forsake the enchantments of summer evenings to rehearse for the annual Broadway musical presented by the Annisquam Village Players, under the long-time direction of Land Court Judge Alexander "Terry" Sands.

Old bridge to Annisquam village, later replaced by a footbridge (much quieter, with no cars rumbling over the wooden planks).

The summer population of Annisquam has included luminaries like playwright Russel Crouse, who arrived by way of parental pride. After an unfortunate first marriage he became a bridegroom again in his fifties, this time to Anna Erskine, daughter of author and editor John Erskine. Where could Russel and Anna take their children to escape the summer heat of Manhattan? Well, Annisquam had proved a tranquil summer haven for other theatre people – Helen Hayes and her family, and Ruth Chatterton, and Boston drama critic Elliot Norton. Russel and Anna bought a comfortable big house near the village church. Howard Lindsay and his actress wife Dorothy Stickney came to stay often, especially when Lindsay & Crouse were at work on a show. Together they crafted some of the most successful plays and musical scripts in the heyday of the Broadway stage: *Anything Goes* built around Cole Porter's melodies and lyrics, *Life with Father*, *Arsenic and Old Lace*, *State of the Union*, *Call Me Madam* and, later, the book for *The Sound of Music*.

Crouse set up the Russel Crouse Award for the encouragement of literary efforts on Cape Ann. The winner in 1954 was S. Foster Damon for his play "The Witch of Dogtown," presented during the Cape Ann Festival of the Arts that summer, and Howard Lindsay and John Kieran came to the show, together with Crouse.

When Damon had been a thin, blond-mustached youth at Harvard he was everywhere in the arts: president of the Harvard Music Society, editor of the *Harvard Music Review*, editor of the *Harvard Monthly* poetry magazine. He organized the Harvard Poetry Society in 1915 and talked up a scheme for an anthology of poetry from the contributors to the *Harvard Monthly*. It was published in 1917 as *Eight Harvard Poets*, and included works by himself, John Dos Passos, and the most successful poet of the group, that eschewer of initial capitals, e. e. cummings. Foster Damon's greatest personal influence was upon Cummings. He taught e. e. to play the piano, and Cummings said Damon opened his eyes and ears to the new European movements in music, poetry and painting. In later years Cummings kept in touch, visiting Damon in Annisquam.

Malcolm Cowley said Foster Damon had a talent for anonymity. Damon encouraged other poets and artists who gained fame in the '20s and '30s, but he himself settled into inquisitive scholarship. He wrote authoritative works on William Blake and James Joyce, and a biography of his friend, cigar-smoking poet Amy Lowell, as well as articles on everything from square dancing to Puccini to Mickey Mouse. Damon married Louise Wheelwright, the sister of a poet friend. He summered in Annisquam all his life, and satisfied his creative urges in later years as impresario of a Punch and Judy show that was a popular component of the annual August Sea Fair.

Malcolm Cowley remembered another Lost Generation figure who could not get Cape Ann out of his blood. In 1930 wealthy Bostonian poet Harry Crosby, a central figure among the American expatriates in Paris and publisher of the Black Sun Press, committed suicide. But seven years earlier in Paris, Crosby had been recuperating from the Quatz' Arts ball of the night before and longing, of all things, " . . . for the sunset at Coffin's Beach . . . I would even like (for me tremendous admission) a small farm near Annisquam with a stone farmhouse looking out over flat stretches of sand toward the sea. The hell you say." But Harry Crosby was too far gone, too desperate in distant absinthe cafes to find his way back.

In the prolific tricentennial year of 1923 that saw publication of Pringle's *History* and Susan Babson's *Along the Old Roads of Cape Ann*, thirty-four-year-old Charles Boardman Hawes was putting the finishing touches to his *Gloucester By Land and Sea*, written at his home "at the Head' the Cove" in Annisquam. It was a leisurely history of the Gloucester villages, rich in anecdote and local color. Somewhere he found old verses about Isaac Dennison, a Revolutionary War veteran who lived in the Dennison homestead (once a tavern) up where Revere Street reverted to a cart track that joined the old Squam Path to Sandy Bay. Isaac's wife Moll, the story went, "traipsed the neighborhood round and round / Telling tales and getting news, / And wearing out old Isaac's shoes." Then,

> In the west when the sun sank low,
> Molly thought it time to go.
> With a cup of tea and a halibut fin,
> Then Molly traipsed home again.

Charles Hawes went in pursuit of old village tales in Lanesville,

Pitt Dillingham
July 11th 1915—

Florence B. Dillingham
July. 11. 1915.

Pauline B. Dillingham
July 11, 1915.

Roger Huntington Sessions
July 31, 1915 – August 1, 1915

August 7-8. 1915
E Estlin Cummings
Philip H. Smith

Aug 9th 1915
Katharine Gordon
Geo Bryant Woods

In 1915, poet e. e. cummings reverted to capital letters when he signed the guestbook as "E. Estlin Cummings" at the Annisquam home of his Harvard chum, S. Foster Damon. Composer Roger Sessions had been a guest a week earlier. *Courtesy Paul Littlefield*

too, and among the fishermen on Bearskin Neck in Rockport, and on Rocky Neck in East Gloucester where other sea dogs shared their well-worn anecdotes with him. Hawes said that his favorite destination at the end of a summer afternoon was to walk to Halibut Point and, "at nightfall, when the lamps are lighting," to sit on one of the heaps of slag rock and "watch the lights of the big hotels across the bay." There he thought of one of the "follies" associated there with Folly Cove, whereby investors had been lured by a scheme to extract gold from sea water. Hawes took a certain satisfaction from the thought: "thus you can med-

For determined Cape Ann vacationers, the setting was what mattered, not the amenities. *Author photo*

itate comfortably upon the labors and vanities and credulities of man."

With his command of neighborhood lore, it seemed as if Hawes must have lived on the island cape all his life. The fact was that he and his wife and two young sons had taken up residence in Annisquam only three years earlier. He had been an editor at *Youth's Companion* magazine until he went out on his own hook to write adventure stories for the young, tales that often had a maritime slant. While waiting for *Gloucester By Land and Sea* to be printed, Hawes and the family took a trip to Northampton in western Massachusetts, the summer home of his wife's parents (her father was George W. Cable, author of Southern novels like *Old Creole Days* and raconteur who had traveled the lecture circuit with Mark Twain). During the visit Hawes contracted meningitis. It was almost invariably a fatal disease in those times, and the family watched helplessly as his life flickered out. Hawes was returned to Annisquam and buried in Mt. Adnah cemetery. His span was so brief that this author who wrote so engagingly about Cape Ann is little remembered.

Beyond Annisquam, off the Bay View shore, sails were seen for forty years that would excite the admiration of every yachtsman. It was the schooner yacht *America*, General Ben Butler's pride and joy, returning to its mooring at the family compound. Built by New York pilot-boat designer George Steers, this was the racing schooner that sailed to victory off the Isle of Wight in 1851 and claimed the Royal Yacht Squadron trophy, renamed in its honor as the "*America*'s Cup." After the race *America* changed hands four times in British registry as *Camilla*, then turned up in Savannah, possibly intended for service as a Confederate blockade runner. Next she was found scuttled in a Florida river, was recovered by the Union Navy and armed to join the blockade fleet off Charleston. After the war the battered vessel was tied up at Annapolis where she sailed on summer training cruises for cadets of the Naval Academy. She was refitted for the *America's* Cup challenge in 1870, but after all those hard years could finish no better than fourth.

In 1873 the Navy put the grand old but weary *America* up for auction. She was purchased for $5,000 by a surrogate for Butler. The general boasted that he had threatened to sue anyone who dared submit a competitive bid. Butler spent handsomely to restore *America* to her old glory, and relished the plaudits of guests he took on sailing outings across Ipswich Bay – they lounging in the cockpit with glasses of cheer, the old general in panama hat and silk gloves braced squarely in undisputed command at the helm.

On May 3, 2003, a scrupulously accurate model of *America*, commissioned by Stevens family descendants of Ben Butler, and crafted by maritime historian and ship model-maker Erik A. R. Ronnberg, Jr., was unveiled at the Cape Ann Historical Museum. General Ben would no doubt have applauded the gesture as a worthy tribute to the celebrated yacht (and to himself).

Lanesville became more attractive as a summer retreat after the thunder from the quarries went silent and the stone dust settled. There were no tourist amenities, but that was all right. The summer boarders liked to meet friends at the post office, and go into Fred Foster's drugstore for an ice cream soda. A few insiders knew that Fred was also a talented amateur photographer who had documented the people, places and happenings of the village between the two world wars. Barbara Erkkila had illustrated her *Village at Lane's Cove* with many of Fred's photos.

But if Lanesville was an innocent, idyllic village, serpents had once lurked in its shadows. There had been, for example, the suave, sophisticated Lotharios from downtown Gloucester who sorely tested the virtue of the local maidens. How could the simple swains of Lanesville hope to compete with the blandishments of those cosmopolitan heartbreakers? That was the complaint of "Sentinel" in "Ye Ballad of Ye Gloucester Lads and Ye Lanesville Lassies" printed in an 1875 issue of the *Cape Ann Advertiser*:

Keep, O keep them out of Lanesville, -
Glo'ster youths with dashing airs,
Sitting on suburban doorsteps
Filling heart and home with cares.

How the hearts of maidens flutter,
When the evening, cool and grey,
With a tender, slow approaching
Dims the glowing golden day.

*****

After sunset, bonnie faces
Close are pressed against the glass;
Pretty girls their eyes are straining,
For, perchance, a friend may pass.

Whistles come in quick succession,
Or a knock sounds at the door;

Lanesville youths look sour and murmur,
"Glo'ster dandies are a bore!"

Tender, gushing sprigs of manhood,
Do your mothers know you're off?
When the midnight moon is shining,
Can they guess what you're about?

Are you "played out" in the city –
Tender shoots yet under age –
That you needs must come to Lanesville,
Or are Lanesville girls the rage?

Dainty Darlings, when you're courting,
Much more careful should you be,
For a shadow on a curtain
One outside can plainly see.

Twice a week the girls are happy,
As they comb out curls and braids,
Weaving dreams of future weddings,
Silly, silly village maids!

For the boys are "only fooling," –
Parents stop 'em while you may!
Else there'll be a sad lamenting
On some not far distant day.

Despite this dire warning, certain downtown Romeos did win the hearts of Lanesville lasses, and often found themselves on the way to the altar shortly thereafter, wondering how it had all happened. The country lads of Lanesville had their revenge – some of them stole alluring maidens from the center of Gloucester out from under the noses of those "Glo'ster dandies."

Eastern Point was the summer magnet for Gloucester's version of the Bloomsbury Set: economist/Assistant Treasury Secretary/Congressman

A. Piatt Andrew, interior designer Henry Davis Sleeper, and portraitist Cecilia Beaux, as well as their enviable roster of weekend guests that included Isabella Stewart Gardner, Henry and William James, and John Singer Sargent, that master of probing portraiture. Piatt Andrew had been introduced to Sargent by "Mrs. Jack" Gardner in Boston, and he pronounced the artist too business-like and not at all "aesthetic." In other words, not someone who would be compatible with Andrew's familiars.

Sargent's father, FitzWilliam, had been born in Gloucester, and wistfully pursued maritime interests throughout his life. But the artist's grandfather, Winthrop, moved the family to Philadelphia after the Sargent merchant trading business collapsed following the loss of several vessels in the Far East. FitzWilliam became a doctor, but his wife came into a little money and decreed that they should lead an expatriate life in Europe, although they did so on a shoestring. There John Singer Sargent was born, in Italy. He spent much of his career in Paris and London, but always called himself an American, and in later life was most at home in Boston. He wrote in letters about his "New England conscience," and might have felt an ancestral twinge when he visited Gloucester. If so, he does not seem to have been moved to paint the lanes and wharves trod by all those Sargent ship owners and sea captains. It is worth noting, though, that one of Sargent's rare marine oils, "Sea Coast with a Wreck," dates from the World War I period when he was photographed as a house guest on Eastern Point and, in two separate years, signed the guest book at the Sargent House Museum.

Of Eastern Point's summer enclave of artists and writers, Cecilia Beaux was the most formidable. A Philadelphian to the core, Beaux was an acclaimed portrait painter and the first woman instructor at the Pennsylvania Academy of Fine Arts. Her 1905 portrait of seven-year-old "Jimmy" (Henry Parsons King, Jr.) hanging in the Cape Ann Historical Museum declares her artistic affinity with Sargent. Cecilia Beaux's early visits to Gloucester were described by admiring friend Thornton Oakley. Oakley could not remember just where it was that his and Cecilia's paths had first crossed. Was it in Philadelphia? "Or was it at Gloucester, at the Fairview? – where gathered, summer after sum-

Sculptor Cecilia Beaux at Beauport, the creation of Henry Davis Sleeper (standing beside her).
Courtesy Cape Ann Historical Museum

mer, the artists, writers, intellectuals of New England ...."

Oakley and Cecilia tramped together to Brace's Cove, and Dogtown, and to the property she had bought on Eastern Point. She would build her villa there and call it "Green Alley." It had a certain Mediterranean charm, Green Alley, with winding paths and lanterns flickering in the dusk. Beaux credited her handsome Italian major-domo, Natale Gavagnin, with helping her achieve her dream. Natale, alas, died young, but remained a vibrant presence for Cecilia among the paths and terraces he helped her create. Oakley could never forget the enchantment of the evenings at Green Alley. He remembered the singing and a violin, a costumed dancer swirling about in the candle light, the faces of guests emerging momentarily from the shadows.

In 1928 Cecilia Beaux began writing her autobiography, *Background with Figures*. She approached the work as she would a commissioned portrait, sketching in and rubbing out phrases, adding new words to her palette, filling in the background with shadings of thought. At one point while crafting this self-portrait in words, she spoke of writing contentedly as the bees buzzed and gulls soared in her splendid view of the harbor. Then an impatient afterthought that may be shared, privately, by many authors: "The only way really to enjoy literary exercises . . . is not to publish."

After a broken hip, Cecilia Beaux did little painting. Thornton Oakley preferred to remember her in the old days, as when he saw her off on the boat to Europe. "So as she waved that day I love to think of her – radiant, clad in crimsons, wealth of greens, scarf blowing, headdress touched with gleams of gold – departing on the culminating adventure of her career."

Cecilia Beaux's niece Catherine Drinker Bowen remembered her aunt less affectionately as an autocratic presence on crutches after the broken hip. In her *Family Portrait* (1970), Bowen said she had never summered at Green Alley while "Aunt Beaux" was alive, and Beaux left the property to Catherine's brother Harry who planned to sell it off. During World War II, with her husband off in the Navy and her children scattered, Catherine Bowen was looking for a place to write the biographies in which she combined well-researched fact with imagined conversations. One of her subjects was the namesake son of author-physician Dr. Oliver Wendell Holmes. She called her book on Supreme Court Justice Holmes *Yankee from Olympus.*

Bowen moved into Green Alley with her books and typewriter, and by the second day decided "this is my place." She was writing *John Adams and the American Revolution.* Bowen heard the gulls and the foghorn "like a cello C string, *basso continuo* in an old, familiar music." The air was scented with bayberry, and at dawn each day she saw the fishing fleet go out.

Everything about the house suited Catherine, and she wrote of her delight to brother Harry, begging him to sell Green Alley to her rather than to a stranger. She should have been more noncommittal about her infatuation with Aunt Beaux's villa. Harry wrote back that if Green Alley was as wonderful as Catherine said it was, he wouldn't think of selling it. So for the next ten summers or so Harry and his wife summered in the studio at Green Alley. Up at the main house were Bowen's sister and brother-in-law, Samuel Barlow. Barlow was author of a book of aesthetic opinion called *The Astonished Muse.* He was a composer, too; his *Mon Ami Pierrot* was the first opera by an American performed at the Paris Comic Opera. Bowen made herself comfortable in a small beach house on the property.

She visited back and forth with other artists and writers on Cape Ann. She dropped over to Walker Hancock's studio in Lanesville sometimes to read aloud from a chapter she was working on, and he would pause from some sculpture in progress to offer his suggestions. One who sat to him was Chief Justice Warren Burger who told Hancock that Catherine Bowen's *Miracle at Philadelphia* was the book he liked best about the framing of the United States Constitution. Another time Catherine Drinker Bowen told Walker Hancock what Cape Ann meant to her. "When I die, if I see a sign ahead of me saying 'Route 128 North,' I'll know I'm on my way to heaven."

It was a prolific mix: a noble maritime heritage; connections to the sea reaching as far as the quarries behind Rockport and into the haunted tracks of Dogtown; seductive but capricious natural splendors; untidy independence that repelled some but converted other discerning visitors into lifetime devotees. Somehow – worked upon by this brew of influences – painting, sculpture, music, decorative arts, poetry, fiction and narrative prose have, over time, burst forth from every seam on Cape Ann.

CHAPTER 15

A Special Luminosity

IT WAS 1973 and Gloucester Mayor Robert L. French was convinced that recognition of Gloucester as a center of American painting of the first order was sadly overdue. French approached Hyde Cox, president of the Cape Ann Historical Association, and proposed that an exhibition of significant artists associated with Gloucester be mounted in the Historical's museum, to coincide with the 350th anniversary of the founding of the town.

Hyde Cox agreed to make the museum available, and approached sculptor Walker Hancock about the mayor's idea. Hancock liked the plan, and suggested that an ideal candidate for organizing the show would be James F. O'Gorman, a young art scholar at Wellesley College who had recently moved to Bay View. O'Gorman accepted the challenge and headed a selection committee that included Annisquam's A. Hyatt Mayor, a grandson of marine biologist Alpheus Hyatt. Hyatt Mayor was Curator of Prints at New York's Metropolitan Museum of Art and author of works on art, including an absorbing tour through printmaking technology and artistry called *Prints & People: A Social History of Printed Pictures.*

The committee set about gathering together the works of notable American artists who had painted on Cape Ann. Up on the walls went works by Winslow Homer, William Morris Hunt, Frank Duveneck, John Twachtman, Childe Hassam, Maurice Prendergast, John Sloan, Edward Hopper, Stuart Davis and Marsden Hartley. It proved to be a landmark show. James Mellow, writing in the *Boston Globe*, called it "a striking . . . exhibition of the depth of painting in and around Gloucester."

The theme was "Portrait of a Place: Some American Landscape

Painters in Gloucester." In the show catalogue O'Gorman critiqued a number of the paintings that were hung. He also apologized that lack of time, money and space forced the omission from the exhibition of a number of other outstanding artists, among them Cecilia Beaux, Gifford Beal, Stephen Parrish, George Harvey, Frederick Mulhaupt and Edward Potthast. The omissions were rectified in 2001 when works by these and other notable artists who painted Cape Ann – Leon Kroll, Anthony Thieme, Max Kuehne, Milton Avery, Jane Peterson, Gordon Grant, Stow Wengenroth – were reproduced in *Artists of Cape Ann* by Kristian Davies.

The "Portrait of a Place" show broke new ground in demonstrating that the art of a maritime area could be strikingly individual and infinite in its variety. A number of important painters had interpreted the fisheries of Gloucester and the coastal beauties of Cape Ann according to their differing styles, ranging from the Munich-school realism of Duveneck and Twachtman to the Cubist-influenced Modernism of Stuart Davis.

Prior to the "Portrait of a Place" show, the only painter Gloucester was known for was Fitz Hugh Lane (as he was known in error from 1938 until 2005, when Sarah Dunlap and other members of the Gloucester Archives Committee, including Stephanie Buck of the Cape Ann Historical Museum, discovered that the artist born Nathaniel Rogers Lane had legally changed his name to Fitz *Henry* Lane). Lane had only been newly appreciated in the 1960s, largely thanks to Alfred Mansfield Brooks.

Gloucester native Brooks had retired to Gloucester in 1937 from his career as Professor of Fine Arts at Swarthmore, and remained in his home town until his death in 1963 when he was ninety-three. Throughout those latter years Brooks contributed a lively flow of articles on Cape Ann history and the fine arts that appeared in the *Essex County Historical Collections* and elsewhere, supplementing his scholarly works on Dante and the architectural heritage of Greece and Rome. (He was also jotting down those family reminiscences that Joseph E. Garland later sorted out and edited as *Gloucester Recollected*.)

Brooks had many interests, but the one which most engaged him was the museum of the Cape Ann Historical Association. His aim was

"Old Stone Jug," the house artist Fitz Henry Lane built, from which he could view Gloucester harbor in every light. *Author photo*

to make it a repository, not only of the artifacts, but of the art of Gloucester. He set about bringing together under its roof the Fitz Henry Lane paintings he had seen on the walls behind the tea sets in the old houses of his Mansfield relatives and their friends – those glowing marine paintings that captured the balance and harmony of light and shapes in Gloucester harbor in the mid-1800s.

Lane had enjoyed some distinction during his lifetime. An article in the *Cape Ann Weekly Advertiser* in 1862 said that "Mr. Lane, as a marine painter, ranks first in the country." The piece, titled "Visit to Lane's Studio," began "We called at the studio of this artist a few days ago, and found several new paintings had been added to his collection since our last visit." These included a view of Good Harbor Beach, and a scene outside Eastern Point in which "a brig and schooner are running before the wind, under full sail, while others are running in to make a harbor." Also a sketch in which "a ship lies near the rocks, at anchor, rolling about at a fearful rate. The whole scene is wild in the extreme, and gives a faithful idea of a storm on our rock-bound coast, in Winter." Clearly, the more action the better in the opinion of the *Advertiser* reporter.

A hundred years later, in the 1960s, Lane paintings were selling for less in buying power than they had when he was alive. He was dismissed as a decently competent disciple of Robert Salmon in the British tradition of marine painting (Salmon had been resident in Boston when Lane was working as a lithographer there). But Lane had not learned to paint the luminosity of sky and ocean from Salmon, nor from Hudson River School artists. He learned it from observing Gloucester harbor in all its seasons and lights and moods. A very few people recognized that Lane's paintings represented a rare, high level of art. Charles Childs was one, at the Childs Gallery in Boston. Also Maxim Karolik, the Russian tenor who married into the Boston Codman family, money from the union financing the purchase of much American art for the Boston Museum of Fine Arts.

Alfred Brooks's belief in the artistic merit of Fitz Henry Lane was persistent and persuasive. In 1949, when the Sawyer Free Library directors voted to sell off the library's collection of Lanes donated by philanthropist Samuel Sawyer, Brooks made an impassioned plea to save the paintings for the community. A judge blocked their sale.

One of those infected by Brooks's enthusiasm for Lane paintings was a young graduate student, John Wilmerding. In his *Fitz Hugh Lane, 1804–1865, American Marine Painter*, Wilmerding demonstrated that Lane, besides being a superb Luminist, took care to paint every sheet and stay of a vessel with scrupulous accuracy. And like Brooks, Wilmerding recognized that Lane was a visual historian who captured with his brush the Gloucester that John J. Babson was recording in print at about the same time. Lane's lithographs of the harbor, too, Wilmerding said, "have a special documentary value."

John Wilmerding's book on Lane, published in 1963, marked a

turning point in the critical appreciation and market value of the artist's paintings and prints. In 1967 Wilmerding also wrote "Interpretations of a Place – Views of Gloucester, Massachusetts, by American Artists," an article printed in the *Essex Institute Historical Collections*. Here Wilmerding pointed out the consistent appeal of Gloucester to major artists like Lane, and attributed the attraction as due not only to Gloucester's rugged shoreline framed against inland hills, but to the "almost . . . tangible qualities of light and air."

Wilmerding went on to become a distinguished authority on American art – curator of American art at the National Gallery of Art, professor of American art at Princeton and visiting curator in the department of American art at New York's Metropolitan Museum of Art. Along the way he wrote perceptive books on American marine and landscape painting and studies of the artists. In 2004 Wilmerding donated to the National Gallery in Washington, D.C. two Fitz Henry Lane masterpieces, as well as enough works from his private collection of other major American artists to stock, it was said, a creditable small museum.

In that same year, the Cape Ann Historical Association marked the 200th anniversary of Fitz Henry Lane's birth with lectures by Wilmerding and Theodore Stebbins, former curator of American art at Boston's Museum of Fine Arts. The museum also marked the anniversary with publication of a series of papers by Erik Ronnberg in which that maritime historian analyzed Lane's subject matter and techniques in his paintings of the busy commerce of Gloucester harbor in the 1840s.

Soon thereafter, in 2006, James Craig, Associate Curator for Permanent Collections at the Cape Ann Historical Museum, built upon Wilmerding's pioneering study with *Fitz H. Lane: An Artist's Voyage through Nineteenth-Century America*. Written with scholarly attention to detail, the work provides a wealth of new information on the life and career of the artist, as well as fresh interpretations of the paintings, and provocative speculations on how social and intellectual movements in 19th century America might have influenced Lane's work.

Alfred Mansfield Brooks drew many, artists and others, into the cause of transforming the Cape Ann Historical Museum into a first-class small art museum. Edward Hyde Cox carried forward his mentor's vision for the museum and contributed generously of his time and wealth. Harold Bell next took over as president. From a family that got its start in Gloucester making heavy outerwear for the fishermen, Bell remained at the helm of the museum until succeeded by John Cunningham in 2004. The quarter-century Harold Bell era saw the continued expansion and evolution of the institution, with frequent exhibitions showcasing the work of artists who painted Cape Ann, beginning with exhibitions of the paintings of Alfred Wiggin, Marsden Hartley and Frank Duveneck, later presenting shows on contemporary interpreters of the Cape Ann scene like Bernard Chaet.

The tradition of plein air painting in Gloucester harbor begun by Fitz Henry Lane was taken up again in the 1870s by Winslow Homer, and by William Morris Hunt in whose "Gloucester Harbor" the water and sky reflect sunlight that seems to radiate from within the painting. Late in the '80s Frank Duveneck arrived, followed soon after by other artists, mainly from the Cincinnati area, drawn by Duveneck's charismatic personality to paint Gloucester harbor and the shorescapes of Cape Ann. Most notable of these "Duveneck's boys" was John Twachtman, who painted Gloucester settings in bold, bright colors before his sudden death there in 1902.

Childe Hassam, just returned from study in Europe, was staying summers on Grapevine Road in East Gloucester. (Frederick Childe Hassam was of the Salem Horshams. They changed the spelling of the family name perhaps after hearing too many mischievous mispronunciations.) The atmospheric light and color of Gloucester harbor seduced Hassam as it had Lane and Homer. He painted iridescent scenes of the harbor and the town in which he sought to capture the light filtering through air between the viewer and objects in the distance. Maurice Prendergast painted frequently in Gloucester, too, over a span of years reaching from before until well after World War I. His Gloucester scenes are typically colorful, busy, full of people.

In those decades other notable American artists, most of whom wintered in New York and other big cities, began to set their easels before Gloucester views in the summer – and the intense artistic activity reflected in the "Portrait of a Place" show was under way. John Sloan

Frank Duveneck, "Horizon at Gloucester." *From a private collection*

and his wife Dolly shared a "red cottage" in East Gloucester with the Davis clan that included budding Modernist Stuart Davis. Sloan, originally from Philadelphia, was best known for painting scenes of El structures and New York slums with unblinking realism (he was labeled as one of the "Ashcan School"). Biographer John Loughery says that Sloan, in his first summer in Gloucester in 1914, had "the most productive ten weeks of his life." Much of the work was experimental, with Sloan striving to capture "the fluidity of the water and of the sky." Best known from Sloan's Gloucester summer stays from 1914 to 1918 are lively street scenes with busy little trolley cars and carefree open autos, and sun-drenched yellow flowers seen against the harbor. Sloan and Davis were invited to show their works at the Gallery-on-the-Moors in East Gloucester, as were other Cape Ann summer artists Maurice

Prendergast, Anna Hyatt, Cecilia Beaux, Charles Grafly, Theresa Bernstein and her husband William Meyerowitz, and William Glackens.

Meantime, Edward Hopper was pursuing his own solitary, idiosyncratic path to artistic self-realization. Fifty summers after Winslow Homer had turned seriously to watercolors on Gloucester harbor, Hopper discovered watercolor himself as the liberating medium for depicting the special luminosity of the locale. Generally shunning boat and wharf themes, he painted the Greek Revival houses with their severe wooden cornices and strong angles that he thought must reflect the independent spirit of the fishing captains who built them. Critics noticed that watercolor then became Hopper's most spontaneous medium. He

John Sloan, "Glare on the Bay" (1915). *From a private collection*

Edward Hopper, "Cemetery at Gloucester." *From a private collection*

joined the select company of Childe Hassam, Winslow Homer and Fitz Henry Lane in experiencing a transforming insight while painting under Gloucester skies.

In the tercentenary Gloucester summer of 1923, Hopper also fell in love with his wife-to-be when he and Josephine Nivison were painting on Bass Rocks. Hopper began reciting a poem by Verlaine in the French he had learned in his art student days in Paris, and Josephine took up from where he left off and finished the poem in equally facile French. Hopper was dumfounded; there was obviously nothing left to do but marry the girl. Years later they returned and Hopper said they "fell in love with Gloucester again."

Maine-born artist and poet Marsden Hartley arrived in Gloucester on the Boston ferry in 1931, and found his subject matter not along the waterfront but back in Dogtown, where the landscape made him think of Stonehenge. There he painted the glacial erratic boulders as dark,

From 1916 to 1922, the Gallery-on-the-Moors was a showplace for the works of John Sloan, Stuart Davis and many other Cape Ann summer artists.

heavy, molten forms. Hartley was a poet of repute, too; his Gloucester poems include "Soliloquy in Dogtown" and "Beethoven (in Dogtown)."

In his research for the "Portrait of a Place" exhibit of 1973, James O'Gorman's scholarly curiosity led him down some obscure painterly and architectural avenues. He prospected among the records of the Universalist Society, stored in the basement of the Cape Ann Bank & Trust. There he found conclusive evidence that housewright Jacob Smith, who had designed and built the Cape Ann Historical Museum's core building, the Captain Elias Davis house, had also been the architect-builder of the soaring Universalist church of 1806, now the Independent Christian Church. Erik Ronnberg and others have concluded that the church was built tall so that, with a reflective lantern in its belfry, it could serve as a lighthouse (the first in Gloucester harbor).

O'Gorman found artistic merit in a Gloucester cemetery. He cites Oak Grove as a landmark of the mid-19th century movement to design cemeteries as urban parks for the living as well as dignified surroundings for the departed. Mount Auburn in Cambridge was an early example of this radical departure from the old bare graveyards, and Oak Grove was not far behind, designed by Robert Morris Copeland and Horace William Shaler Cleveland. Cleveland published books on landscape architecture and moved on to Chicago where he became the leading landscape architect in that part of the world.

Among Oak Grove's tenants O'Gorman found the graves of artists Fitz Henry Lane and John Twachtman, as well as "Centennial" Johnson, the first to make a transatlantic crossing alone under sail; racing schooner skipper and entrepreneur Ben Pine; library angel Samuel E. Sawyer; and philanthropist Addison Gilbert, whose name is on the

Marsden Hartley, "Summer Outward Bound, Dogtown."
From a private collection

local hospital that all of Gloucester is jealous to preserve, now that it has been absorbed into a regional medical complex. O'Gorman might have added to his list of those with a final Oak Grove address the names of highline skippers Captains Sylvanus Smith and Solomon Jacobs. And John Jay Watson, Gloucester's "fiddling fisherman."

At the urging of *Gloucester Daily Times* editor Paul Kenyon,

O'Gorman wrote up his findings in a series of articles that were published in *North Shore Magazine*, a weekend supplement to the Essex County Newspapers. In 1976 these were collected into a volume called *This Other Gloucester*. James O'Gorman went on to become a professor of the history of American art at Wellesley and authority on the architecture of H. H. Richardson. His dozen other books are rich in stimulating insights akin to those that enliven his little volume on the art and architecture of Gloucester.

In Rockport, the Rockport Art Association was founded in 1921 by a group of summer artists including baseball aficionado Aldro T. Hibbard, Antonio Cirino and Anthony Thieme. The oldest member of the Association was Gilbert Margeson, who had set up the first artist's studio in Rockport in 1873 (but paid his bills by operating a stationery shop, serving as Rockport tax collector, and running the Western Union telegraph office in Gloucester). William Lester Stevens was the first Rockport native in the group to achieve national status as an artist, and a local reputation as an eccentric, indifferent to the elements, who painted outdoors in all kinds of weather. Rockport's first resident sculptor was Richard Recchia, friend of Lanesville sculptor George Demetrios and husband of painter-poet Kitty Parsons Recchia. Richard Recchia's bas relief "Architecture" was carved on the Fenway façade of the Boston Museum of Fine Arts.

Notable artist-illustrators explored outdoor subjects during their Rockport summers, including Carl Peters, Gifford Beal, Lester Hornby, Harrison Cady (best known as the illustrator of Thornton Burgess's Peter Rabbit books). It was Cady who said that "nearly all of the leading names in American art have at one time or other been found as temporary or permanent residents of either Gloucester, Annisquam, Pigeon Cove, or Rockport." Stow Wengenroth summered in Rockport, and managed to support himself selling his quietly austere lithographic prints, mainly of the New England coast.

Norway-born Jonas Lie was, like John Sloan, popularly known as an "Ashcan School" painter in New York. But while Sloan chose Gloucester, Lie painted summer life in Rockport. Max Kuehne later took over Lie's studio, and brought into his full-colored Cape Ann scenes the influences of his early training under William Merritt Chase and Robert Henri. The Rockport Art Association continues to be the coalescing center of activity for the Rockport art colony.

The village of Lanesville, with its granite quarries, attracted a set of preeminent American artists in stone. Philadelphia sculptor Charles Grafly set up his summer atelier there first, and following him came Walker Hancock. Hancock had rattled out to Lanesville on the trolley to introduce himself to Grafly, but at Grafly's door turned tail in panic and fled Gloucester. Hancock returned, though, worked at Grafly's studio summers, wintering in New York and commuting to Philadelphia to teach.

Hancock could not stay away from Cape Ann. He immersed himself in the Finnish community where he met and married Saima Natti. He bought a quarry and built his own studio, and made Lanesville his home. He ranged over all of Cape Ann, shuttling between the beau monde of Eastern Point and the granite pits and Finnish community of Lanesville, marveling at the general sociability. And the absence of formality. Charles Grafly had warned him severely: "Walker, if you ever wear a dickey [tuxedo] on Cape Ann, I'll come back and haunt you."

Walker Hancock was a good neighbor and in-law to the people of Lanesville. In the Depression, after the quarry companies folded, the Finns of Lanesville were especially hard up. Hancock lobbied the Chamber of Commerce to provide a storefront in downtown Gloucester, and there the Finnish women displayed the mats and rugs they wove by tradition, and sold their fresh-baked nisu bread. The carpenters among the Finnish men displayed in the window the violins and kayaks they crafted while looking for work, and the ship models. The storefront did not make enough to cover the hardships of the time. But it helped. Robert Frost would approve of Hancock's efforts to promote the skills and values of the community. "Locality gives art," Frost had said.

During World War II Walker Hancock distinguished himself in the service of civilization half a world away, in Europe as the German Wehrmacht was collapsing. In his autobiography, *A Sculptor's Fortunes* (1997), he tells how, as a U.S. Army officer assigned to the British-American Monuments, Fine Arts and Archives organization, he worked on the fringes of warfare to preserve classic works of art from casual vandalism on both sides. Sometimes it was not easy to get unit officers to take his concerns seriously, until he flashed an authorizing directive from Supreme Allied Commander Dwight Eisenhower, decreeing that all measures were to be taken to protect objects of cultural or historic value.

And then Walker Hancock returned to Lanesville for another half century of shaping monumental portraiture in stone, of Eisenhower, Douglas MacArthur, Warren Burger, the elder George Bush. His work was commissioned for the U.S. Military Academy, U.S. Capitol, Library of Congress, and National Cathedral. Hancock remained mild and modest in manner to the end, but granite-hard in artistic honesty.

Hancock had fellow sculptors near at hand: Paul Manship, another Grafly protégé best known for his "Prometheus" in New York's Rockefeller Center, and Katharine Lane Weems. Hancock and Weems had been friends since student days. She had studied under Grafly too, when that master was critiquing at the Museum of Fine Arts in Boston. When Weems published her recollections in 1985, Hancock wrote the Foreword. Her book was "told to" Edward Weeks, editor of the *Atlantic Monthly*. Weeks persuaded her to call the book *Odds Were Against Me*. It was an unusual title for a book by someone who inherited a tidy fortune from her moneyed Boston father, who at one time was president of the Museum of Fine Arts. Katharine shuttled between her Fifth Avenue apartment and waterfront estate in Manchester, and finally married a fellow just as rich as she.

But Weems did have to overcome the pressures of a mother who expected this vivacious, attractive daughter to take her place in Park Avenue society of the early 1920s. Katharine, instead, knew her real talent lay in sculpting animals: elephants, leopards, a classic jet-black whippet, dolphins in front of the Boston Aquarium, two great bronze rhinos to guard a biology lab at Harvard.

She tells of getting together with her kind of people in Lanesville – artists Hancock, Manship, George Demetrios. The artist who shared her interests most was Annisquam's Anna Vaughn Hyatt. Weems regularly stopped by that other woman sculptor's studio by the Goose Cove bridge (Hyatt's father, marine scientist Alpheus Hyatt, had built the studio for Anna and her sister Harriet on the family property when both daughters had been budding sculptors). It was in this studio that

Anna Hyatt had begun to work out the design for her Joan of Arc equestrian statue, in which Joan holds her new sword aloft in an appeal that it be blessed from the Heavens.

Anna completed a plaster cast of the work during her early years in Paris when she was proving that she could make ends meet as a sculptor, and a female one at that. To shape Joan's steed she visited the stables of an elegant department store, the Beaux Arts, that maintained handsome horses to deliver merchandise to its customers. The stablemaster appreciated Anna's interest, she said, and he sent one of his finest examples of horseflesh over to Anna's studio, which fortunately was at street level and of a height to admit large animals.

With this live model before her, Anna completed her Joan, and it was exhibited in the Paris Salon. There it was seen by a member of a New York City committee, and the work was commissioned in 1911 for a park site on Riverside Drive. Later, castings of the statue were installed in dramatic settings on the Plains of Abraham in Quebec, overlooking the city of Blois in France – and, in 1921, opposite the American Legion Building (the old town hall) in Gloucester. A year after that installation, Anna Hyatt married Archer Huntington, and Katherine Weems could no longer drop in on her inspiring friend. Anna moved off into wealth unimaginable even by Katherine's standards.

Most of the sculptors of Cape Ann were of the classical mold. But not George Aarons, who moved flexibly among the artistic trends of the 20th century. Russian-born, trained in Boston, Aarons summered and taught on Cape Ann for years before moving in for his final thirty years in 1950. His work reflected deep concern for mankind, especially for the Jewish victims of Nazi genocide. George Aarons was a strong formative influence for David Black, a Gloucester-born sculptor with Wonsons and Tarrs in his family background. Black has become best known for monumental sculptures installed on campuses and in plazas in the Midwest, Japan, Germany and Alaska. Bearing titles like "Coastline" and "Breakers," they evoke Black's Gloucester beginnings, and in them he consciously incorporates Cape Ann forms and architectural details. In 1996 Black won an international competition to design the memorial to the Wright Brothers in Dayton, Ohio, with a soaring structure he called "Flyover."

George Demetrios bust of Scottish émigré John Murray, long-time violinist with the Boston Symphony Orchestra and, in the 1950s, with the Cape Ann Symphony.
From a private collection

Charles Grafly, Walker Hancock's mentor, unknowingly initiated another pocket of artistry in Lanesville. After Grafly's death, his student George Demetrios inherited use of his studio on Folly Cove, and taught summer classes there in painting and sculpture. When he married the irrepressibly creative Virginia Lee Burton, they soon settled in the neighborhood year-round, and Virginia began writing and splendidly illustrating children's books, like *Mike Mulligan and His Steam Shovel*, *The Little House*, and *Choo Choo*. (In 1999, sixty years after the publication of *Mike Mulligan*, the Boston Public Library celebrated "Mike Mulligan Day" to kick off National Children's Book Week.)

Virginia Lee Burton was also the flame that attracted other local designers to what became the Folly Cove Designers, creating distinctively original and often humorous graphics they incised onto linoleum blocks and stamped onto fabrics as dress materials, curtains, towels, napkins, placemats, scarves. In time the Folly Cove Designers were instanced as a flowering of the Arts & Crafts Movement.

The group had begun to make some sales, then Roger Babson brought them national attention with one of his magazine articles. Babson's piece celebrating the creativity and quality of fabrics designed by Virginia Lee Burton and her fellow artisans in their barn on Folly Cove appeared in 400 newspapers and was read into the *Congressional Record*. Articles in other newspapers and magazines followed, the most influential of which was a *Life* magazine photo story. Responding to the demand from readers, major department stores placed orders, and proceeds flowed in for all to share. In the end, though, the Folly Cove Designers had second thoughts about the publicity stirred up by well-meaning Roger Babson, and sustained by their own creative efforts. One of them was quoted as saying that the work became too demanding, intruding into the lives of the artists. After Burton's death in 1968, the group disbanded.

The lineage of musical performance on Cape Ann reached back to the days of the fiddler William Bentley spoke of who had brought his instrument along to "pick up a few coppers" at Eastern Point, and was carried on by musicians of the fleet like John Jay Watson. Then, in the early 20th century, came Lanesville's Waino Band. The musicians were mostly Finns, and they traveled around Cape Ann in open trolley cars, stopping to play in the villages along the way. Members of the band included a saxophonist who went on to join march-king John Philip Sousa, as well as three musicians who would play in Navy and Coast Guard bands.

The most notable alumnus of the Waino Band was Sylvester "Hooley" Ahola, "The Gloucester Gabriel." His ringing trumpet wowed British dance band crowds in the 1920s and '30s, when he was the leading horn in Bert Ambrose's swinging orchestra at London's May Fair Hotel. Hooley recorded scores of records with the top American and British dance bands of the day. Then, at age forty, Ahola gave it all up to return to Lanesville and quiet village life, playing occasional gigs in local hotels with a small group he put together as "Sylvester's Music." He brought music to children in the schools, too, riding on stage on a tricycle, carrying drums and horns and playing his

"Lanesvillen Suomalinen Band" (Socialist Working Men's Band) of 1912. Boy with trumpet at far right is Sylvester Ahola, sitting next to his instructor, Jacob Soltti. *From the Sylvester Ahola Collection, via Dick Hill*

trumpet. Eminent Gloucester jazz trumpet player and Berklee College music instructor Herb Pomeroy remembered playing in a band with Ahola in downtown Gloucester in the pre-television times when, as Pomeroy said, there could be fifteen swinging groups playing around town for listening and dancing pleasure on a Saturday night.

Later on there was classical music on Cape Ann as well. In 1952, Sam and Helen Gordon spearheaded the formation of the Gloucester Civic Symphony Orchestra, mainly so that they and other amateur musicians could play together. They gave concerts and invited the public. No admission was charged, so it was unimportant to the players whether or not audiences liked what they heard. In the 1980s the orchestra, by then known as the Cape Ann Symphony Orchestra, was reorganized on a paid admission basis. Twenty years later, with Yoichi Udagawa as conductor and most of the chairs in the orchestra occupied by professional musicians, the Cape Ann Symphony had become an outstanding community orchestra that plays a subscription concert series and, free to all when funding is forthcoming, a summer pops evening of music and fireworks at Stage Fort Park.

Many were responsible for putting the orchestra on a solid footing, most notably David Benjamin, who plays in the woodwinds section

Sylvester Ahola, third from left in the Ruby Newman society orchestra in 1925, before his days as featured trumpeter with the Ambrose dance band in London.

From the Sylvester Ahola Collection, via Dick Hill

Cape Ann Symphony Orchestra plays a pops concert at Stage Fort Park, 1999. An audience of hundreds crowded a slope at left, out of view. *Photo by Wendy Morgan*

and for years has doubled as the orchestra's tireless hands-on manager. Benjamin is also with the Gloucester school system, and each year introduces a fresh wave of children to the joys of music. A scholarship program has been established in David Benjamin's name to further the studies of promising young performers.

In Rockport, audiences are drawn from afar to that town's Chamber Music Festival, presented each year under the aegis of pianist-impresario David Deveau. Programs featuring celebrated ensembles from around the globe have made the Rockport Festival a respected venue for the performance of classical music in small groups.

Musical technology in Gloucester has evolved considerably from the barrel organ that privateersman Captain Somes donated to the Universalist church. A very different keyboard plays the carillon bells today at Our Lady of Good Voyage church. Marilyn Clark or guest carillonneurs strike the console keys with soft fists and work their feet to play selections that chime from one of the twin bell towers. Weekly summer concerts fill the church parking lot with audiences sitting in their automobiles, and after each number the listeners honk their car horns in applause.

A pipe organ installed on the opposite shore of Gloucester harbor had an eccentric history. The scientific interests of the younger John Hays Hammond had led him into musical acoustics. As his mansion, Abbadia Mare, took form, Hammond built its towers eighty-five feet tall to accommodate a 10,000-pipe organ. After Hammond's death, flamboyant virtuoso organist Virgil Fox owned Abbadia Mare for a year (it had become known as Hammond Castle). There, on Hammond's organ, Fox recorded for RCA Victor the complete Brahms Chorale Preludes.

But the most notable in the lineage of Gloucester organs have been those built by the Fisk organ company. Physicist Charles B. Fisk had spent his boyhood summers in Gloucester, and in 1961 returned with a dream of building great pipe organs. He had apprenticed himself to other builders and was now ready to set up his own shop – in an old ropewalk building where strands of hemp had once been woven into trawl lines for the vessels. Fisk gathered a cadre of craftsmen about him who came to share his vision, which was to draw upon the experience of centuries of master organ-builders in the construction of modern pipe organs.

Charles Fisk kept his company small and his output limited, but in time C. B. Fisk became recognized as a premier American organ-builder. Fisk died in 1983 at fifty-eight. The people who had worked with him, steeped in his collegial style, continued the tradition of excellence. And built organs of distinction for churches, universities and concert halls across America.

Then Europe. The Cathedral at Lausanne, Switzerland, completed in 1275, is generally conceded to be the finest example of French gothic architecture in Switzerland. The time had come to replace its 1955 organ, and Fisk was one of five organ-builders invited to bid. After the selection commission had evaluated concepts and designs, Fisk was the unanimous choice, and the decision was confirmed by the Swiss Parliament (after some nationalistic grumbling). The Fisk team proposed to build the organ in the tradition of the romantic-style French instruments of the late 19th century, but with the flexibility to do justice to music of the earlier baroque period.

When work was completed in 2003, the instrument became the

Lausanne Cathedral, Switzerland. Construction begun in 1175, pipe organ by C. B. Fisk of Gloucester installed in 2003.

first American-built organ installed in a European Cathedral. In the course of subsequent music festivals and recitals, distinguished organists from around the world have put the "Great Fisk Organ" of Lausanne Cathedral through its paces, and found it worthy.

The first settlers, and all those who followed through Gloucester's tallest years as a fisheries center, had resolutely settled in to make the most of what they had: a remote shore close to rich fishing grounds. They would mind their nets and their gear and hope to feed the mouths ashore and live to tell about it. Tell them that the maritime culture they shaped would one day influence some of the nation's most accomplished outdoor painters and sculptors, as well as makers of and performers on musical instruments, and they would level a piercing glare of disbelief. But so it was to be.

Tell them that a number of skilled wielders of the written word would also find subjects worth serious attention on Cape Ann, and they would be even more skeptical. But that, too, came to pass.

for his concepts of the geodesic dome and "Spaceship Earth."

But, with Olson nominally in charge, Black Mountain dissolved angrily in 1956. Olson moved to Gloucester where he presided over conversation late in the night among stacks of books in an overheated, smoke-filled, airless apartment in the Fort neighborhood. Still, Olson found time for *Maximus*. It evolved as an epic poem about Gloucester as a place and as an idea. Olson compared Gloucester with Tyre, the chief port of the ancient Phoenicians. Tyre had stood alone, facing the sea, joined to the mainland by a causeway that discouraged all invaders – until Alexander's legions swept through. In the same way Gloucester was on and of the sea, visited by only a trickle of traffic from the mainland, until construction of the Route 128 bridge opened the way to hordes invading by automobile. (John Wise had made a more hopeful analogy between Gloucester and Tyre three centuries earlier.)

Olson began by digging into the published histories of Cape Ann, but the scholar in him could not settle for the research of others. He progressed to original sources – probed local records in Gloucester City Hall, traveled to Salem to ferret deeds and wills from the archives of the Essex County Court House, viewed microfilm documents at Salem's Essex Institute, borrowed family papers.

Olson's method in shaping his *Maximus* can be glimpsed from one of the better-known individual poems, "April Today Main Street" (*Maximus* I.155). His intention here was to communicate directly the Gloucester of three centuries mingling together on an April day on Main Street. (Others had been at this thought before Olson. T. S. Eliot spoke of literature in all the ages of man as having a simultaneous existence.)

Olson did not explain the sources for this or any of his work, in fact took a mischievous satisfaction in covering the tracks of his scholarship. If readers were not informed enough to understand all of his allusions, Olson certainly was not going to enlighten them. Much of "April Today Main Street" would be lost on the modern reader if it were not for the scholarship of George F. Butterick, a colleague of Olson's at Black Rock College. Butterick tracked Olson's sources tirelessly, and published his findings as *A Guide to the Maximus Poems of Charles Olson* (1978). Butterick is a virtually indispensable aid when attempting to follow Olson's cascading of historical arcana, genealogy and local references throughout *The Maximus Poems*.

Leafing through Butterick's annotations the reader gets some sense of the burrowing research into Gloucester's written memory that lay behind Olson's poems, and the links Olson explored between widely separated people and places and happenings on Cape Ann, and the profound significance he found in it all. If even a Butterick could not keep up with the obscure references, the poems remain. Future searchers will find it rewarding to pursue Olson's spelunking trips through the caverns of Gloucester's antiquity.

This was Charles Olson the poet, and then there was Charles Olson the activist. The letters he wrote to the *Gloucester Daily Times* between 1962 and 1969, the year before his death, were given special prominence in the newspaper by editor Paul Kenyon. In 1997, Gloucester writer Peter Anastas issued a collection of the letters in *Charles Olson – Maximus to Gloucester*.

Some of these were letters of praise, as when Olson sought to make the public aware of the achievements of Fitz Henry Lane (he insisted that Lane and even Marsden Hartley were more deserving of being honored with a postage stamp than was Winslow Homer). More often the letters were outcries at the planned destruction of one city landmark after another. Olson's letters caught the attention of Gloucester but made people nervous with his attacks on bankers and businessmen reminiscent of left-wing diatribes of the 1930s. Cries of "Oh city of mediocrity and cheap ambition" antagonized more than they mobilized civic pride. In the long run, though, Olson probably helped give impetus to a growing consensus that the city should think twice and look for alternatives before losing more of the old Gloucester.

Charles Olson was always stirring people up with his poems and opinions, but in Gloucester they listened to him. And he knew they listened, which is why he stayed in Gloucester until he saw his end approaching. His first intimations of mortality are suggested in his poem, "Cole's Island," in which, walking with his son on that island in the Great Marsh, he met a man dressed as a "country gentleman," who was indeed Death, but it was a casual encounter. The acquaintanceship had become much more intimate by the time Olson looked down on the street activity from his top floor apartment in the Fort, maybe repeating his comment, "I'll miss this earthly paradise." Some thought it was a cynical remark. But maybe Charles Olson was not being cynical at all.

Olson had many literary predecessors on Cape Ann. In the early 1840s, two of the new American nation's most promising men of letters had ventured out to Pigeon Cove for boarding-house stays. William Cullen Bryant and Richard Henry Dana, Sr. both stayed at John Wheeler's "Old House." They were charmed by the wild coast briefly subdued by summer, and were lulled by the somnolence of the back lanes. And by the fishing fleet, which toiled at a picturesque distance off-shore.

Bryant was celebrated as America's first home-grown poet of any importance, largely on the basis of his *Thanatopsis*. It had a tongue-tying title but was a work acclaimed in its day as hopeful evidence that America could, after all, produce its own Wordsworths and Shelleys. Bryant had already settled into his half-century role as liberal editor of the New York *Evening Post*.

Dana had written a novel or two, and some poetry, including "The Pleasure Boat," very likely inspired by a summer day's sailing off Pigeon Cove. But his friend Bryant had warned him that "Poetry may get printed in the newspapers but no man makes money at it, for the simple reason that nobody cares a fig for it." Thereafter Dana suppressed his poetic muse and turned to editing journals and writing essays.

Bryant and Dana eventually cast their summer anchors elsewhere – Bryant on Long Island, New York (he had family there), and Dana farther down the Cape Ann shore, in Manchester, at the invitation of his namesake son. Richard Henry Dana, Jr. was building a solid reputation as a lawyer in Boston. He had started late, though, dropping out of Harvard to rest weak eyes and signing on as an ordinary seaman aboard the brig *Pilgrim*, bound around Cape Horn to the coast of California.

Young Dana returned to Harvard with his eyesight improved and his ambition admirably focused. He finished first in his class and wrote of his Pacific adventures in *Two Years Before the Mast*. It remains a classic of blue water memoirs, not only of life aboard a square-rigger but of adventures along a spectacularly wild California coast sparsely inhabited by Mexicans before the Gold Rush.

There was some of Gloucester in *Two Years Before the Mast*. It was a welcome day for Dana and his crewmates when, at San Pedro on the Pacific Coast, they met the ship *California*, owned by Gloucester merchant George H. Rogers. Seven months out from Boston, the *California* had mail for Dana and his crewmates, and newspapers full of dated but welcome news.

Two Years Before the Mast was a work of boisterous youth. But, for all his enthusiasm, Dana also saw the dark side of life on merchant vessels – the mistreatment of crewmen by tyrannical captains. After Harvard Dana devoted himself to maritime law, and wrote *The Seaman's Friend*, which became a standard work on the rights and recourses of sailors aboard vessels of United States registry.

The younger Dana was familiar with Cape Ann. He and his wife had honeymooned in Pigeon Cove at William Norwood's boarding house in 1841, the year *Two Years Before the Mast* was published. Four years later, young Richard Henry ventured from his Boston law office down to Manchester where he closed on thirty acres of choice property off Summer Street. There he built a summer retreat for his family, including his scholar father.

After Bryant and the elder Dana, the next literary personages to visit Cape Ann were drawn by speaking fees for appearances at the Gloucester Lyceum. In 1830 a group of Gloucester clergymen and men of affairs had formed the Lyceum for "the diffusion of useful knowledge and the advancement of popular education." It was confidently believed that audiences made up of sea captains wise to the ways of far reaches of the world, and of cosmopolitan traders, and of the intellectually curious women of their households, would welcome authorities on a wide range of topics. The subject chosen for the first Lyceum debate was "Does the mechanic, the mariner, the merchant, or the farmer enjoy the greatest amount of happiness?" After spirited arguments for each calling were heard, the farmer was judged happiest. Perhaps, in the minds of sea-going Gloucester, the farmers had an easy time of it, living safely ashore, doing most of their outdoor work in warm weather, loafing by the fire all winter.

Gloucester's appetite for enlightenment from the podium had been whetted. Lyceum patrons cheerfully dug down for series subscriptions priced at a dollar for gentlemen, seventy-five cents for ladies. There were lectures on medical subjects, as when Dr. Eben Dale spoke on "the good effects of sea bathing." And science, when the principal of a female academy in Derry, New Hampshire spoke on "the philosophy of light." During those glory years of the American lyceum movement, eminent figures from Boston and the literary groves of Concord ventured to Gloucester to deliver their talks. Ralph Waldo Emerson gave a Gloucester Lyceum lecture almost every year between 1845 and 1853, even on Christmas Eve in 1851.

Emerson's early subjects were personalities, as in his talks on Napoleon Bonaparte and Montaigne. Later he took on broader topics as when, on February 13, 1850, he spoke to Gloucester on "The Spirit of the Age." In that lecture he expressed optimism about the 19th century, confident that mankind would master the machine for the ultimate well-being of all. Emerson told his audience that "The great lesson which science is teaching the age is improvement. It convinces man that every age makes its impress upon matter, and impels him to a higher destiny."

The review in *The Gloucester News* was effusive: "The whole lecture was a chain of striking thoughts, ornamented with sparkling gems of wit, humor, and quaint sarcasm." The *Gloucester Telegraph* was distinctly more restrained: "For while there are many here who would travel several miles afoot, in any weather, to hear Emerson, there are good people who scout him as an infidel." John S. E. Rogers was "Editor & Proprietor" of the *Telegraph*, and stood behind everything that appeared in the paper. Its masthead slogan read: "Devoted to Patriotism, Sound Morals, Temperance, Literature and News." Last but not least, the news.

Emerson, being a celebrity, was paid $12 for a single speaking engagement in Gloucester. Lesser literary luminaries had to commit to grueling lyceum tours, tossed about in stagecoaches for hours between destinations, for what they ruefully called F.A.M.E. ("Fifty And My Expenses").

Henry David Thoreau was booked for a Gloucester Lyceum appearance after his lecture on "Economy – Illustrated by the Life of a Student" had been well received at the Salem Lyceum in 1848. The ever-acerbic critic for the *Gloucester Telegraph* was not impressed when Thoreau repeated the lecture in Gloucester: "The lecturer spoke at considerable length of society, men, manners, travelling, clothing, etc., often 'bringing down the house' by his quaint remarks .... With all deference to the sagacity of those who can see a great deal where there is little to be seen . . . we would take the liberty of expressing the opinion that a certain ingredient to a good lecture was, in some instances, wanting." Thoreau did not speak before a Gloucester audience again.

The notion of Thoreau "bringing down the house" and telling "humorous anecdotes" may seem out of character, but his letters and *Journal* reveal that he took more of an interest in local characters and village humor than did the other Concord men and women of letters. Fellow writers were confounded by Henry David Thoreau. Salem's Nathaniel Hawthorne described him to editor Epes Sargent as "a wild, irregular, Indian-like sort of fellow." Sometimes Hawthorne found Thoreau downright exasperating: "He is the most unmalleable fellow alive – the most tedious, tiresome, and intolerable – the narrowest and most notional . . ." And yet: "and yet, true as all this is, he has great qualities of intellect and character."

Hawthorne and Thoreau were compatible sociopaths. When they were neighbors in Concord and Hawthorne heard visitors at his front door, he would slip out the back to go boating on the Concord River with Henry David. Consummate Yankees both, they were at ease sharing taciturn silences.

Another ornament of the lecture circuit who held forth at the Gloucester Lyceum in mid-century was Edwin Whipple, unmistakable with his massive head atop a slender frame. Whipple was, in fact, a Gloucester boy by birth, but had been raised in Salem and eventually found himself superintending documents at the Merchants' Exchange in Boston. He was a literary man at heart, though, and was fortunate enough to marry into the Beacon Hill circle ornamented by Dr. Oliver Wendell Holmes, author and alter ego of *The Autocrat of the Breakfast Table*. Whipple produced a prodigious number of essays and reviews spiced with crisp wit – such as his assessment that Walt Whitman's *Leaves of Grass* had "every leaf but the fig leaf."

The Lyceum lectures were discontinued in 1864 after a fire in the old town hall. By then the Lyceum had evolved into a library. Indeed, only a few weeks after its founding the Lyceum had received its first gift of a book, Rollin's *Ancient History*. After some fragile early years, the library came to be buttressed by regular infusions of cash from merchant Samuel E. Sawyer, who in 1884 bought the house since incorporated into the library's present structure. A grateful citizenry named the institution the Sawyer Free Library.

The Gloucester Lyceum was vigorously revived in the 1990's. The goal of David R. Ellis, the Chairman, was to re-acquaint Gloucester with its rich cultural heritage. With the support of Library Director David McArdle, Board President and Library benefactor Arthur Ryan, and other members of the Lyceum Committee, multi-event programs were presented on Rudyard Kipling, T. S. Eliot and Charles Olson. Subsequent to Ellis's death the Lyceum Committee has continued to present a lively schedule of informative programs presented by specialists on Cape Ann topics, as well as authorities from distant parts, as was the practice with the original Lyceum lectures.

One long-time member of the Lyceum Committee also brings local authors to the attention of the community via cable TV. Educator-poet-filmmaker John Ronan interviews them on his "Writer's Block" program that is carried on the local public access channel. From the same studio, Sinikka Nogelo, who has long fought the good battle to keep public television alive on Cape Ann, interviews musicians, artists, stage performers and other newsmakers on her "Cape Ann Report" show.

During the palmy days of the "New England Renaissance" in the 19th century, there were strong connections between maritime Gloucester and the Boston publishing world. One of the most influential of Boston literary gatekeepers during the '40s and '50s was Gloucester's Epes Sargent, another of those Epes's the Sargent family named at least once every generation, heaping confusion upon the genealogists. This Epes was the son of none other than Captain Epes, whom we met in old Canton, haggling over parasols and tea sets for his sisters back home in Gloucester. The Epes now under discussion spent his first five years in Gloucester before his father decided to try his hand at foreign trade out of Boston. Those five years were enough to imprint the sea upon the boy, and he wrote a number of poems on maritime topics, some of them gathered into *Songs of the Sea,* published in 1847. In one of the poems in that collection, "Midsummer in the City," he yearned, in hot midsummer Boston, for his boyhood, sporting in the flashing breakers with other lads in "that rugged, sea-side hamlet" where, beyond the waves,

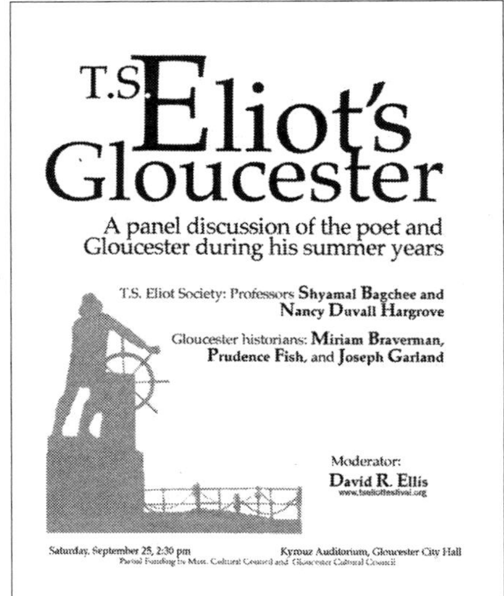

The Gloucester Lyceum's 1999 celebration of T. S. Eliot in Gloucester filled three days with presentations, panel discussions, music, dance and children's events.
Poster courtesy Gloucester Lyceum and Sawyer Free Library

"with their snow-white canvass idly drooping, / Stood the tall vessels." His best-known sea poem was "A Life on the Ocean Wave," which was set to music by Henry Russell in 1838, and was popular as a rousing encore for bandstand concerts throughout the century.

Sargent's prolific output included plays. *Velasco* was boffo at the Tremont Theatre in Boston in 1839, and even enjoyed some success in London. Sargent had written it specially for the lead actress, Helen Tree. Newspapers of the day offered up the usual romantic gossip about stage people, hinting that Sargent had been felled by that lovely Tree.

It was as editor of the *Boston Transcript* between 1847 and 1853 that Epes Sargent rounded into top journalistic form. The *Transcript* was for generations Boston's uncompromisingly civilized newspaper. Under Sargent's direction it printed lengthy disquisitions upon literature, drama and music, including extracts in French where appropriate (a subscriber to the *Transcript* was assumed to be fluent in French). There were those who lamented the passing of the Sargent era at the *Transcript*. It was said to be the end of genteel, classical journalism in

Boston, of leisurely observations that began "as we were walking around the Common last evening."

Epes Sargent was a regular at the Old Corner Bookstore of publishers Ticknor & Fields, their "Parnassus Corner" at the crossroads of commercial and cultural Boston. There he might run into Henry Wadsworth Longfellow, whose accessible poems like "Wreck of the Hesperus" had earned him popular acclaim. According to Gloucester summer author Elizabeth Stuart Phelps, Longfellow said he had never actually seen the Reef of Norman's Woe, his "Wreck of the Hesperus" setting, until he visited her years later at her home in East Gloucester. Perhaps, but Longfellow's summer digs at Nahant were not all that distant from Manchester, where his publisher and friend, James T. Fields, spent his summers.

This was the Fields of Ticknor & Fields; he was a welcoming presence at the Old Corner Bookstore. James Fields entertained, lavished praise upon, consoled and prodded creative output not only from Longfellow but from Emerson, Thoreau, Hawthorne, Dr. Oliver Wendell Holmes, James Russell Lowell, John Greenleaf Whittier – most of the Massachusetts authors who became household names in the mid-19th century. Fields had much to do with establishing their lit-

Epes Sargent, Gloucester-born poet, playwright, and editor of the *Boston Transcript* in its most genteel era.
Courtesy Sargent House Museum

James T. Fields, the Boston & Manchester-by-the-Sea publisher of Longfellow, Hawthorne, Elizabeth Stuart Phelps and Dr. Oliver Wendell Holmes.

erary credentials by publishing their books under Ticknor & Fields's prestigious "Riverside Press" imprint. And he kept their names before the public by printing their poems, fiction and essays in *The Atlantic Monthly*, which he edited throughout the 1860s.

Early in the '60s Fields and his wife Annie had, in the steps of Bryant and the Danas, vacationed at one of the plain and hearty boarding houses at Pigeon Cove. But beginning in 1865 James and Annie became regular summer denizens of Manchester. They rented cottages that served as one "Parnassus East" after another, to which Fields could invite his authors to discuss the arts and, ever so delicately, the terms of their contracts. After Fields retired in 1871, he and Annie built their own Manchester cottage, "Thunderbolt Hill," indulging even more in literary hospitality.

Many of Fields's pride of literary lions were attracted to Cape Ann. Salem's Nathaniel Hawthorne and family fell in love with a farm for sale in Manchester, but were not quick enough to make an offer. They then moved to the Berkshires where Hawthorne was uncomfortable in the summer heat and yearned for a sea breeze. "Oh that Providence would build me the merest little shanty, and mark me out a rood or two of garden-ground near the sea-coast." Manchester might have made a great difference in Hawthorne's life, or at least in his spirits. When he was close to death, his wife Sophia wrote "He needs the damp sea-air for health, comfort and enjoyment."

Among other distinguished almost-Cape Anners, William Dean Howells would have set up his summer domestic establishment in Rockport – except that low water was against him. The author of *The Rise of Silas Lapham*, literary arbiter, and editor of *The Atlantic Monthly* after Fields and through the 1870s, Howells was well pleased with the accommodations when he stayed at the Headlands boarding house. When he learned the establishment was on the market, he rushed back to Boston to bring his wife, Elinor, down to see for herself, no doubt extolling all the way the wonders of the locale and how this was an opportunity not to let slip by. But when they arrived at the old inn, the tide was out and the aroma of stranded fish was in. Elinor inhaled deeply from downwind and, in one glance, eloquently conveyed to Howells her opinions as to his taste, judgment and business instincts.

The literary associations linked under James T. Fields extended to the next community beyond Manchester, Beverly Farms. That was where Dr. Oliver Wendell Holmes summered. Dr. Holmes had little salt water to tip out of his boots, but when he was just twenty-one he had written a powerful poem against the planned scrapping of the frigate *Constitution* – "Old Ironsides." The public outcry raised by the young law student (soon to switch to medicine) with his impassioned lines that began "Ay, tear her tattered ensign down!" saved the patriarch warship of the American Navy. If it was Annie Fields who amplified Manchester to "Manchester-by-the-Sea," it was Holmes who, in his character as Autocrat of the Breakfast Table, riposted that his summer residence was situated in "Beverly-Farms-by-the-Depot." (The doctor's was not the only attempt to make humor with much-hyphenated descriptive titles; the unkindest was "Gloucester-by-the-Smell.")

As to Holmes's winter digs, the author-physician moved his brood from one desirable neighborhood in Boston to another, and finally to Beacon Street, after his parental home in Cambridge had been torn down for Harvard buildings – an act he pardoned as "justifiable domicide." But even Beacon Street eventually fell prey to advancing urbanization. In the 1890s the "electric cars" were rattling down that fashionable avenue. These were the original little trolleys with a single pole reaching up to the overhead power line. As he watched the trains sparking and grinding along the tracks newly set into the cobblestones, eighty-one-year-old Dr. Holmes burst into verse with "The Broomstick Train, or The Return of the Witches." The electric cars betrayed no visible means of propulsion, and he imagined them operating under witch power. The tracks being laid across the countryside he fantasized as evidence that His Satanic Majesty was spreading demonic influence anew across Essex County, even to fair Cape Ann, of which he asked, "Where is the Eden like to thee?"

Sometimes when he wandered down to the village in Beverly Farms, Dr. Holmes would run into Lucy Larcom and they would have a chat. Both were published regularly in the *Atlantic Monthly*. Larcom had spent her early girlhood on the Beverly shore known as "Cape Ann-Side," but when her father died her mother moved the children to Lowell. There Mrs. Larcom kept a boarding house for the young women "operatives" of the textile mills. Lucy herself, at age eleven, worked from five in the morning till seven at night in a mill, changing bobbins on the spinning frames. She shared fantasies with the other children at work, gazed out the windows at freedom and the river, and pasted poems on the wall to memorize. She found time at night to write the poems she contributed to *The Lowell Offering*, that urgently literate journal of the thoughts and fancies of the mill girls.

But there was always the longing to return to the little girl exploring the shore. Later Larcom distilled her yearnings into *Wild Roses of Cape Ann*. In it she rhymed of an old cow path, become a lane, that skirted the seashore above Salem, to "Pigeon Cove, and sheltered Annisquam." But the old rural charm was lost, she said, now that the coastal countryside of Beverly and Manchester had been domesticated by wealthy outsiders:

The ubiquitous French roof, the shaven lawns,
The modern villas posing on the verge
Of roadside-precipices, consciously,
In the Rhine-castle manner, - everything
That hints of Nature closely taken in hand
By patronizing wealth, and stroked and smoothed
Into suburban elegance.

James and Annie Fields were representative of the element in Manchester that "stroked and smoothed" nature into "suburban elegance." But James was not offended by Lucy Larcom's bucolic nostalgia. He appointed her the only salaried editor of one of his magazines, *Our Young Folks*, and she solidified that juvenile periodical's circulation and revenue. In gratitude, Fields put Larcom in charge of the magazine, which she ran successfully for almost a decade. By the time she was fifty she had been mill girl, schoolteacher, poet, essayist and magazine editor.

Confidant, pen-pal and mentor to Lucy Larcom was John Greenleaf Whittier, the Quaker poet. Although the Merrimac Valley was home ground to Whittier, he ranged down to coastal Essex County in search of grist for his poetic mill. In "The Garrison of Cape Ann," Whittier rhymed of ghostly specters and shrieks plaguing a remote outpost, the "Old Castle" in Pigeon Cove. "The Swan Song of Parson Avery" was a tribute to Reverend John Avery who, with his wife and six children, perished in 1635 in the shipwreck that spared only Reverend Anthony Thacher and his wife on what would be known as Thacher's Island.

Many on the Fields roster besides Lucy Larcom were women, including Isles of Shoals poet Celia Thaxter, and Elizabeth Stuart Phelps. Fields, said Phelps, "was incapable of that literary snobbishness that undervalues a woman's work because it is a woman's." Fields was also well aware that a hefty percentage of *Atlantic Monthly* readership was female. And Elizabeth Stuart Phelps was a money-maker. Fields sold 58,000 copies of her first romantic novel, *The Gates Ajar*, published in 1868. With that opus Phelps was only just hitting her stride. She wrote fifty-some books before she was done, plus a staggering quantity of poems, pamphlets and magazine articles. Ministers had been scattered through Phelps's family, and this ecclesiastical climate could help account for the missionary fervor Elizabeth brought to her writings. She herself said her chief causes were heaven, homeopathy, and women's rights. Belatedly she married a minister herself, one seventeen years her junior, and thereafter styled herself Elizabeth Stuart Phelps-Ward.

A few years after publication of *The Gates Ajar* Phelps, by then a well-established author, first dared the unknown and visited Gloucester, which she found "The noisiest and dustiest and fishiest of little cities." But, once past that dreadful waterfront, she found her heaven. "Out of the salt dust, out of the narrow, scorching streets, by the fish-flakes and the fish-teams, past the rude roads . . . we came upon the fairest face of all the New England coast, - the Eastern side of Gloucester Harbor." Elizabeth Stuart Phelps became a seasonal resident from May to November, and took a well-intentioned, if not widely appreciated, interest in the fishing population she regarded as primitive and misguided. She conducted Sunday services in grog shops, delivered temperance lectures at the Reform Club. Her novels *Madonna of the Tubs*, *Jack the Fisherman* and *A Singular Life* were moralistic tales of fishermen addicted to drink, to the ruin of their families. Not surprisingly, Phelps attracted few readers on the docks. Thirsty schoonermen, congratulating themselves that they had survived another trip to Georges Bank, did not take kindly to the forces of righteousness, in the person of Mrs. Phelps, seeking to divert their steps from saloon to chapel.

And she meddled in navigation. A summer visitor should know better than to interfere with the vessels. She used her influence to silence the whistling buoy off Brace's Rock (it had inconsiderately kept her awake), and schooners were wrecked and lives put at risk when there was no groaner to help vessels find their way in thick weather around to the harbor mouth.

Though obsessed with causes and out of touch with working Gloucester, Elizabeth Phelps could respond to the splendors of the place. There was the time she was in a carriage with a friend, clip-clopping through East Gloucester. "It was after tea, and a sky, translucent overhead, was burning down towards the west, preparing for one of the famous Gloucester sunsets."

Elizabeth Stuart Phelps. She forgave Gloucester its fish, and Gloucester forgave her those novels about fishermen addicted to drink, to the ruin of their families.

She wrote of another sunset after a storm:

> All Gloucester harbor tossed against it. The bows of the anchored fleet rose and sank angrily. The head-lights came out one by one, and flared, surging up and down. Ten Pound Island Light flashed out for the night; but her blinder was on, towards us. The little city, glorified now, forgiven of her fish, and her dust, and her bouncing roads, loved and dreamed over, and sung in heart and pen, melted all through her pretty outlines against the massive colors of the west.... The fishermen's children are in their beds; the rocks are quiet, but for the cannonade of the surf. Shut away from the world, shut in from the sea, I light my lonely fire, and thank God for my own hearth, and for Gloucester shore.

As she forgave Gloucester its fish, Gloucester forgave Elizabeth Stuart Phelps her reformist zeal, and tolerated her for her devotion to the town. Her status as a major author prevailed to the turn of the century. As late as 1923, when James R. Pringle's Gloucester Tercentenary Pageant was performed at Stage Fort Park, Phelps's poem "Gloucester" was recited as the Epilogue.

James T. Fields, orchestrating the publication of Phelps and his other writers, was ever genial and cultivated, quick to reassure a self-doubting author and resuscitate his or her morale. On the practical side, book reviewers like Edwin Whipple and editors like Epes Sargent at the *Transcript* were made to understand that advertising dollars and other rewards would flow to those who responded favorably – better, effusively – to the latest masterpiece from one of Fields's authors.

Fields could be a hard bargainer, but his fair dealing and personal warmth won over even suspicious English authors like William Thackeray and Charles Dickens. Fields actually paid them royalties, at a time when it was common practice for American publishers to simply pirate the works of foreign authors. To Dickens, Fields was more than just his American publisher. James and Annie Fields were two of Dickens's closest American friends. Whenever they were in England he insisted they come stay with him at Gad's Hill Place near Rochester, the country house Dickens had dreamed of owning from the days of his Oliver Twist boyhood.

In Boston, needing diversion after a harrowing reading tour, Dickens challenged Fields to enter an American contender against his own English favorite for a walking race. Dickens had drawn up elaborate rules for the contest, and insisted that first Fields and he must test the course. The two of them marched thirteen miles out of Boston in brisk weather, pausing only at the half-way mark to take a breather. The locals in Newton Centre were unaware that the two gentlemen sitting on a shop doorstep and devouring oranges were, respectively, the summer literary squire of Manchester, and the creator of Mr. Pickwick, Little Nell and David Copperfield. On the appointed day the race was run with partisans of the American and British entrants noisily cheering on their favorite. That evening all parties adjourned to a high-spirited dinner hosted by Dickens at the Parker House.

Dickens and Thackeray would not have visited James and Annie on Cape Ann; lecture tours by eminent foreign authors were not scheduled for the summer months. But they would be there in spirit when the brotherhood (and sisterhood) of Ticknor & Fields authors socialized on Manchester summer afternoons with James and Annie Fields.

Befriending and encouraging writers was not just business for James T. Fields – he took it as his mission. Elizabeth Stuart Phelps pronounced the final word on the publisher after his death in 1881: "He had life's fine wine."

A century passed from the days of veranda chit-chat between Fields and his authors. It was 1953 and Hyde Cox was talking Robert Frost into taking part in a Gloucester Festival of the Arts. Frost was at the time America's most revered and popular poet, four-time winner of the Pulitzer Prize. An eager Gloucester audience filled the high school auditorium to hear him speak. No stranger to the area, Frost regularly spent the Christmas holidays at Crow Island, Hyde Cox's estate in Manchester. Cox had become almost a second son to Frost after the poet's own troubled son committed suicide.

Three years before Frost spoke in Gloucester, Hyde Cox had shuttled him out to Lanesville to have his head modeled by sculptor Walker Hancock. Hancock remembered that Frost did most of the talking during the sittings. Hancock took Frost and Cox for walks in the woods and Frost was particularly interested in "The Ledges," a stretch of granite, laid bare by quarrymen, that revealed the scourings of boulders during the Ice Age. Frost mixed references to these ice scratches and to quarries and cellar holes, and New Hampshire abandoned farm allusions, in "Directive," which Frost biographer Jay Parini calls "one of Frost's most central poems . . . a map of his inner landscape." Hancock found Frost a mix of the genial and pugnacious, but kind. One Christmas day Frost had come along from Crow Island with Cox with words of cheer when Hancock was laid up with pneumonia.

Crusty as he was, Robert Frost knew and liked certain people on Cape Ann. Historian-naturalist Elliott Rogers was ushering Annisquam fisherman "Bunt" Davis into a select gathering at which Frost was the guest of honor. Rogers was about to risk introducing the rough man of the sea to the distinguished poet, when Frost recognized Bunt and rushed over to greet him. Bunt was a long-time friend of Hyde Cox, and the three of them had cruised in Bunt's boat on Ipswich Bay.

Robert Frost was a frequent guest at the Crow Island, Manchester home of his friend Hyde Cox, president of the Cape Ann Historical Association. *Courtesy Cape Ann Historical Museum*

These then, along with Rudyard Kipling and T. S. Eliot, were some of the not inconsiderable authors who had written of Cape Ann before Charles Olson put his poetic stamp on the area in the mid-20th century. Olson had become the dominant literary figure in Gloucester, and he attracted other writers to his circle. Peter Anastas, in addition to his *Charles Olson - Maximus to Gloucester*, energized the panelists and audience in Gloucester City Hall during a Charles Olson Festival sponsored by the Gloucester Lyceum in 1995. Anastas, in conjunction with Peter Parsons, also compiled the oral history of Gloucester, *When Gloucester Was Gloucester*. He would later write personal reminiscences:

in *At the Cut* (2002) he told of growing up near the Cut Bridge that separates island Cape Ann from the mainland; in *Broken Trip* (2004) he spoke of his years with a local relief agency.

Close to Olson's own work was that of Vincent Ferrini. In 1949 Olson liked a poem of Ferrini's he had read in the magazine *IMAGI*. Olson dropped in on Ferrini, and Ferrini was hypnotized by "his manner of ease and his candid quality . . . he talked like I did, at the center of things." Often in the evening, Ferrini said, Olson and he would meet for coffee at the old Cape Ann Diner, then they would walk along the waterfront, talking all the way.

Olson learned Ferrini's history. Vincent told it to the public in 1988 in his earthy autobiography, *Hermit of the Clouds*. It tells how Ferrini rented a storefront in Gloucester from his brother, and opened shop in 1950 as a maker of picture frames. That year Charles Olson began addressing the first of his *Maximus* poems to Ferrini, calling him "my brother poet, my twin." He said Ferrini's was his body on Cape Ann when he was not there, he contributed to Ferrini's poetry magazine, *Four Winds*, and encouraged Vincent's writing.

But in *Maximus* letter No. 5, in 1955, Olson was suddenly harsh on *Four Winds*, and was disparaging to Ferrini personally as a poet. Ferrini's wife and mutual friends felt betrayed by Olson's treatment of his most tireless advocate in Gloucester. Ferrini, although wounded, was forgiving. He owed Olson so much for helping him believe in himself, he said. And he had happy recollections of Olson's apartment at the Fort. Ferrini remained a loyal friend and wrote poems invoking Olson's spirit long after the other poet's death.

By Ferrini's count, he himself published some forty volumes of poetry. The most representative collection is *Know Fish*, incorporating many poems written after Gloucester City Council meetings. In those poems Ferrini was often abusive toward officials and civic notables. Snarled then-Mayor Leo Alper, "He's never done anything for the city of Gloucester except write those lousy poems." The mayor was showing commendable restraint, after Ferrini pilloried him again and again, in one poem calling him a "somber bomballo buffoon." It seems remarkable that Ferrini was not assassinated by one of the many targets of his verbal assaults, or at least sued for serial libel and defamation of character.

Nevertheless, this maker of picture frames and poems had many defenders. Ferrini might have lacked Olson's scholarly apparatus, but he often transformed unexpected perceptions into illuminating turns of phrase and thought. And Ferrini could be generous in his poems to the people he admired, like preservationist Betty Smith, fishermen's advocate Angelina Sanfilippo, editor Paul Kenyon. And Peggy Sibley, war bride wife of Captain Bill Sibley, she indelibly English, warm-hearted gadfly, irrepressible. Wandering through the warrens of her English Book Store on Rocky Neck was a bibliophile's delight. Ferrini paid tribute to her in "Fisherwoman: Peg Sibley."

Prominent Gloucester citizens would shift uneasily when they saw Vincent Ferrini fix his gaze upon them. They might be graciously praised in his next poetic profile. Or they might be skewered.

For summer theatre, Gloucester has the Gloucester Stage Company, founded by Israel Horovitz in 1980. Horovitz sometimes performs in his own plays in this intimate theatre, which once served as winter quarters for the town cars of wealthy summer residents. Horovitz grew up in the north-of-Boston suburb of Wakefield, which may help to explain why this playwright of international stature picked Gloucester for the site of his summer productions. He and his family live between New York and London. Aside from Eugene O'Neil, no American has had more plays translated into French and produced in France. A perennial contributor to the off-Broadway repertory, Horovitz wrote "The Indian Wants the Bronx" that introduced Al Pacino, and a "Growing Up Jewish" trilogy that included "Today I Am A Fountain Pen."

Several of Horovitz's fifty-some plays – "Gloucester Fish," "Park Your Car in Harvard Yard," "Fighting Over Beverly," "Strong Man's Weak Child" – were set amid the economic stagnation of Gloucester in the early 1990s. Horovitz's Gloucester plays are fraught with blasted dreams and betrayals and simmering resentments, from which his troubled characters struggle through to a degree of acceptance and dignity.

The implications reverberate as the patrons leave the Gloucester Stage Company theatre and step into the softness of an East Gloucester summer evening. The tensions between the personalities and the subtleties of the play recede as the senses take in a medley of August harbor smells, with laughter and idling engine sounds rising from Smith Cove.

*****

George Procter, publisher and author of the first books on Gloucester as a fishing port said, "there is more here than can be pictured by the most ingenious pen." Or by the most ingenious brush, for that matter. For some of the creative spirits the inspiration was the maritime heritage, the nobility of a people struggling to make a living from the sea. For others it was the sheer beauty of sea and granite ledge under puffs of cloud set in deep blue sky, or accidental arrangements of schooner sails and wharf sheds, with maybe a punctuating lighthouse. For others it meant an escape to remote, wild shores where all of nature seemed to suggest clues to an ultimate enigma. Many others could not define exactly why they responded, but knew a certain magic was working upon them, poking at them until they wrote it all down or put it on canvas.

That pact with the sparkling, rippling, murmuring, thundering, procreative sea? It has cost Cape Ann dearly in lives and fortune. But it has paid remarkable dividends of a sort never imagined by those first few fishermen the Dorchester Company left to winter over in Gloucester Harbor in 1623.

Epilogue

GLOUCESTER'S CONTRACT with the sea is up for renewal again, as it always is. The challenges are out there. Fishing stocks have declined, making it necessary to find new ways to make money from the fisheries, and refine the old ways.

Those on Cape Ann who earn their livelihood from one of the many sea trades feel most threatened by commercial ventures proposed to invade the sea bed for non-maritime purposes. Such as ranks of wind turbines that would rise over 400 feet from the ocean surface to generate electricity. Or an enormous liquefied natural gas depot that would offload tankers square in the most abundant fishing grounds.

Those are the most apparent challenges. A more insidious threat to the comfortable small-scale life along the shores of Cape Ann is simply the irresistible modern proliferation of humankind, especially with technology dispersing work away from major cities. As more houses are built, there is the fear of population pressures spreading the same tidal wave of urbanization that has overwhelmed other areas, leaving only a few landmarks poking up through the amorphous flood.

But stroll down Main Street in Gloucester, and you get the sense that its citizens will not accept being consigned to any soulless sameness if they can help it. Gloucester today is basically small-town in attitude, accommodating with easy-going grace all its ethnic, occupational and social diversity. It is risky to make generalizations about a population, especially of a port like Gloucester because ports see a constant traffic of people as well as goods from all over the world. But on the streets of Gloucester, you get a sense of a people going their own way, thank you very much. In front of the towering city hall a meter maid is in animated discussion with a man wearing a Red Sox cap and shrugging his shoulders with a resigned grin. In the center of town the owner of a beauty products shop is out on his sidewalk as usual, discoursing and gesturing in Italian to a barrel-chested man braving November in shorts. A bank vice president crosses the street calling out to them both, and to a woman who is vigorously sweeping the sidewalk outside her shop.

Passersby will often greet one another, recognized or not. They are like the vessels Joshua Slocum spoke of in *Sailing Alone Around the World.* "The time was," said Captain Slocum, "when ships passing one another at sea backed their topsails and had a 'gam' .... it is a prosy life when we have no time to bid one another good morning." For people with Gloucester deep in their bones, there is always time for a "Good Morning." And they enjoy talking, having a "gam," unlike the stereotypical taciturn Yankee. Maybe about family, friends, high school hockey. Mostly about the weather. They tend to make light of their own misfortunes, and are genuinely concerned over the hard luck of others.

There are, to be sure, certain behaviors that are contrary to their code, and which will elicit a sardonic lifted eyebrow. There is little toleration for whining self-pity or snobbishness of any sort. The most prosperous man in town may drive a rusted-out pickup truck, because he knows his affluence may go out on the next tide. In a town with a long tradition of the sea as a great leveler, the emphasis is on getting along together. And enjoying life, as best you may.

Many in Gloucester persist in making a living from the ocean in one way or another. In a recent issue of the List of Residents the people of Gloucester listed their occupations not only as commercial fisherman (many), but as clammer, fish cutter, lobsterman, lobsterwoman, lumper [dock worker], lobster broker, fish hauler, drawbridge operator, marine surveyor, ship's carpenter, compass assembler, dockmaster, fish biologist, shrimp packer. Others are engaged in the relatively benign eco-tourism of the whale-watch fleet. The development of a cruise ship terminal suggests new opportunities for squeezing a day's pay out of the harbor.

With any luck the fishermen of Gloucester, and their neighbors who work at all the associated trades of maintaining and outfitting the vessels, and those active in other pursuits who are part of the same economy and heritage, will persevere in the same independent spirit that has kept so many families afloat for centuries. May these people continue to find ways to make a living one way or another, and to enjoy the satisfactions of life on Cape Ann, at the margin of "old ocean." And may they keep the spirit alive that, contrary to every reasonable expectation, has fostered so much excellence in works of the mind and imagination.

Bibliography

Anonymous:

- *Essex: The Shipbuilding Town*, issued by The Essex Bicentennial Committee and Essex Historical Society; printed by The Cricket Press, Manchester, 1976
- *Folly Cove Designers, May 7 through October 31, 1996*. Catalogue. Cape Ann Historical Association
- *Outline of History and Dedication of the Sawyer Free Library of Gloucester, Mass., Tuesday, July 1, 1884 – Sermon, Press Notices, Etc.* Gloucester: Cape Ann Bulletin Steam Book and Job Print, 1884 (Copy in New England Genealogic Society, Boston reads "Compliments of Samuel E. Sawyer, Brookbank, November 6, 1884")
- *Photographic History of Gloucester*. Gloucester: 4 Vol., issued by Gloucester Historical Reproductions, 1976
- *St. Peter's Fiesta Through the Years*. Gloucester: The Young Men's Coalition, 2001
- *Rockport As It Was - A Book of Pictures*. Rockport: Sandy Bay Historical Society & Museums, 1975; reprinted 1992

Abbott, Gordon, Jr. *Jeffrey's Creek: A Story of People, Places and Events in the Town That Came to Be Known as Manchester-By-The-Sea*. Manchester: Manchester Historical Society, 2003

Ackroyd, Peter. *T. S. Eliot – A Life*. New York: Simon and Schuster, 1984

Adams, William T. (See Optic, Oliver)

Addison, Daniel Dulany. *Lucy Larcom – Life, Letters, and Diary*. Boston: Houghton, Mifflin, 1895

Ambler, Edward Vassar. *Know Cape Ann*. Gloucester: printed by North Shore Press, 1931

Anastas, Peter. *When Gloucester Was Gloucester – Toward an Oral History of the City* (co-author Peter Parsons). Gloucester: Gloucester 350th Anniversary Celebration, Inc., 1973

- *Charles Olson and Gloucester: The Poet, the Poetry, the Place*. Gloucester: typewritten manuscript of lecture delivered at Sawyer Free Library, 1984
- *Charles Olson – Maximus to Gloucester*. Peter Anastas, ed., Gloucester: Ten Pound Island Book Company, 1992
- *At the Cut*. Gloucester: Dogtown Books, 2002
- *Broken Trip*. Thetford, VT: Glad Day Books, 2004

Babson, John J. *History of the Town of Gloucester, Cape Ann*. Gloucester: Procter Brothers, 1860. Reprinted by Peter Smith Publisher, Inc., with introduction and historical review by Joseph E. Garland, 1972

- *Additions to the History of Gloucester: Part 1 – Early Settlers.* Gloucester: printed by M. V. B. Perley, Telegraph Office, 1876. *Second Series* published by Salem Press Publishing and Printing Co., Salem, 1891

Babson, Roger W. *Dogtown – Gloucester's Deserted Village.* Address by Roger W. Babson before Gloucester Rotary Club, September, 1927. Published by the Historical House, Pleasant Street, Gloucester, 1927

- *Actions and Reactions – An Autobiography of Roger W. Babson.* New York: Harper & Brothers, 1935, 1949

- *Cape Ann Tourist's Guide* (with Foster H. Saville). Rockport: Sandy Bay Historical Society and Museum, 1936. Revised 1946, 1952

Babson, Susan: *Along the Old Roads of Cape Ann.* Gloucester: Cape Ann Literary and Historical Society, 1923

Babson, Thomas E. "Evolution of Cape Ann Roads and Transportation, 1623-1955." *Essex Institute Historical Collections,* Vol. 91, October, 1955, pp. 302-28. Also in "A Talk Before the Cape Ann Historical Association, April 11, 1955"

Babson, W. Warren, M.D. and Brooks, Laurence F. *As They May Need – A History of the Addison Gilbert Hospital.* West Kennebunk, ME: Phoenix Publishing, 1989

Barbour, Philip L.: *The Three Worlds of Captain John Smith.* Boston: Houghton Mifflin, 1964

- *The Complete Works of Captain John Smith,* ed. Philip Barbour. Chapel Hill, NC: University of North Carolina Press, c1986

Barrow, Julia Paxton. "William Bentley: An Extraordinary Boarder," *Essex Institute Historical Collections,* Vol. 97, April, 1961, pp. 129-50

Bartlett, Kim. *The Finest Kind – The Fishermen of Gloucester.* New York: Avon Books, 1977. Re-issued by W. W. Norton, 2002

Bayliss, Jonathan. *Gloucesterbook, Gloucestertide, Prologos.* A self-published trilogy available from Basilicum Press, Ashburnham, MA

Beaux, Cecilia. *Background With Figures – Autobiography of Cecilia Beaux.* Boston: Houghton Mifflin, 1930

Benét, William Rose. *The Stairway of Surprise.* New York: Knopf, 1940, 1957

Bennett, Mary Angela. *Elizabeth Stuart Phelps.* Philadelphia: University of Pennsylvania Press, 1939

Bentley, Rev. William. *The Diary of William Bentley, D.D.*. Salem, MA: The Essex Institute, 1907. Reprinted by Peter Smith, Gloucester, 1962

Bishop, John H. *AYC* (Annisquam Yacht Club) *1896-1988.* Gloucester: 1988

Bowen, Catherine Drinker. *Family Portrait.* Boston: Little Brown, 1970

Brigham, Chester. *The Stream I Go A-Fishing In: Musical Adventures of Gloucester Schoonerman John Jay Watson.* Gloucester: Whale's Jaw Publishing, 2003

Brooks, Alfred Mansfield. *Gloucester Recollected – A Familiar History,* ed. Joseph E. Garland. Gloucester: Peter Smith, 1974

Brooks, Laurence F. and Babson, W. Warren, M.D. *As They May Need – A History of the Addison Gilbert Hospital.* West Kennebunk, ME: Phoenix Publishing, 1989

Brown, Robert F. *Bibliography of Cape Ann Literature*, in "Cape Ann Summer Sun," July, 1952; Updated with annotations by G. Gibson, Gloucester Arts and humanities, November 1978

Buell, Lawrence. *New England Literary Culture – From Revolution Through Renaissance*. Cambridge, England: Cambridge University Press, 1986

Burgess, Thornton. *Now I Remember*: Boston: Little Brown & Co., 1960

Bush, Ronald. *T. S. Eliot, A Study in Character and Style*. New York: Oxford University Press, 1983

Butler, Gen. Benjamin F. *Butler's Book*. Boston: A. M. Thayer, 1892

Butterick, George F. *A Guide to the Maximus Poems of Charles Olson*. Berkeley, CA: University of California Press, 1978

Cahill, Bill. *From the Lumper's Picnic to the Hospital Ball: Bill Cahill's Gloucester*. Manchester: The Cricket Press, 1979

Carrington, C. E. *The Life of Rudyard Kipling*. Garden City, NY: Doubleday, 1955

Carter, Robert. *A Summer Cruise on the Coast of New England*. Boston: Crosby & Nichols, 1864. Abridged and illustrated edition, entitled *Carter's Coast of New England*, edited by Daniel Ford and published by New Hampshire Publishing Company, Somersworth, NH, 1969. Reprinted in paperback, 1977.

Chamberlain, Allen. *Pigeon Cove, Its Early Settlers and Their Farms, 1702-1740*. Pigeon Cove: Village Improvement Society of Pigeon Cove, Inc., 1940. Second Edition published by Sandy Bay Historical Society and Museums, 1999

Chamberlain, Samuel. *Gloucester and Cape Ann – A Camera Impression*. Madison, NJ: Stanley F. Baker, 1938

\- *Cape Ann Through the Seasons – A Photographic Sketchbook*. New York: Hastings House, 1953

Chamberlin, Joseph Edgar. *The Boston Transcript – A History of its First Hundred Years*. Boston: Houghton Mifflin, 1930

Champlain, Samuel de. *Voyages du Sieur de Champlain*. Paris: Imprimé au Frais du Gouvernment, 1830

\- *Voyages of Samuel de Champlain 1604-1618*, ed. W. L. Grant, M.A (Oxon.). New York: Scribner's, 1907

Chapelle, Howard I. *American Sailing Craft*. New York: Kennedy Brothers, 1936

\- *The American Fishing Schooners, 1825-1935*. New York: W. W. Norton, 1973

Chipley, Louise. "William Bentley, Journalist of the Early Republic," *Essex Institute Historical Collections*, Vol. 123, No. 4, January 1987, pp. 331-347

Clark, Tom. *Charles Olson – The Allegory of a Poet's Life*. New York: W. W. Norton, 1991

Colby, Larry. *Gloucester Fire Department - A Pictorial History, 1847-1947*. Gloucester: printed at The Pressroom, Inc., 1994. Volume II printed 1996.

Collins, Capt. Joseph W. *Fearful Experience of a Gloucester Halibut Fisherman*. Boston: Printed by F. A. Varnum, shortly after 1883. Reprinted by Ten Pound Island Book Company, Gloucester, 1987

Connolly, James B. *The Seiners*. New York: Scribner's, 1904

- *Fishermen of the Banks*. Preface by T. S. Eliot. London: Faber & Gwyer, 1928
- *Gloucestermen: Stories of the Fishing Fleet*. New York: Scribner's, 1930
- *The Book of the Gloucester Fishermen*: New York: John Day, 1930
- *Port of Gloucester*. New York: Doubleday, Doran, 1940
- *Sea-Borne – Thirty Years Avoyaging*. Garden City, N.Y.: Doubleday, Doran, 1944

Cooley, John L. *Rockport Sketch Book: Stories of Early Art and Artists*. Rockport: Rockport Art Association, 1965
- *The Granite of Cape Ann*. Rockport: Rockport National Bank, 1974

Copeland, Melvin T. and Rogers, Elliott C. *The Saga of Cape Ann*. Freeport, ME: Bond Wheelwright, 1960

Cowley, Malcolm. *Exile's Return*. New York: W. W. Norton, 1934
- *New England Writers and Writing*. Hanover, NH: University Press of New England, 1996

Cox, Frank L. *The Gloucester Book*. Gloucester: printed by White & Gaffney, 1921

Craig, James A. *Fitz H. Lane: An Artist's Voyage through Nineteenth-Century America*. Charleston, SC: The History Press, 2006

Crowell, Rev. Robert. *History of the Town of Essex, from 1634 to 1868*. Springfield, MA: Samuel Bowles, 1868

Currier, Guy C. *Around Cape of Islands: Cape Ann*. 1955

Dandola, John. *Living in the Past, Looking to the Future: The Biography of John Hays Hammond, Jr.* Glen Ridge, NJ: Quincannon Publishing Group, 2004

D'Andrea, Cheslie. *Gloucestermen, Their Fishing and Their Boats*. Highline Publications, 1975

Davies, Kristian. *Artists of Cape Ann*. Rockport: Twin Lights Publishers, 2001

Davis, Solomon H. *Journal of Captain Solomon H. Davis, A Gloucester Sea-Captain, 1828-1846*. Privately printed at The Plimpton Press, Norwood, MA, 1922

Davison, Peter. *Half Remembered: A Personal History*. New York: Harper & Row, 1973. Revised edition published 1991 by Story Line Press, Brownsville, OR

Dexter, Ralph W. "Two Centuries of Naturalists on Cape Ann, Massachusetts," *Essex County Historical Collections*, Vol. 122, April, 1986, pp. 246-58
- "The Scientific Period of the Cape Ann Scientific and Literary Association and its Successors, 1873-1952," *Essex County Historical Collections*, Vol. 109, April, 1973, pp. 165-74

Dow, George Francis. *Two Centuries of Travel in Essex County, Massachusetts – A Collection of Narratives and Observations Made by Travelers, 1605-1799*, collected and annotated by George Francis Dow. Topsfield, MA: The Topsfield Historical Society, 1921

Dresser, Thomas. *Dogtown, A Village Lost in Time*. Littleton, NH: third printing by The Ink Spot, 1996

Dunlap, Sarah V. *The Jewish Community of Cape Ann*. Gloucester: Cape Ann Jewish Community Oral History Project, 1998

Dunlop, Marianne. *Judith Sargent Murray: Her First 100 Letters*. Gloucester: The Sargent House Museum, 1995

Eddy, Rev. Richard. *Universalism in Gloucester, Mass.* Gloucester: Procter Brothers, 1892

Eldredge, David S. "The Gloucester Fishing Industry in World War II," *The American Neptune*, Vol. 27, July 1967, pp. 53-65

Eliot, T. S. *Collected Poems 1909-1935*. New York: Harcourt, Brace, 1952

- *The Complete Poems and Plays, 1909-1950*. New York: Harcourt Brace Jovanovich, 1967

Eliot, Valerie, ed. *T. S. Eliot: The Waste Land, A Facsimile and Transcipt of the Original Drafts Including the Annotations of Ezra Pound*. New York: Harcourt Brace Jovanovich, 1971

Elleman, Barbara. *Virginia Lee Burton: A Life in Art*. Boston: Houghton Mifflin, 2002

Emerson, Everett H. *Captain John Smith*. Boston: Twayne Publishers, 1971

Erkkila, Barbara H. *Hammers on Stone: A History of Cape Ann Granite*. Woolwich, ME: TBW Books, 1980

- *Village at Lane's Cove*. Gloucester: Ten Pound Island Book Company, 1989

Falt, Clarence M. *Wharf & Fleet: Ballads of the Fishermen of Gloucester*. Boston: Little, Brown, 1902

- *Souvenir Poems of Points of Interest of Gloucester in Song*. Boston: Alfred Mudge, 1894

Ferrini, Vincent. *Know Fish*. Storrs, CT: The University of Connecticut Library, 1979. Book III, The Navigators, 1984; Books IV & V, The Community of Self, 1986; Books VI & VII, 1991

- *Hermit of the Clouds – The Autobiography of Vincent Ferrini*. Gloucester: Ten Pound Island Book Co., 1988

Fields, James T. *Yesterdays With Authors*. Boston: Houghton, Mifflin, 1871

Fifield, Charles Woodbury, Jr. *Along the Gloucester Waterfront, 1938 to 1946*. Gloucester: Cape Ann Ticket & Label Co., 1955. Second printing by Eagle Printing Company, Northbridge, MA, 2001

Fisher, Capt. R. Barry. *A Doryman's Day*. Gardiner, ME: Tilbury House; Bath, ME: Maine Maritime Museum, 2001

Floyd, Frank L. *"Manchester-by-the-Sea"*. Manchester: Floyd's News Store, 1945

Foote, Mark and Ingersoll, Larry. *Behind the Badge: The History of the Gloucester Police Department*. Gloucester: Dogtown Books. Vol. 1, 2003; Vol. 2, 2004, Vol. 3, 2005

Fowler, William M., Jr. *Rebels Under Sail: The American Navy during the Revolution*. New York: Scribner's, 1976

Garland, Joseph E. *Lone Voyager*. Boston: Little Brown, 1963. Revised edition published by Nelson B. Robinson, Rockport, 1978. Reprinted as *Lone Voyager: The Extraordinary Adventures of Howard Blackburn*, published by Touchstone, London, 2000.

- *That Great Pattillo*. Boston: Little, Brown, 1966. Reprinted as *Bear of the Sea: Giant Jim Pattillo and the Roaring Years of the Gloucester-Nova Scotia Fishery*, published by Commonwealth Editions, Beverly, MA, 2001.
- *Eastern Point*. Peterborough, NH: Noone House, 1971. Revised edition published by Commonwealth Editions, Beverly, MA, 1999
- *The Gloucester Guide – A Retrospective Ramble*. Gloucester: Gloucester 350th Anniversary Celebration, Inc., 1973. Reprinted as *The Gloucester Guide – A Stroll through Place and Time*, published by Protean Press, Rockport, 1990. Reprinted 2004 by History Press, Charleston, SC
- *Guns Off Gloucester*. Gloucester: Essex County Newspapers, 1975
- *Down to the Sea – The Fishing Schooners of Gloucester*. Boston: David R. Godine, 1983
- *Adventure – Queen of the Windjammers*. Camden, ME: Down East Books, 1985
- *Eastern Point Revisited – Then and Now: 1889-1989*. Gloucester: Association of Eastern Point Residents, 1989
- *Beating to Windward – A voyage in the Gloucester Daily Times through the stormy years from 1967 to 1973*. Gloucester: The Curious Traveller Press, 1994
- *Gloucester on the Wind – America's Greatest Fishing Port in the Days of Sail*. Dover, NH: Arcadia Publishing, 1995
- *Beam Reach*. Gloucester: The Curious Traveller Press, 1997
- *The North Shore*. Beverly, MA: Commonwealth Editions, 1998

Garrett, Edmund H. *Romance & Reality of the Puritan Coast*. Boston: Little Brown, 1897

Gilligan, Edmund. *White Sails Crowding*. New York: Scribner's, 1939

- *The Gaunt Woman*. New York: Scribner's, 1943

Gordon, Lyndall. *Eliot's Early Years*. New York: Oxford University Press, 1977

- *Eliot's New Life*. New York: Oxford University Press, 1988

Gott, Lemuel, M.D. *History of the Town of Rockport, as Comprised in the Centennial Address of Lemuel Gott, M.D.* Rockport: printed at Rockport Review Office, 1888

Grant, Robert. *The North Shore*. New York: Scribner's, 1896

Greenlaw, Linda. *The Hungry Ocean: A Swordboat Captain's Journey*. New York: Hyperion, 1999

- *The Lobster Chronicles*. New York: Hyperion, 2002

Gummere, Richard M. "John Wise, A Classical Controversialist," *Essex Institute Historical Collections*, Vol. 92, July, 1956, pp. 265-78

Gustafson, Eleanor H. "Fitz Who Lane?," *Antiques Magazine*, June, 2005

Hahn, Ina. *Windhover*. Rockport: Twinlights Publishers, 2000

Halsted, Isabella. *The Aunts*. Manchester: The Sharksmouth Press, 1992

Hammond, John Hays. *The Autobiography of John Hays Hammond.* New York: Farrar & Rinehart, 2 Vol., 1935

Hancock, Walker. *A Sculptor's Fortunes – Memoir by Walker Hancock.* Gloucester: Cape Ann Historical Association, 1997

Harding, Walter. *The Days of Henry Thoreau, a Biography.* New York: Knopf, 1966

Hartt, Hildegarde T. *Magnolia, Once Kettle Cove.* 1962

Hawes, Charles Boardman. *Gloucester by Land and Sea.* Boston: Little, Brown, 1923

Hayden, Sterling. *Wanderer: An Autobiography.* New York: Knopf, 1963

- *Voyage: A Novel of 1896.* New York: G. P. Putnam's Sons, 1976

Hayes, David F. "The Role of the Finnish Immigrant in the History of Lanesville, Massachusetts, 1870-1957," *Essex Institute Historical Collections*, Vol. 95, October, 1959, pp. 313-47

Heyrman, Christine Leigh. *Commerce and Culture – The Maritime Communities of Colonial Massachusetts, 1690-1750.* New York: W. W. Norton, 1984

Higginson, Rev. Francis. *New-Englands Plantation, with the Sea Journal and Other Writings* (1630). Reprinted by The Essex Book and Print Club, Salem, 1908

Higginson, Thomas Wentworth. *Oldport Days.* Boston: James R. Osgood, 1873

Hill, Dick. *Sylvester Ahola – The Gloucester Gabriel.* Metuchen, NJ.: The Scarecrow Press, and The Institute of Jazz Studies, Rutgers – The State University of New Jersey, 1993

Hill, Robert W. "Our Coastal Pioneers," *Essex Institute Historical Collections*, Vol. 78, January, 1942, pp. 24-40

Hodgkins, Pierce N. *That Is the Way It Was – An Autobiographical Novel.* New York: Carlton Press, 1977

Holzman, Robert S. *Stormy Ben Butler.* New York: Macmillan, 1954

Horovitz, Israel. *Three Gloucester Plays.* Garden City, NY: The Fireside Theatre, 1992

Howe, Henry F. *Prologue to New England.* New York: Farrar & Rinehart, 1943

Howe, M. A. DeWolfe. *Holmes of the Breakfast-Table.* New York: Oxford University Press, 1939

Hoyt, William D. *Hanging On: The Gloucester Waterfront in Change, 1927-1948.* Gloucester: Martin J. Horgan, Jr., 1987

Hubbard, Rev. William. *A General History of New England from the Discovery to MXCLXXX.* Boston: Little Brown, 1848. Revised second edition, 1878.

Ingersoll, Larry and Foote, Mark. *Behind the Badge: The History of the Gloucester Police Department* [see entry for Foote, Mark]

Johnson, Irving and Electa. *Yankee's Wander World: Circling the Globe in the Brigantine Yankee.* New York: W. W. Norton, 1949

- *Yankee's People and Places* (with Lydia Edes). New York: W. W. Norton, 1955

Junger, Sebastian. *The Perfect Storm – A True Story of Men Against the Sea.* New York: W. W. Norton, 1997

Kenny, Herbert A. *Suburban Man.* New York: The Monastine Press, 1965

- *Cape Ann, Cape America.* Philadelphia: J. B. Lippincott, 1971. Reprinted by The Curious Traveller Press, 1998

Kenyon, Paul B. *Roger W. Babson, A Reminiscence* (with Philip S. Weld). 1982

- *People & Books, The Story of the Gloucester Lyceum and Sawyer Free Library, 1830-1980.* Gloucester: Sawyer Free Library, 1980

Kieran, John. *Not Under Oath.* Boston: Houghton Mifflin, 1964

Kipling, Rudyard. *Captains Courageous: A Story of the Grand Banks.* London and New York: Macmillan, 1897

- *Something of Myself – For My Friends, Known and Unknown.* London and New York: MacMillan, 1937

Kirk, Russell. *Eliot and His Age.* LaSalle, IL: Sherwood Sugden, c1984

Lamson, Rev. D. F. *History of the Town of Manchester, Essex County, Massachusetts, 1645-1895.* Manchester: Town of Manchester, 1895

Larcom, Lucy. *Wild Roses of Cape Ann, And Other Poems.* Boston: Houghton Mifflin, 1881

- *A New England Girlhood.* Boston: Houghton Mifflin, 1889

Laughery, John. *Joan Sloan: Painter and Rebel.* New York: Henry Holt, 1995

Leonard, Rev. Henry C. *Pigeon Cove and Vicinity.* Boston: F. A. Searle, 1873

Lescarbot, Marc: *Nova Francia – A Description of Acadia* (1606). Translated by P. Erondelle, 1609. London: George Routledge & Sons, 1928.

Low, Gorham P. *The Sea Made Men – The Story of a Gloucester Lad, "presented" by Roger W. Babson, edited by Elizabeth L. Alling.* New York: Fleming H. Revell, 1937. Also published as *The Sea Made Men – Memoir of An American Sea Captain, 1826-1840.* London, John Lane, 1939

Lowe, Charles A. *Portrait of Gloucester – Charles A. Lowe Photos.* Gloucester: Gloucester Daily Times, 1983

Lyons, Louis. *Newspaper Story: One Hundred Years of the Boston Globe.* Cambridge, MA: The Belknap Press of Harvard University Press, 1971

MacKaye, Percy. "Dogtown Common." New York: MacMillan, 1921

Manchester-by-the-Sea 350th Anniversary Committee: *Manchester by-the-Sea, 1645-1995.* Manchester: 1995

Mann, Charles Edward. *The Sargent Family and the Old Sargent Homes.* Printed by Frank S. Whitten, Lynn, MA, 1919

- *In the Heart of Cape Ann; or The Story of Dogtown.* Gloucester: Procter Brothers, 1896

Marchalonis, Shirley. *The Worlds of Lucy Larcom, 1824-1893.* Athens, GA: University of Georgia Press, 1989

Marriner, Ernest C. *Jim Connolly and the Fishermen of Gloucester – An Appreciation of James Brendan Connolly at Eighty.* Waterville, ME: Colby College Press, 1949

Martin, Roger. *Rockport Remembered.* Gloucester: The Curious Traveller Press, 1997

- *A Rockport Album: Photographs of Bygone Days*. Gloucester: The Curious Traveller Press, 1998
- *Rockport Recollected*. Gloucester: The Curious Traveller Press, 2001

Matthiessen, F. O. *The Achievement of T. S. Eliot*. New York: Oxford University Press, 1935, 1958

Maud, Ralph. *Charles Olson's Reading – A Biography*. Carbondale and Edwardsville, IL: Southern Illinois University Press, 1996

McAveeney, David C. *Gloucester & Rockport – A Curious Traveller Guide*. Gloucester: The Curious Traveller Press, 1990

- *Kipling in Gloucester – The Writing of Captains Courageous*. Gloucester: The Curious Traveller Press, 1996

McClure, W. Raymond. *They That Go Down to the Sea in Ships*. Rutland, VT: printed by Sharp Offset Printing, 1968

McCullough, David. *John Adams*. New York: Simon & Schuster, 2001

McElroy, Paul Simpson. "John Wise: The Father of American Independence," *Essex Institute Historical Collections*, Vol. 81, July 1945, pp. 201-26

McFarland, Raymond. *A History of the New England Fisheries*. Philadelphia: University of Pennsylvania, 1911

- *The Masts of Gloucester – Recollectons of a Fisherman*. New York: W.W. Norton, 1937

McLane, Merrill F. *The Adventure of Blueberrying*. Cabin John, MD: Carderock Press, 1994

- *Place Names of Old Sandy Bay*. Bethesda, MD: privately published by Helene Orbaen, 1998

Mears, Sherman. *Essex Electrics*. Essex: Essex Historical Society, 1981

Meltzer, Milton and Harding, Walter. *A Thoreau Profile*. Concord, MA: Thoreau Foundation, c1962

Merrill, Ben. *A History of Twentieth Century Manchester*. Manchester: The Cricket Press, 1990

Moody, William Vaughn. *Selected Poems of William Vaughn Moody*, ed. Robert Morss Lovett. Cambridge, MA: Houghton Mifflin – Riverside Press, 1931

Moorhouse, Geoffrey. *The Boat and the Town*. London: Hodder and Stoughton, 1979

Morison, Samuel Eliot. *Builders of the Bay Colony*. Boston: Houghton Mifflin, 1930, 1964

- *The Intellectual Life of Colonial New England*. Second edition, New York: New York University, 1956. First published in 1936 as *The Puritan Pronaos*.
- *John Paul Jones: A Sailor's Biography*. Boston: Little Brown, 1959
- "The Dry Salvages and the Thacher Shipwreck," *The American Neptune*, Vol. 25, October 1965, pp. 231-41
- *The European Discovery of America: The Northern Voyages*. New York: Oxford University Press, 1971
- *Samuel de Champlain – Father of New France*. Boston: Little Brown, 1972

Morris, Rob. *Alfred "Centennial" Johnson: The Story of the First Solo Atlantic Crossing from West to East in 1876*. Pembrokeshire, Wales: Y crofft, 2003

Morse, Capt. Tom. *All My Girls*. Gloucester: printed by The Pressroom, 2000

Murray, Rev. John. *The Life of Rev. John Murray, Written by Himself, with Notes and Appendix by Rev. L. S. Everett*. Boston: A. Tompkins, 1858

Murray, Judith Sargent: *The Gleaner – A Miscellaneous Production*, by "Constantia." Boston: I. Thomas and E. T. Andrews, 3 volumes, 1798

Naismith, Helen. *Walking Cape Ann*. Gloucester: Ten Pound Island Books, 1994

- *The Hermit of Ravenswood*. Gloucester: printed by The Pressroom, 1997

Nicastro, Charles G. *Iron Men, Wooden Ships*. Gloucester: 1998

Oakley, Thornton. *Cecilia Beaux*. Philadelphia: Henry Biddle Printing Company, 1943

Oaks, Martha. *The Gloucester Fishermen's Institute, 1891-1991*. Gloucester: Gloucester Fishermen's Institute, 1991

O'Gorman, James F. *Portrait of a Place: Some American Landscape Painters in Gloucester*. Gloucester: Gloucester 350th Anniversary Celebration, 1973

- *This Other Gloucester – Occasional Papers on the Arts of Cape Ann Massachusetts*. Boston: Nelson B. Robinson, 1973. Reprinted by Ten Pound Island Book Company, Gloucester, 1990

- "Two Granite Tents at Bay View on Cape Ann: An Architectural Note on the B. F. Butler and J. H. French Houses," *Essex Institute Historical Collections*, Vol. 118, October, 1982, pp. 241-47

Olson, Charles. *The Maximus Poems*, edited by George F. Butterick. Berkeley, CA: University of California Press, 1983

Optic, Oliver (William T. Adams). *The Starry Flag, or, The Young Fisherman of Cape Ann*. Boston: Lee and Shepard, 1869

Orlando, Joseph M. *The Fisherman's Son*. Xlibris, 2004

Parsons, Eleanor C. *Hannah and the Hatchet Gang*. Canaan, NH: Phoenix Publishing, 1975

- *Thachers: Island of the Twin Lights*. Canaan, NH: Phoenix Publishing, 1985; reprinted 2000

- *Fish, Timber, Granite & Gold*. Rockport: Sandy Bay Historical Society and Museums, 2003

Parsons, Peter and Anastas, Peter. *When Gloucester Was Gloucester – Toward an Oral History of the City*. Gloucester: Gloucester 350th Anniversary Celebration, Inc., 1973

Patch, Isaac. *Growing Up in Gloucester*. Gloucester: The Curious Traveller Press, 2004

Pattillo, James W. *The Autobiography of James William Pattillo, 1806-1887*. Dictated by him to W. J. Rakey in 1884 or '85 (typed manuscript in Cape Ann Historical Association library)

Peckham, Courtney Ellis. *Essex Shipbuilding*. Charleston, SC: Arcadia Publishing, 2002

Phelps, Elizabeth Stuart. *Chapters from a Life*. Boston: Houghton, Mifflin, 1896

Piraino, Thomas. *The Sicilian Fisherman's Son*. Braintree, MA: Thomas Piraino, 1992

Pope, Eleanor. *The Wilds of Cape Ann*. Boston: The Nimrod Press, 1981 ("A publication of Resources for Cape Ann, a project of the Massachusetts Audubon Society and the Essex County Ecology Center, Inc.")

Pringle, James R. *History of the Town and City of Gloucester, Cape Ann, Massachusetts*. Printed in Lynn, MA by G. H & W. A. Nichols, 1892. Indexed edition published by City of Gloucester Archives Committee and Ten Pound Island Book Company, 1997

- *The Book of the Three Hundredth Anniversary Observance of the Foundation of the Massachusetts Bay Colony at Cape Ann in 1623 and the Fiftieth Year of the Incorporation of Gloucester as a City*. Compiled and edited by James R. Pringle. Gloucester: Three Hundredth Anniversary Executive Committee, 1924

- *Gloucester: A Pageant Drama*, presented at Stage Fort Park, Gloucester, August 28th and 30th. Manchester: North Shore Press, 1923

Procter, George H. *The Fishermen's Memorial and Record Book*. Gloucester: Procter Brothers, 1873 Reprinted 2004 by The History Press, Charleston, SC

- *The Fisheries of Gloucester - from 1623 to 1876*. Gloucester: Procter Brothers, 1876

- *The Fishermen's Own Book*. Gloucester: Procter Brothers, 1882

Prybot, Peter K. *White-Tipped Orange Masts: Gloucester's Fishing Draggers – A Time of Change, 1970-1972*. Gloucester: The Curious Traveller Press, 1998

- *Lobstering off Cape Ann: A Lifetime Lobsterman Remembers*. Charleston, SC: The History Press, 2006

Ray, Waino T. *A Young Finn on Cape Ann*, ed. Sally Ray Bennett. New Brighton, MN: Sampo Publishing, 1997

Raffel, Burton. *T. S. Eliot*. New York: Frank Unger, 1982

Recchia, Kitty Parsons. "Dogtown Common." 1936

- *Gloucester Sea Ballads*, Gloucester: Fermata Press, 1981

Reilly, John C.; Kippen-Smith, Priscilla O.; Sparling, Edith M. *Historical Gleanings from the Gloucester Archives*. Gloucester: City of Gloucester Archives Committee, 1995

Reynolds, Joseph D., M.D. *Peter Gott, The Cape Ann Fisherman*. Boston: John P. Jewett, 1856.

Rich, Hiram. *Leaves on the Tide*. Boston: J. S. Lockwood, 1913

Robbins, Sarah Fraser and Yentsch, Clarice. *The Sea Is All About Us*. Salem, MA: The Peabody Museum of Salem, and The Cape Ann Society for Marine Science, Inc., 1973

Robey, Harriett. *Bay View: A Summer Portrait*. Boston: Howland, 1979

Robinson, F. J. G. *Tragabigzanda, or Cape Ann – The Romance, Legend and History of Cape Ann, Past and Present*. 1935

Rogers, Elliott C. and Copeland, Melvin. *The Saga of Cape Ann.* Freeport, ME: Bond Wheelwright, 1960

Rose, Arthur K. *Portagee Hill and a People.* Gloucester: 1991

- *A Place in Time.* Gloucester: 2002

Rose-Troup, Frances. *John White – The Patriarch of Dorchester (Dorset) and The Founder of Massachusetts.* New York and London: G. P. Putnam's Sons, 1930

Rowse, A. L. *The Elizabethans and America.* New York: Harper & Brothers, 1959

Sargent, Emma Worcester and Sargent, Charles Sprague. *Epes Sargent of Gloucester and His Descendants.* Boston: Houghton Mifflin, 1923

Sargent, Capt. Epes. *Reminiscences of Epes Sargent, 1784-1853, written to his Grandson Epes, 1841-1857.* Typed copy of manuscript in Cape Ann Historical Association library, Gloucester

Sargent, Epes. *Songs of the Sea, with Other Poems.* Boston: James Munroe, 1847

- *The Light of the Light-House, and Other Poems.* No. 1 of "The Drawing Room Library"

Saville, Foster H. and Babson, Roger W. *Cape Ann Tourist's Guide.* Rockport: Sandy Bay Historical Society and Museum, 1936. Revised 1946, 1952

Sedgwick, Ellery. *The Atlantic Monthly, 1857-1909.* Amherst, MA: University of Massachusetts Press, 1994

Sencourt, Robert. *T. S. Eliot, A Memoir,* ed. Donald Adamson. New York: Dodd, Mead, 1971

Sewall, Samuel. *The Diary of Samuel Sewall,* ed. M. Halsey Thomas. 2 volumes. New York: Farrar, Straus and Giroux, 1973

Shaler, Nathaniel S. "The Geology of Cape Ann, Massachusetts," *Ninth Annual Report,* U.S. Geological Survey for 1887-1888, pp. 537-618

- *The Autobiography of Nathaniel Southgate Shaler.* Cambridge, MA: Houghton Mifflin – The Riverside Press, 1909

Slocum, Capt. Joshua. *Sailing Alone Around the World.* Cornwall, NY: printed by The Cornwall Press. Copyright 1899, 1900 by The Century Co.

Smith, Bonnie Hurd. *From Gloucester to Philadelphia in 1790: Observations, anecdotes, and thoughts from the 18th-century letters of Judith Sargent Murray.* Judith Murray Society, Cambridge, MA and The Curious Traveller Press, Gloucester, 1998

- *Letters I Left Behind: Judith Sargent Murray Papers, Letterbook 10.* Salem, MA: Judith Sargent Murray Society, 2005

Smith, Earl. *Yankee Genius – A Biography of Roger W. Babson.* New York: Harper, 1954

Smith, Capt. John. *A Description of New England; or, Observations and Discoveries in the North of America in the Year of Our Lord 1614.* Boston: William Veazie, 1865 (true copy of original)

- *The Complete Works of Captain John Smith (1580-1631),* ed. Philip C. Barbour. Williamsburg, VA: Institute for Early American History & Culture, Vol. 1, 1986

Smith, Capt. Sylvanus. *Fisheries of Cape Ann.* Gloucester: Press of Gloucester Times Company, 1915

Solley, George Willis. *Alluring Rockport.* Manchester: North Shore Press, 1924. Revised edition published by Walkabout Press, Rockport, 1986

Somes, John J. *The Gloucester Fire Department – Its History and Work from 1793 to 1893.* Gloucester: The Steam Fire Association, printed by Procter Brothers, 1892

Story, Dana. *Frame Up! - The Story of Essex, Its Shipyards and Its People.* Barre, MA: Barre Publishers, 1964

- *The Building of a Wooden Ship.* Barre, MA: Barre Publishers, 1971
- *Hail Columbia! The Rise and Fall of a Schooner.* Gloucester: Ten Pound Island Book Company, 1985
- *Building the Blackfish.* Gloucester: Ten Pound Island Book Company, 1988
- *Growing Up in a Shipyard – Reminiscences of a Shipbuilding Life in Essex Massachusetts.* Mystic Seaport Museum, Inc., Mystic, CT, in association with the Essex Shipbuilding Museum, Inc. Essex, MA, 1991
- *The Shipbuilders of Essex – A Chronicle of Yankee Endeavor.* Gloucester: Ten Pound Island Book Company, 1995
- *Daily Except Sundays: The Diaries of a Nineteenth Century Locomotive Engineer.* Edinborough Press. Copyright 2005 by Walker Transportation Collection, Beverly Historical Society and Museum, Beverly, MA

Sutherland, John Lester. *Steamboats of Gloucester and the North Shore.* Charleston, SC: The History Press, 2004

Swan, Marshall W. S. *Town on Sandy Bay: A History of Rockport, Massachusetts.* Rockport: Town of Rockport, Massachusetts, 1980

- "Emerson and Cape Ann," *Essex Institute Historical Collections*, Vol. 121, October 1985, pp. 257-68
- "Cape Ann at the Nadir (1780)", *Essex Institute Historical Collections*, Vol. 119, October 1983, pp. 252-59

Tagney, Ronald N. *The World Turned Upside Down – Essex County During America's Turbulent Years, 1763-1790.* West Newbury, MA: Essex County History, 1989

Testaverde, R. Salve. *Memoirs of a Gloucester Fisherman.* Rockport: Rockport Publishers, 1987

Thayer, Lydia Prescott. *Annisquam (Peaceful Harbor).* Annisquam: Annisquam Historical Society, 1994

Thomas, Gordon W. *Builders of Gloucester's Prosperity.* Gloucester: Cape Ann Savings Bank, 1952

- *Fast & Able: Life Stories of Great Gloucester Fishing Vessels.* Gloucester: Historic Ships Associates (owners of Schooner *Caviare*), 1968; re-issued by Gloucester 350th Anniversary Celebration, Inc., 1973; re-issued by Commonwealth Editions, 2002
- *Wharf & Fleet.* Gloucester: Nautical Reproductions of Gloucester, 1977

Thompson, Carolyn and Jim. *Cape Ann in Stereo Views.* Charleston, SC: Arcadia Publishing, Images of America series, 2000

Thoreau, Henry David. *The Writings of Henry David Thoreau.* Boston: Houghton Mifflin, 1906

- *The Journal of Henry D. Thoreau*, ed. Bradford Torrey and Francis H. Allen. New York: Dover, 1962

Thornton, John Wingate. *The Landing at Cape Anne. ; or, The charter of the first permanent colony on the territory of the Massachusetts company.* Boston: Gould & Lincoln, 1854

Tibbetts, Frederick W. *The Story of Gloucester, Massachusetts, An Address Prepared by Frederick W. Tibbetts and Given Before the Convention of the Massachusetts State Firemen's Association at City Hall, Gloucester, September 21, 1916.* Copyright Fred W. Tibbetts, 1917

Tougias, Michael. *Ten Hours Until Dawn: The True Story of Heroism and Tragedy Aboard the Can Do.* New York: St. Martin's Press, 2005

Tryon, W. S. *Parnassus Corner – A Life of James T. Fields, Publisher to the Victorians.* Boston: Houghton Mifflin, 1963

Tucker, Louis Leonard. *The Massachusetts Historical Society: A Bicentennial History, 1791-1991.* Boston: Massachusetts Historical Society, 1996

Vickers, Daniel. *Farmers & Fishermen – Two Centuries of Work in Essex County, Massachusetts, 1630-1850.* Chapel Hill, NC: Published for The Institute of Early American History and Culture by University of North Carolina Press, 1994

Wallace, Mary. *Summer Magic.* Garden City, NY: Doubleday, 1967

Walton, Mason A. *A Hermit's Wild Friends, or Eighteen Years in the Woods.* Boston: Dana Estes, 1903

Waters, Thomas Franklin. *Ipswich in the Massachusetts Bay Colony.* Ipswich, MA: The Ipswich Historical Society, 1905

- "Two Ipswich Patriots," *Publications of the Ipswich Historical Society XXVI*, Ipswich, MA, 1927 (section on John Wise by Thomas Waters)

Webber, John S. Jr. *In and Around Cape Ann: A Hand-Book of Gloucester, Mass., and Its Immediate Vicinity, for the Wheelman Tourist and the Summer Visitor.* Gloucester: printed at the Cape Ann Advertiser Office, 1885

Webber, William S., Jr. ("Doc Walker"). *Waterfront – Around the Wharves of Gloucester in the Last days of Sail.* Gloucester: Cape Ann Savings Bank, 1973

Weems, Katharine Lane. *Odds Were Against Me* (as told to Edward Weeks). New York: Vantage Press, 1985

Weld, Philip S. *Moxie: The American Challenge.* Boston: Little, Brown, 1981

West, Richard S., Jr. *Lincoln's Scapegoat General – A Life of Benjamin F. Butler, 1818-1893.* Boston: Houghton Mifflin, 1965

White, Rev. John. *John White's Planters Plea – 1630.* Rockport: Printed in facsimile by The Sandy Bay Historical Society and Museum, 1930

Wilmerding, John. *Fitz Hugh Lane, 1804-1865 – American Marine Painter.* Salem, MA: Newcomb & Gauss, 1964; re-issued 2005 by Cape Ann Historical Association as *Fitz Henry Lane*

- *Fitz Hugh Lane: The First Major Exhibition* De Cordova Museum, Lincoln, MA and Colby College Art Museum, Waterville, ME, 1966

- "Interpretations of A Place: Views of Gloucester, Mass. by American Artists," *Essex Institute Historical Collections*, Vol. 103, January 1967, pp. 53-65

Wilson, Angus. *The Strange Ride of Rudyard Kipling – His Life and Works*. New York: The Viking Press, 1977

Winship, George Parker. *Sailors Narratives of Voyages Along the New England Coast, 1524-1624*. Boston: Houghton, Mifflin, 1905

Wright, John Hardy. *Gloucester and Rockport*. Charleston, SC: Arcadia Publishing, Images of America series, 2000

Wright, Louis B. and Fowler, Elaine W., ed.: *West and by North: North America as Seen Through the Eyes of its Seafaring Discoverers*. New York: Delacorte, 1971

Yentsch, Clarice and Robbins, Sarah Fraser. *The Sea Is All About Us*. Salem, MA: The Peabody Museum of Salem and The Cape Ann Society for Marine Science, Inc., 1973

Young, Alexander. *Chronicles of the First Planters of The Colony of Massachusetts Bay*. Baltimore, MD: Genealogical Publishing Company, 1975

Index